Values and Knowledge

The Jean Piaget Symposium Series
Available from LEA

SIGEL, I. E., BRODZINSKY, D. M., & GOLINKOFF, R. M. (Eds.)
• New Directions in Piagetian Theory and Practice

OVERTON, W. F. (Ed.) • The Relationship Between
Social and Cognitive Development

LIBEN, L. S. (Ed.) • Piaget and the Foundations of Knowledge

SCHOLNICK, E. K. (Ed.) • New Trends in Conceptual Representation:
Challenges to Piaget's Theory?

NEIMARK, E. D., De LISI, R., & NEWMAN, J. L. (Eds.)
• Moderators of Competence

BEARISON, D. J., & ZIMILES, H. (Eds.) • Thought and Emotion:
Developmental Perspectives

LIBEN, L. S. (Ed.) • Development and Learning: Conflict or Congruence?

FORMAN, G., & PUFALL, P. B. (Eds.) • Constructivism in the Computer Age

OVERTON, W. F. (Ed.) • Reasoning, Necessity, and Logic:
Developmental Perspectives

KEATING, D. P., & ROSEN, H. (Eds.) • Constructivist Perspectives on
Developmental Psychopathology and Atypical Development

CAREY, S., & GELMAN, R. (Eds.) • The Epigenesis of Mind:
Essays on Biology and Cognition

BEILIN, H., & PUFALL, P. (Eds.) • Piaget's Theory: Prospects and Possibilities

WOZNIAK, R. H., & FISCHER, K. W. (Eds.) • Development in Context:
Acting and Thinking in Specific Environments

OVERTON, W. F., & PALERMO, D. S. (Eds.) • The Nature and
Ontogenesis of Meaning

NOAM, G. G., & FISCHER, K. W. (Eds.) • Development and Vulnerability
in Close Relationships

REED, E. S., TURIEL, E., & BROWN, T. (Eds.) • Values and Knowledge

Values and Knowledge

Edited by

Edward S. Reed
Franklin & Marshall College

Elliot Turiel
University of California at Berkeley

Terrance Brown
Chicago, Illinois

LEA LAWRENCE ERLBAUM ASSOCIATES, PUBLISHERS
1996   Mahwah, New Jersey

Lawrence Erlbaum Associates, Inc., Publishers
10 Industrial Avenue
Mahwah, New Jersey 07430

Library of Congress Cataloging-in-Publication Data

Values and knowledge / edited by Edward S. Reed, Elliot Turiel, Terrance Brown.
        p.   cm.
    Includes bibliographical references and index.
    ISBN 0-8058-1521-X
        1. Moral development. 2. Values—Psychological aspects. 3. Social values—Psycho-
logical aspects. I. Reed, Edward (Edward S.). II. Turiel, Elliot. III. Brown, Terrance.
    BF723.M54V34   1996   95-25505
    155.2'5—dc20   CIP

Books published by Lawrence Erlbaum Associates are printed on acid-free paper, and their bindings are chosen for strength and durability.

Printed in the United States of America
10   9   8   7   6   5   4   3   2   1

Contents

Preface

David Hume pointed out long ago that values are simultaneously the easiest and the most difficult topic on which to reach agreement. He noted that everyone everywhere agrees that we should strive for good and avoid evil. That is the easy part. The difficult part is knowing what is good and what is evil. And what about those gray areas in between? Hume's truism still resonates for us, both concerning the politics of values and concerning our psychological or pedagogical theories of the role of valuation in development.

Whenever values are discussed at a general or abstract level, there is a tendency for *deceptive agreement*. For example, many in the United States had taken it for granted that the values of tolerance and respect for the rights of individuals were widely agreed to be a basic tenet of American life. Yet in the last few years, attempts to implement this set of values as an organizing principle for social studies education have met with considerable resistance from many Americans in any number of school districts across the country. Tolerance in general is one principle, it would seem, but specific kinds of tolerance —toward non-Christians, or non-heterosexuals, for example—are perceived as something else again. This political fact may be uncomfortable and distressing, but we must reach beyond our discomfort to see the psychological truth revealed by such phenomena.

This psychological truth has profound consequences. To state it simply— no doubt oversimply—we must come to understand that the "values" animating human behavior and thought are not only abstractions that are applied, with varying degrees of success, to different situations; values are also particularistic, emerge from particular, complex situations, and are often brought to bear on other, far less appropriate situations.

The rational principles we state in our attempts to describe a value system cannot be assumed to be the actual values by which others operate. Such an assumption leads to what William James called the *psychologist's fallacy:* the fallacy of taking our *hypothetical descriptions* of another's mental state as being completely equivalent to that mental state. The mental state that we hopefully describe as a belief in tolerance may be little more than a pragmatic maxim to try to be civil to others. To confront a person operating with such a pragmatic maxim and argue that he or she is being "intolerant" or "inconsistent" misses the point that "tolerance" was never a living value for that person in the first place. When we commit the psychologist's fallacy in this way, we lay the groundwork for far worse educational, social, and political fallacies.

To avoid such fallacies we must study values, not as they are represented in the idealized worlds of discourse, but as they live within and among communities of human beings. Values have an odd life cycle, one that transcends the dichotomy between the individual and the social. Values are never born solely within one person, but they can only thrive—or fail—within the development of individuals. The chapters in this book emerged from a set of concerns with values and developments articulated by the editors in the 23rd Annual Symposium of the Jean Piaget Society in 1993, with guidance from the Society's Board of Directors. For the Symposium we brought together speakers covering a broad range of concerns, but whose work focused on the power values exert to organize psychological development. The questions we asked speakers to address were: Where do values come from, and how are they appropriated within individuals? What role do values play in the psychological adaptation of humans to their physical and social environments? Can some values be considered more or less rational? Why do values seem so often to come into conflict, even the values held by a single individual?

All of these questions were addressed by Piaget. As Terrance Brown explains in the concluding chapter of this volume, Piaget struggled with the difficult problem of how to construe values and their relation to knowledge. In two well-known books, Piaget presented analyses of *the moral judgment of the child* and of *intelligence and affectivity.* Beyond these two works, however, Piaget attempted to come to grips with issues revolving around the subjective and objective aspects of values, the relativity and universality of emotions and morality, and especially, relationships between values and the construction of knowledge. These are issues unresolved by Piaget, and they continue to animate research on the role of values in development.

In the context of those influences, Piaget's ideas have been extended, modified, and taken in new directions. In chapter 3, Larry Nucci takes a serious look at Piaget's insight that the development of concepts of self, autonomy, and personal freedom is linked to the development of moral judgments, and especially judgments concerning the points of view and needs of others. Ina Užgiris (chapter 2) examines the earliest phases of value formation, high-lighting representations in infancy and the social and affective nature of in-teractions in the earliest years of life. In chapter 5, Elliot Turiel takes the cen-trality of individual–environmental interactions in moral, social, and personal judgments as a challenge for theories of the role of culture in development. His focus is on variations within cultures, and the conflicts and struggles that can ensue from conflicting values.

Other contributors bring perspectives different from but closely allied to the developmental perspective. Susan Moller Okin, a political scientist and philosopher, discusses the role of the family as a site for the formation of val-ues and the practice of moral judgment in chapter 4. She notes the gendered basis and biases of the institution of the family and shows how moral philoso-phers and psychologists have failed to pay sufficient attention to gender dif-ferences in how justice is manifest in daily life. She argues that, because fam-ilies are sites within which all of us develop our values, it is imperative that a clear understanding of justice and injustice within families be developed. In chapter 6, Lee Ross and Andrew Ward bring the perspective of experimental social psychology to an understanding of values, subjective judgments, social contexts, and social conflict. They show how commonplace subjective infer-ences can produce "naive realism," or the assumption that others share one's attitudes and values, thus resulting in false beliefs and misleading consensus. The social consequences of naive realism are far-reaching, as it can give rise to misunderstandings, conflict, and make difficult the resolution of disputes.

Following Hume's advice, the contributors to this volume address questions of value not in general terms, but in the light of particular areas of develop-ment, thought, and judgment with which they have been concerned. A broad range of topics are covered, making the case that that valuation plays a role in many areas of human development.

—*Edward S. Reed*
—*Elliot Turiel*
—*Terrance Brown*

1

Selves, Values, Cultures

Edward S. Reed
Franklin & Marshall College

A central concept in Piaget's theory is that behavior and thought function as parts of a regulatory system facilitating an individual's adaptation to his or her environment. From this perspective, *values* stand for the diverse patterns of regulation entered into by all persons in a given environment and incorporated into their thoughts and actions. Because our human environment is largely organized through interaction with other people, many—but not all—values emerge within a social context. Values thus mediate between self and world, including the social world, and any theory of value must necessarily tackle the extremely difficult problems of the growth of the self and the socialization of individuals. The attempt to formulate such ambitious theories is useful because it forces us to consider whole persons as agents and as recipients, a salutary change from the fragmentary view of the person so common in modern psychology. Although such ambitious theorizing is fraught with intellectual peril, contributors to this volume have been willing to at least point us in the direction of such a theory. Indeed, much of the research and thinking reported here derives from a small set of problems which—if one could ever solve them— would lead to such a general theory of development. This set of problems can be divided into three issues: (a) What role does valuation play in the growth of individuals into integrated persons, each with a unique suite of predilections and capacities? (b) How are values embodied in the activities, feelings, and thoughts of individuals? (c) How does self individuation and differentiation from others occur within a culture without loss of self-identification with that culture and its values?

This chapter cannot pretend to offer a theory of values and their role in human development, but it does try to set the stage for thinking about such a theory by discussing the last of these three issues in the light of the various contributions to this volume. This focus on self-development is of central importance for psychologists and developmentalists, and should also help to shed light on the other two issues. The goal of the chapter is to outline some of the major perspectives that have been taken concerning the relationship between selves and cultures, as well as to offer some suggestions about promising directions for coming to grips with some of these issues. This historical-conceptual review is enlightening because in many ways, developmental psychology is forced to recapitulate many of the foundational problems of the social sciences.

THE SELF:
AUTONOMOUS, CONSTRUCTED, OR GROWN

Developmental psychology is still fighting an old intellectual battle, one bequeathed to us by that self-described solitary dreamer, Jean-Jacques Rousseau. It was Rousseau more than anyone else who pushed Western thinking about child development away from Christianity and toward modern science (Hendel, 1934; Riley, 1986). Like so many intellectual revolutionaries—and not unlike many of the subjects in Ross and Ward's (chapter 6, this volume) experiments—Rousseau was more influenced by those he opposed than he realized. Thus, in rejecting the idea that original sin has a central place in human development, Rousseau almost went to the other extreme. And, whether or not Rousseau himself truly propounded the doctrine that society is corrupt and the child pure and angelic, there is no question that many subsequent thinkers fell under the spell of this idyll and called their views Rousseauian.

Those who have argued for or against Rousseau's ideal of childhood have tended to focus on whether it is the child or society that carries the seeds of later corruption. Amidst all the noise generated in that debate it is easy to miss another difficulty bequeathed to us by Rousseau. If society is based on a "social contract" and the newborn is essentially outside of society, then all children must "enter" their societies, perhaps even by making some revised form of the original social contract themselves. Yet this implies that the child exists as a more or less complete self despite his or her independence from society. Rousseauians often treat the child as a virtually autonomous individual, engaging the society and others on his or her own terms. This confuses a state of autonomy—a highly differentiated and socialized personality—with a state of being outside of and independent of society. This notion of an unsocialized autochthonous self is one of those ideas that few would defend but nevertheless keeps surfacing as an assumption in many theories. Despite many attempts, those of us interested in explaining how the self develops have not succeeded in overcoming this Rousseauian framework.

Several of the chapters in this book help us to move beyond a simplistic Rousseauian perspective. Užgiris (chapter 2) shows how even the earliest stages of selfhood emerge from a complex network of social relations within the family. Nucci (chapter 3) offers a theory of how each person growing within such networks strives to negotiate a domain of self-determination. Okin (chapter 4) reminds us forcefully that many social ills and prejudices, such as unfair treatment of females, reproduce themselves precisely because individuals become selves within the context of real (and often imperfect) families. Other recent work has also greatly facilitated our understanding of the development of the self through early interaction. The work of Fogel (1993), Stern (1994), and Trevarthen (1994) has shown that the newborn comes into the world not as a full-fledged but unsocialized person—as a potential partner in some social contract—but as an undifferentiated, yet social, agent. Through the intensely interpersonal social developmental process of human infancy, neonates slowly become selves, adapting to their environment, both natural and social.

The first great challenge to the notion of the autonomous self was Hegel's attempt at a developmental account of the self, which he called a "phenomenology" (Hegel, 1807/1977; Pippin, 1989). Freed from the doctrine of an immutable soul, Hegel emphasized that the self undergoes historical development and change. However, in many ways he went to the opposite extreme from Rousseau, arguing that the self is in fact a construction of the self. How this self-creation ex nihilo might be accomplished is, as one might imagine, not exactly clear. Worse, Hegel sometimes seems to have believed that only God is a true self, and so applied this "dialectical" account to Him alone. At other times, Hegel seems to have suggested that each of us shares some elements of the Godhead and therefore somehow participates in this dialectical development. However, when he came down from abstractions to discuss the events of everyday life, Hegel gave an extremely prosaic account of the family and the separate roles of its members (in his *Philosophy of Right*) that differed hardly at all from *Burgerlich* common sense.

In an attempt to reconcile Rousseauian individualism with Hegel's monolithic attempt to embed us all in a Godhead, the young Marx and Engels (1845/1974; Reed, 1995a) suggested that we all make ourselves, but not under conditions of our own choosing. In other words, they demythologized Hegel's theological view of self-creation and at the same time emphasized Rousseau's insight that becoming a member of a society is a key element of self-formation. In many ways the young Marx and Engels thus enunciated the question that stands at the intersection of all the social sciences: How does the human neonate grow into being a unique personality, socialized into a specific culture, according to specific rules and roles? This is not a matter of a pre-existing self acknowledging the values of those around him and signing on (however powerful such myths are when we tell stories about ourselves). But neither is it a matter of self-creation, in which a creature that is somehow outside of the normal constraints of life organizes itself. Marx and Engels never even published this fundamental text for a new social science, *The German Ideology,* leaving it (as they said) for the mice to gnaw as they made themselves into revolutionary intellectuals not under conditions of their own choosing. Ultimately, of course, Marx and Engels came to have a very different kind of influence on anthropologists, sociologists, and psychologists, an influence now quite tattered by the sharp teeth of the rats of history.

Early in the 20th century the American thinker John Dewey—under the influence of both Hegel and Marx—rethought this problem of the growth of the self. A self-described naturalist and pragmatist, Dewey (1938/1991; Westerbrook, 1992) emphasized that selves grow only in specific environing situations. Time and again Dewey used quasi-botanical metaphors to try to get across this perspective: The self begins as a seed that can grow only when nourished, but that will grow in certain ways (for good or ill) depending on the environing factors. As with Marx, it is not a matter of a Rousseauian self negotiating with a separate society, but of some kind of self-creation in which constraints come from both nature and culture. But these "constraints" are not merely negatives (as Užgiris emphasizes)—each constraint is equally an opportunity for growth and development under specific conditions. From this philosophy of development Dewey fashioned an educational theory that emphasized what he considered to be democratic self-development as a central value. For Dewey, education is a kind of sharing of the self-creation process, one that emphasizes opportunity and discovery more than mere transference of information. Dewey never abandoned the centrality of skill and information acquisition in education—as some of his detractors claimed—but he insisted these must be embedded in the process of self-creation, so that the skills and information are made part of the values of the growing individual, not artificially added on.

Although Dewey's influence on later thought in philosophy, psychology, and pedagogy is widespread, it has tended to be piecemeal, and his emphasis on self growth and valuation is one of the pieces that has tended to be lost. Yet it is clear that Dewey had a significant impact on Piaget's thinking and it may be that when one is attempting to sketch a general model of human development—as one is forced to do in discussions of values—Dewey's "garden" metaphor may be required to supplant Piagetian "construction zone" thinking. Nucci, echoing Habermas (1984), suggests that neither of these metaphors is adequate, insisting on the centrality of communication and negotiation in the differentiation of persons from their social contexts.

In Rousseauian theory the growth of the self is inevitably accompanied by conflict, but these are conflicts between the self and society. Hegel has a great deal to say about conflicts within the "Geist" but he seemed to be more interested in applying these to his speculative history than to a psychological account of individuals—a criticism one might equally aim at Marx and Engels. Dewey always emphasized the role of "tension" in individual development, but said little about it that went beyond the metaphorical. Piaget made the issue of "tension"—of contradiction and conflict—central to his account of the mechanisms of developmental change, an insight we would do well to follow when trying to understand the role of value in development.

PLURALITY, MORAL THEORY, AND DEVELOPMENT

Hegel, Marx, and Dewey notwithstanding, theorizing about the development of values has tended not to acknowledge the plurality and incoherence of real value systems. Indeed, this resistance to acknowledging inconsistency is a characteristic of nearly all Western ethical philosophy (Stocker, 1990). Consider Rawls' (1973, 1992) theory of justice, which, as Okin (chapter 4, this volume) notes, has been enormously influential. According to Rawls, the very concept of justice requires us to imagine what he called the *original position*. This is a hypothetical social arrangement in which individuals are all equal in power and prestige and in which information is shared equally. Decisions made by this hypothetical jury not only will be just, Rawls suggested, but *define* what we mean by justice.

Rawls' theory is thus, literally, idealistic, in the sense that it rests on what has been, still is, and probably always will be a totally hypothetical and idealized set of social arrangements. Not only that; these arrangements are so idealized that they do not include the kinds of internal conflicts of values so characteristic of difficult everyday decisions. It would seem to be one of the main points of Rawls' work (and that of so many other philosophers) to try to come up with a *mechanism* that would obviate the need for working through difficult decisions over which we are conflicted. As an ideal case and even as a thought experiment this can have considerable use, but it also has very real limitations. This is because many of the questions that we real people have about justice cannot be resolved mechanically; their resolution in part requires a process whereby they be deliberated on and debated by real people who can empathize with both sides of an issue.

Consider, for example, affirmative action, which is a topic of current concern and controversy. The problem stems from a conflict between the principle of seeking an individual most suited for a position and the principle of distributing good positions across different groups of individuals. When the number of positions is limited relative to the candidates then any attempt to follow both these principles necessarily runs into conflict. At least some of those opposed to affirmative action can nevertheless understand the background that makes this conflict poignant (viz., the benefits of good positions and the degradation of being a member of an "outgroup") even while arguing that the conflict is insufficient to warrant the kind of remediation called for by affirmative action policies. Conversely, some of those who support affirmative action may well find themselves conflicted about what would be the best method of resolving such conflicts. Much of the poignancy of this issue comes from genuine disagreement over concepts of fairness and especially judgments concerning the appropriateness of making reparations for previous wrongs. One group judges that remediation of past errors is of the highest value, whereas others hold that creation of a current fair situation is the highest value. Many others are caught in the middle. No one who grew up amidst the original position can have all the feelings and second thoughts such circumstances create in real people, and the concept of a single "just" solution to all situations tends to downplay the very real complexities that make the process of valuation what it is. It is fascinating to read Ross and Ward's chapter, in which they give evidence for social processes that tend to produce more extreme and less nuanced public positions on controversial topics (not unlike Rawls' people in the original position) and find, in the same subjects at the same time, considerable private ambivalence about such strong positions and an implicit interest in more flexible, nuanced thinking.

One response to the idealization inherent in Rawls' way of thinking about moral judgment is what I would call a "transcendental" approach, which is characteristic of Kohlberg (1983) and Habermas (1984; McCarthy, 1991). Instead of looking for the ideal case under which people would make just decisions, these thinkers try to ascertain the actual conditions that allow for moral debate and judgment to occur. Habermas in particular is very clear about this: He is searching for the actual conditions in actual society that facilitate moral thought and actions.

However, like Rousseau, Habermas and Kohlberg tend to think of this set of possibilities in terms of wholly formed individuals coming into contact with other individuals. Habermas' theory is based on a search for what might be called Kantian regulative ideals of communication. These assume persons who can make demands, statements, request information and, in general, assert themselves in a social context. Kohlberg of course is interested in how these communicative competencies might develop, but does so from what appears to be a Rousseauian perspective, in which the individual child at all its stages of development is considered essentially as a complete microcosm, even prior to socialization.

However, even the conditions of communication have to be created and undergo development. Nucci argues that this development is neither imposed on a child from society, nor does it emerge from some innate propensity on the part of human children. Instead, it is a negotiated, or dialectical process, in which concepts of self, autonomy, and respect for others emerge—or should emerge—from basic everyday actions of children and parents. I would go further and argue that the child's acquisition of the ability to produce speech acts—statements, requests, questions, demands, promises, and so on—itself emerges from the dialectical interplay of children with their caretakers in the first 3 years of life. Dialogue inevitably involves some conflict, as anyone who has raised children can attest. It is only when children come to be able to assert their needs and point of view in contrast to the needs and perspectives of those around them that they master the production of speech acts (Reed, 1995b). One way, then, in which we become ourselves, is by learning to communicate our own unique viewpoint and concern to others, something that happens mostly when we do not immediately succeed in getting what we want. Piaget's fundamental insight about conflict as the motive force in development is especially relevant to the analysis of communication.

Again, the chapter by Ross and Ward perhaps most effectively undermines the abstractions of thinkers like Rawls, Kohlberg, or Habermas. All of these theorists treat communication about values as if it could be made unproblematic—something which is psychologically impossible. For example, Rawls' (1973) concept of the original position assumes not only that individuals have perfect information, but also that they acknowledge that others have such perfect information as well. Yet, as Ross and Ward show, such assumptions are unrealistic, to put it nicely. Communication about values is *intrinsically* fraught with opportunities for false attribution, bad faith, ill will, and worse. The philosophers' trick of "bracketing" these "merely" contingent facts and postulating some ideal community (Rawls) or a transcendental presupposition of charitable communication (Habermas) is unhelpful at best. As Ross and Ward suggest, what is really needed are strategies whereby real, fallible, social agents can nevertheless be encouraged to *develop* a kind of interpretive charity and openness. If social psychological research has demonstrated anything, it has shown that merely hoping that better communication will occur, or can occur under some ideal conditions, is wishful thinking.

COOPERATION AND CONFLICT: FROM AFFORDANCES TO VALUES

If it is true that we make ourselves but not under conditions of our own choosing, then one of the key aspects of any environment is whether some of the resources it contains are scarce relative to the needs or demands of the people living there. Where conditions of relative scarcity are found, there is opportunity for either conflict or cooperation. Consider an extreme case of scarcity, such as a famine. Under these circumstances there will be cases of direct and aggressive physical conflict, such as fighting over food; but there will also be cases in which groups of people organize themselves to make decisions about who should get the available food, and how much (e.g., rationing, provisioning for the ill, triage). Although famine is an extreme example, it nevertheless serves to illustrate that human cultures function in large part as arenas for conflict among people and its resolution.

Throughout human history and across all known cultures there has been this pattern of both cooperation and conflict being elicited by changes in available resources. But resources for human beings are in part created by human beings. Wood has been available in the environment for millions of years, yet only in the past 400,000 years have humans turned wood into a resource for warmth, into *fuel* for fires (Perles, 1977). However, the modification of the environment is largely a product of groups of people: Tools and techniques can be used by individuals, but technologies and procedures are only maintained and developed by cultures (Basalla, 1989). Thus, to paraphrase Marx, individual humans assimilate their environments in part through the mediation of their cultures.

The resources used by individuals as they encounter their surroundings are what James Gibson (1979/1986; Adolph, Eppler, & E. Gibson, 1994; E. Gibson, 1982/1991; Reed, 1988; Rochat & Reed, 1987) called the *affordances* of the environment for behavior. Affordances are the *use values* of objects, places, and people. As such they are not merely properties of the environment, but properties of the environment as they relate to human use and abilities. A tree that may afford climbing for a small primate might not afford climbing for a human being. Notice that a use value need not be used: Although that tree may afford climbing to a human I might not be skilled enough or brave enough to climb it. Affordances, like resources in general, are *opportunities* for action, not causes of action. Affordances are the values available in an environment for an individual.

Yet to say that the tree affords fuel for my fire is to skip over an important set of facts: that without the technology for cutting wood and controlling fire, the tree would not afford fueling my fire. In general, my *capacities* for resource use as an individual human are greatly affected by my cultural milieu as well as my ecological niche. Each of us lives in a populated environment, and this significantly affects both what values are available to us and our ability to take advantage of those values (Reed, in press). The cutting down of trees to burn or to make houses and other things is something only groups of humans have done, but it has literally changed the face of the earth (Goudie, 1989; Goudsblom, 1994). The differences in affordances available from one culture to another may be as great, or greater, than the differences in affordances available from one primate species to the next. Moreover, because humans learn and develop within these cultural contexts, my *proclivities* of affordance usage—what affordances I am inclined to use, when and where I use them, and the skilled procedures I deploy in order to use them—are also greatly affected by my cultural milieu. To take a simple but powerful example, in a great number of cultures, such as traditional Hindu India, the grasping of food must always be done with the right hand, because the left hand is reserved for personal hygiene. Obviously, food items afford being picked up with either hand (as we do in our culture), but people who grow up in certain places have a taboo on using the right hand for getting food.

As J. Gibson (1950) put it, cultures include both techniques and taboos. *Techniques* are socially developed (even when individually realized) ways of acquiring use values. *Taboos* are socially developed (even when individually realized) selected ways of applying those techniques. J. Gibson (1950; see Reed, 1988, ch. 10) suggested that individual behavior is thus divided into *expedient ways* and what he called *proper ways*. These are not separate behavioral acts, but often merely distinct facets of a given behavior. One may learn many expedient ways for using affordances, but one must also learn the proprieties of one's own culture, which constitute selected constraints on affordance use—on what one uses, when one uses it, and where and how one does so.

Thus there are at least *two kinds of conflict* experienced by children growing into their cultures: conflicts over resources and conflicts over mores—or, to use the terms given earlier, conflicts over expediencies versus conflict over proprieties. That is, the child's behavior can fail to be adaptive (in Piaget's sense of the term) in two quite different ways. First, the child's behavior can fail to meet the needs that were the goal of that activity. The conflict thus brought about is between the child and his or her own needs, in which the child's behavior fails to be expedient. Second, even though meeting his or her needs, the child's behavior can fail to meet the norms of the culture in which the child lives. Here the conflict is between the child and the culture's selective ways of gaining access to resources, and the child's behavior fails to be proper. Note that these are two separate spheres of needs that intersect but are not identical. A behavior that meets my needs may not be acceptable within my cultural milieu (e.g., grabbing all objects or food, defecating wherever I care to); but it is equally true that a culturally proper action may not meet my needs (e.g., limiting the food given to females and children in a family in order to feed the father or the boys). Developing selves in any culture thus have to grow and make themselves under conditions not of their own choosing *both* vis-à-vis available affordances *and* vis-à-vis proper ways of using those affordances. Scarcity of resources for an individual can be (and often is) as much a function of cultural organization as of natural resource limitations. From the point of view of a culture or a family (at least of a nurturing one) each new child is surrounded by all the available and appropriate resources for a new human being. However, from the point of view of the developing person there will inevitably be conflicts over both the availability and appropriateness of those resources. Furthermore, not all children's situations are nurturing (Sylvester-Bradley, 1991).

Stated in this way, and with a focus on cultural variation, the question naturally arises as to which cultures are the "best" in terms of expediencies, proprieties, or both, and which cultures are the "best" in terms of nurturing developing selves. Kohlberg's influential work on the development of moral thinking actually goes so far as to try to specify a more or less universal set of developmental stages toward the best set of proprieties. Many popular discussions of values have tended to hover around these questions of which set of mores is better (Bennett, 1993). However as Turiel (chapter 5, this volume) stresses, these concerns start from a mistaken equation between the values embodied in a culture and those of the individuals in that culture. The assumption that an individual's values simply mirror his or her culture's is overly simple, to say the least. Indeed, as Turiel emphasizes, a culture's values may literally force some individuals into ambivalence or conflict. Part of the problem here is that few thinkers have taken the issue of conflict seriously in trying to understand how selves appropriate their culture's proprieties.

TAKING CONFLICT SERIOUSLY

One domain in which conflict over values has been taken seriously is in the study of psychological issues surrounding prejudice and the integration of minorities into majoritarian practices and culture. To some degree, this focus on conflict with regard to minorities is misleading because it can lead to the false assumption that individuals who are in the majority group are never conflicted. Nevertheless, a focus on minority integration has the advantage of bringing conflict onto center stage, so to speak. An important case in point is W. E. B. DuBois. A student of William James, and widely known among African Americans for his sociological and psychological theorizing, DuBois' work is almost unknown among "mainstream" psychologists (Gaines & Reed, 1994, 1995; cf. Lewis, 1993). One of DuBois' central concerns is precisely the development of the self under conditions of conflict and tension. In particular, in his classic *The Souls of Black Folk* (1903/1990), DuBois formulated the theory that each individual necessarily internalizes some of the cultural divisions within which he or she grows up. DuBois was primarily concerned with self-image and self-esteem in African American children, arguing that some form of division within a person's value system is inevitable for Black Americans, or, more generally, for any person in a subaltern position within a culture. The argument is simple, but profound: In an explicitly racist society, the success of subaltern individuals requires that that individual explicitly renounce pride in those aspects of his or her person that the local culture deems to be associated with the inferior race. For an African American to succeed in the Jim Crow South, the (White) powers that be in that culture required a demeanor that signaled renunciation of all pride in one's African heritage. Turiel and Okin both discuss related examples concerning internal conflicts over values in girls and women who are forced to play subordinate roles in their family and society.

To this day, the distinction between White and Black criteria for success is a major factor in the personality development of all individuals American society deems to be Black. (Notice that this account presupposes a cultural definition of race—those who can "pass" are treated in a completely different way from their brothers and sisters.) Just as many African Americans learn to speak one way to other African Americans and a different way to White Americans (Labov, 1972), so , I would speculate, many African Americans probably learn how to regulate their thought and actions in accordance with two or more value systems.

As DuBois emphasized, for most individuals these conflicts of value are extremely powerful and painful. In many aspects of work, personal relations, and play there can be no unalloyed "good" or "bad" for such dual personalities. How can there be, when what society treats as "good" for people of a certain type is precisely what it treats as "bad" for other people, or vice versa? What is assertive and positive for Whites and males is often deemed aggressive and negative for Blacks and females. Anyone who is socialized into this society and belongs to even one outgroup will thus find themselves conflicted over at least some instances of good and bad, right and wrong. Writing more than 90 years ago, DuBois presciently explained how it was that African Americans who are proud of their African heritage necessarily confront the fact that that heritage is considered debased by mainstream American society. Those African Americans who try to take pride in their American heritage find themselves objects of suspicion within their own community, and are rarely granted full status as Americans by the mainstream. For such "dual personalities" there is always an alternative way of evaluating a given situation, character, or action. No fully developed subaltern self can possibly avoid such intrinsic duality.

The case of African Americans is perhaps an extreme one, based on literally centuries of cruel cultural history, but the psychological point made by DuBois is almost surely applicable in many other instances. Wherever selves grow up and identify with multiple aspects of their social milieu there should be some internal division of their value systems. After all, one may identify very closely with one's religion, one's gender, one's ethnic group—or all three together.

Antonio Gramsci—another intellectual from a highly marginalized group (in this case, Sardinians in Italy)—discussed the duality of values embodied in each individual's worldviews in his influential discussions of "hegemony" (Bocock, 1986). Gramsci, a political activist, was especially concerned with the question as to why subaltern individuals might come to internalize as "common sense" beliefs that could be demeaning to their selves (or worse). "One might almost say," Gramsci wrote of the average person, "that he has two theoretical consciousnesses (or one contradictory consciousness): one which is

implicit in his activity and which in reality unites him with all his fellow workers . . . ; and one, superficially explicit or verbal, which he has inherited from
the past and uncritically absorbed" (cited in Forgacs, 1988, p. 321). Gramsci
was one of the first social theorists to emphasize the role played by schools and
the media in reproducing not the entire range of values of a society, but a restricted subset of that range, a subset typically in line with the needs and as-
pirations of the dominant, not the subaltern members of the society.[1] And, like
DuBois, Gramsci emphasized the debilitating psychological effects of such internalized dual perspectives on right and wrong, good and bad: It is often the
case, he emphasized, that this "contradictory state of consciousness does not
permit of any action, any decision, or any choice, and produces a condition of
moral and political passivity" (Forgacs, 1988, p. 321). In my opinion, this is
one of the most incisive analyses of the problem of studying valuation in the
late 20th century. Having acknowledged the ubiquity and even necessity of plu-
ralism in values, we are not at all sure how to go about seeking a satisfactory
integration of often conflicting values.

As our century draws to a close, we all are increasingly aware of the fact that
no society is completely homogeneous. (Indeed, as Durkheim, 1894/1934,
long ago argued, all societies necessarily involve complex divisions of labor, but
modern postindustrialization has perhaps exacerbated these divisions.) Therefore, children growing up in any culture are exposed to multiple sets of values.
As Okin points out, referencing John Stuart Mill's (1869) trenchant analysis,
in traditional Western families there are often striking double standards in the
treatment of males and females, systematic and powerful differences that must
have profound effects on both boys and girls. Further, because differences
among families and individuals also vary in nonsystematic ways, due to such
variables as social status and temperament, different children in a given culture will often be exposed to different subsets of a culture's values. In modern
complex societies it is thus very likely that children raised in different social
sectors will grow up sharing very few values.

In the early decades of this century, DuBois and Gramsci urged us to start
asking how personalities reflect the complex divisions within societies, a task
that psychology has yet to take up, but that appears increasingly urgent in an
increasingly fragmented and aggressive world. Ambivalence, regret, contradictory thoughts, and impulses are just as much a part of the human personality as single-mindedness and dominant motives. As Ross and Ward suggest,
even people who are fairly strongly committed to an ideology can and do acknowledge doubts, problem cases, and complexities. Isn't it possible that one

---

[1] This is a theme more recently taken up by Chomsky (1989), who argued that, in modern mass
cultures, intellectuals as often as not reflect the ideology of dominant groups more than do ordi-
nary people, precisely because they are "better educated" and therefore have been exposed to
more of the (self-serving) rationales of those groups.

of the major contributions developmentalists could make is to understand what developmental factors tend to favor rigidity or versatility in an individual's approach to valuation?

CONCLUSION

If we are to truly overcome the Rousseauian framework that has so hobbled thinking about the development of the self we will need to learn how to treat self-development not as "receiving values instruction" or even "finding the values of one's culture," but as a genuine, often conflict-ridden, developmental process. Self-development is a complex process of appropriation and transformation of some of the values available in one's milieu, often under conditions of conflict, either over expediencies ("needs") or proprieties ("choices") or both. Under such conditions, individuals do not develop coherent systems of values, but clusters of valuations, some of which may undermine others. Indeed, as I have argued, many individuals will feel considerable ambivalence, even concerning their own core values. Throughout the course of development, these conflicts and ambivalences fuel developmental change. Within early development, the family setting can both structure basic patterns of evaluation (Užgiris) and create long-lasting conflicts (Okin, Turiel). As Nucci points out, the development of a personal domain tends to emerge from such processes of conflict and their resolution. Working with young adults, Ross and Ward found tendencies both toward the crystallization of certain core values and the acknowledgment of ambivalence and conflict concerning values. They also found a disturbing set of social relations that seems to favor the ossification of values and disfavor more exploratory patterns of developmental change.

However, even in what appear to be rigidifying contexts, the need to make concrete decisions about values may ultimately lead to major reorganizations of a person's attitudes and beliefs. For example, as Okin suggests, the traditional male who derogates "women's work" may come to change his mind after negotiation with a female partner and exposure to the benefits of his own performance of such work. I submit that such changes of mind are likely to have repercussions throughout a person's value system As James (1902) long ago emphasized in his discussion of "conversion," such cases of extreme changes in values usually involve the ascendancy of previously minor patterns of feeling and thought into major elements of one's stream of consciousness and action. If this analysis is correct, the major elements in one's stream of consciousness and action cannot be a single, coherent, set of values in most cases, because human social arrangements simply do not allow for such context-independent generalization. Rather, as Stocker (1990) emphasized, most people adhere to sets of plural and even conflicting values, a point especially emphasized by Brown (chapter 7, this volume). Such plurality may be manifest in different patterns of choice in different situations, or simply in various forms of second-guessing or even regret (Landman, 1993; Reed, 1994). As developmental psychologists, we need to understand the factors that serve to keep a personality open to exploration and growth in patterns of valuing.

ACKNOWLEDGMENTS

I thank my co-editors and Stan Gaines for very helpful critical comments on an earlier version of this chapter. The writing of this chapter was supported in part by a fellowship from the John Simon Guggenheim Foundation.

REFERENCES

Adolph, K., Eppler, M., & Gibson, E. J. (1994). Development of the perception of affordances. *Advances in Infancy, 8,* 52–98.

Basalla, J. (1989). *The evolution of technology.* New York: Cambridge University Press.

Bennett, J. (1993). *The book of virtues.* New York: Simon & Schuster.

Bocock, R. (1986). *Hegemony.* London: Tavistock.

Chomsky, N. (1989). *Necessary illusions: Thought control in democratic societies.* Boston: South End Press.

Dewey, J. (1991). *Experience and education, freedom and culture, theory of valuation, & essays: Volume 13 of the Later Works of John Dewey.* Carbondale & Edwardsville: University of Southern Illinois. (Original work published 1938)

DuBois, W. E. B. (1990). *The souls of Black folk.* New York: Library of America. (Original work published 1903)

Durkheim, E. (1934). *The division of labor in society.* New York: The Free Press. (Original work published 1894)

Fogel, A. (1993). *Developing through relationships.* Chicago: University of Chicago Press.

Forgacs, D. (1988). *Selected writings of Antonio Gramsci.* Boston: Schocken.

Gaines, S. O., & Reed, E. S. (1994). Two social psychologies of prejudice: Gordon Allport, W. E. B. DuBois, and the legacy of Booker T. Washington. *Journal of Black Psychology, 20,* 8–28.

Gaines, S. O., & Reed, E. S. (1995). Prejudice: From Allport to DuBois. *American Psychologist, 50,* 96–103.

Gibson, E. J. (1991). The perception of affordances: The renascence of functionalism. In E. J. Gibson, *An odyssey in learning and perception.* Cambridge, MA: MIT Press. (Original work published 1982)

Gibson, J. J. (1950). The implications of learning theory for social psychology. In J. G. Miller (Ed.), *Experiments in social process: A symposium on social psychology.* (pp. 149–167). New York: McGraw-Hill.

Gibson, J. J. (1986). *The ecological approach to visual perception.* Hillsdale, NJ: Lawrence Erlbaum Associates. (Original work published 1979)

Goudie, J. (1989). *The human impact* (3rd ed.). Cambridge, MA: MIT Press.

Goudsblom, J. (1994). *Fire.* New York: Allen Lane/Penguin.

Habermas, J. (1984). *The theory of communicative action.* Boston: Beacon.

Hegel, G. W. F. (1977). *The phenomenology of spirit* (A. V. Miller, Trans.). New York: Oxford University Press. (Original work published 1807)

Hendel, C. W. (1934). *Jean Jacques Rousseau: Moralist*. Indianapolis, IN: Bobbs Merrill.

James, W. (1902). *The variety of religious experiences*. New York: Holt.

Kohlberg, L. (1983). *Moral stages: A current formulation and reply to critics*. Basel: S. Karger.

Labov, W. (1972). *Sociolinguistic patterns*. Philadelphia: University of Pennsylvania Press.

Landman, J. (1993). *Regret*. New York: Oxford University Press.

Lewis, D. L. (1993). *W. E. B. DuBois: A biography* (Vol. 1). New York: Holt.

Marx, K., & Engels, F. (1974). *The German ideology*. Moscow: Progress. (Original work published 1845)

McCarthy, T. (1991). *Ideals and illusions*. Cambridge, MA: MIT Press.

Mill, J. S. (1869). *The subjection of women*. London: Longman.

Perles, C. (1977). *Préhistoire du feu* [The prehistory of fire]. Paris: Masson.

Pippin, R. B. (1989). *Hegel's idealism*. New York: Cambridge University Press.

Rawls, J. (1973). *A theory of justice*. Cambridge, MA: Harvard University Press.

Rawls, J. (1992). *Political liberalism*. New York: Columbia University Press.

Reed, E. S. (1988). *James J. Gibson and the psychology of perception*. New Haven, CT: Yale University Press.

Reed, E. S. (1994). Perceiving is to self as remembering is to selves. In U. Neisser & R. Fivush (Eds.), *The remembering self* (pp. 278–292). New York: Cambridge University Press.

Reed, E. S. (1995a). The challenge of historical materialist epistemology. In I. Parker & R. Spear (Eds.), *Psychology and Marxism: Coexistence and contradiction*. London: Pluto.

Reed, E. S. (1995b). The ecological approach to language learning. *Language and Communication, 15*, 1–29.

Reed, E. S. (in press). *Encountering the world: Towards an ecological psychology*. New York: Oxford University Press.

Riley, P. (1986). *The general will before Rousseau*. Princeton, NJ: Princeton University Press.

Rochat, P., & Reed, E. (1987). Le concept d'affordance et les connaissances du nourrisson [The concept of affordance and understanding in infants]. *Psychologie Française, 32*, 97–104.

Stern, D. (1994). The role of feelings for an interpersonal self. In U. Neisser (Ed.), *The perceived self: Ecological and interpersonal sources of self-knowledge* (pp. 205–215). New York: Cambridge University Press.

Stocker, M. (1990). *Plural and conflicting values*. Oxford, UK: Clarendon.

Sylvester-Bradley, B. (1991). Infancy as paradise. *Human Development, 34*, 35–54.

Trevarthen, C. (1994). The self born in intersubjectivity: The psychology of an infant communicating. In U. Neisser (Ed.), *The perceived self: Ecological and interpersonal sources of self-knowledge* (pp. 121–174). New York: Cambridge University Press.

Westerbrook, R. (1992). *John Dewey and American democracy*. Ithaca, NY: Cornell University Press.

2

Together and Apart:
The Enactment of Values in Infancy

Ina Č. Užgiris
Clark University

Human interactions necessarily partake of both the physical and social worlds, because humans are embodied beings living in spatial and temporal contexts. Nevertheless, research on children's development, especially during infancy, has tended to impose a conceptual split between children's experience with physical objects and their experience with people, suggesting two distinct spheres of understanding. In this context, Piaget's theory is often portrayed as being mainly concerned with the development of understanding in relation to the physical world. One of my goals in this chapter is to show that human actions, especially early in development, encompass both physical and social dimensions and that Piaget's theoretical framework does not preclude consideration of experience in the social realm.

Discussions of children's development with respect to the social world are often still predicated on the assumption that autonomous beings gradually come into relationships and form knowledge of those relationships (Youniss, 1983). The focus is on how the individual child becomes integrated into various social groupings, takes on roles, and learns the rules while maintaining a basic separateness, individual identity, and actualization of personal goals. Rousseau's classic view of the child as needing only benevolent ambience for self-sufficient unfolding forms the background for considerable thinking about human development (cf. Guisinger & Blatt, 1994).

My starting point is similar to that of others who have argued against treating the individual and society as independent entities that are brought together only gradually in the course of development. The central term for me is *inter-*

action, and a foregrounding of interaction requires that both the individual and society be viewed as mutually constructed. In this chapter, I consider how the web of ever-changing ongoing relations in which infants and children partici- pate translates into more lasting, organized dispositions with development. This construction has dimensions not only of structural complexity and prag- matic efficacy, but also of value.

In subsequent sections, I briefly review some conceptions of human infancy, contrasting the view of the infant as a being to be gradually brought into the world of human relationships with a view of the infant as part of interpersonal relationships from the beginning. The latter view gives great importance to communication, and I present some illustrations from the research literature to concretize my case. Finally, I outline some suggestions for how the cultur- ally and interpersonally situated activities of infancy create a foundation for symbolic representations of constructed tacit understandings that are already imbued with the dimension of value.

CONCEPTIONS OF INFANCY

Although infants are currently described as participating in genuinely social interactions (Richards, 1974), their understanding is initially assumed to be di- vided into that pertaining to the world of objects and that pertaining to the world of people (Schaffer, 1984). For example, play with objects is usually stud- ied separately from play with people and perception of objects' characteristics separately from their human uses. Because, in fact, the physical and social do- mains overlap, it is tempting to try to reduce one to the other. Either the in- fant's interest in people is connected with perceptual preferences for visual contrasts, moving forms, and need gratifications, or the infant's interest in shapes and sounds is connected with the inherent presence of such features during social interactions.

This distinction between the physical and the social is deeply ingrained in Western thought, but it is not a distinction that is self-evident. It is constructed in different ways by different cultural communities, and infants need to con- struct it gradually in accord with its understanding in their cultural group. Therefore, an alternative stance is to recognize that the social and physical worlds are intermingled, especially for an infant, and to view the very young infant's actions as directed to a common, complex reality.

It is often claimed that the infant in Piaget's theory is directed toward the world of physical objects, forms an understanding of the physical world, and only slowly, by extension, comes to understand a social reality. Thus, those who consider the social world to be important from the outset, and in a nonderiv- ative way, find Piaget's theory inadequate for treating social development (Tre- varthen, 1980). It is true that in his formal statements, Piaget generally used examples from children's activities with physical objects. However, the actual episodes cited in Piaget's infancy books show a recognition of infants' social engagement. For example, in describing the beginnings of visual exploration, Piaget (1952) commented on Laurent's looking at his mother, his nurse, and Piaget himself, "with a change of attitude when confronted with each new face" and suggested that already in the second month, "the familiar faces have become fraught with meaning" (p. 69). It is claimed that Piaget's neglect of the child's social experience is a real neglect, but not a denial of its relevance. It is a gap in the theory that is not necessitated by the overall framework and can be remedied without changing the theory in a fundamental way. In my view, an examination of early development with respect to the whole nexus of social and nonsocial objects is worthwhile and can be carried forward within the Piagetian perspective.

A recognition that aspects of the social permeate infants' experience from the beginning suggests that considerations of value are not totally inappropriate for understanding development in infancy. Values of whatever kind basically imply standards. Even though there is a large gap between sensorimotor action in the here and now, taken to characterize infancy, and the regulation of action in terms of certain kinds of standards, knowable separately from concrete action, all organized activities entail standards. Value is implied in the directionality of action and in the repetition of action to reduce incongruity. Moreover, if the infant is viewed not as an isolated being, but as a participant in interpersonal relationships, reciprocal feedback between infant and Other can be considered to help structure what becomes known as well as what becomes good.

My general aim is to suggest that considerations of value are quite pertinent to a comprehensive conceptualization of development during infancy. The motivational aspect of Piaget's equilibration theory suggests one starting point; the reciprocal communication at the core of interpersonal relationships among people, including relationships with preverbal infants, suggests another. An assumption that the foundation of tacit knowledge constructed during infancy is relevant to subsequent symbolic and reflective functioning implies a form of continuity across structural transformations that may merit exploration. In these different ways, personal and societal value orientations come together to form the texture of human activities in which infants participate.

INFANT AS BIOLOGICAL ORGANISM

Biological Nature of Early Functioning

In contrast to an interactional perspective, those approaching infancy from psychodynamic and ethological positions (e.g., Als, 1979; Bowlby, 1969; Emde, Gaensbauer, & Harmon, 1976; Mahler, Pine, & Bergman, 1975) emphasize the largely biological nature of infant adaptation and functioning during the first few months of life. This view is implicit in questions such as when does the infant become a self, when does intentional action begin, when does actual rather than imputed communication with caregivers appear, when does the infant become active rather than reactive toward the environment, and so on (McCall, Eichorn, & Hogarty, 1977; Schaffer, 1984). The problem is not the assertion of highly important changes in infant functioning during the first year of life, but the assumption of discontinuity in the relevance of biological and experiential determinants for infant behavior.

This position is also sometimes attributed to Piaget, because he discussed the continuity between biological and psychological functioning and described human intelligence as an instrument of adaptation. Especially in *Biology and Knowledge* (1971), Piaget portrayed human intelligence as functionally related to the instincts and habits of other organisms. At issue is not the functional continuity envisaged by Piaget, but the tendency to think of biological structures largely in terms of constraints. In my view, Piaget himself was quite clear in presenting the biologically organized adaptations not as constraining, but as enabling certain kinds of function; this much is true of any structure. For human infants, the biologically organized adaptations present at birth do not limit the infant to biological reactivity, but enable psychologically distinctive functioning in the context of a human world. These adaptations carry possibilities for action, only some of which may be actualized in specific human contexts.

Because Piaget's theory requires some organized structures for psychological functioning to begin, certain biologically organized behavioral patterns are singled out as the initial structures for infant functioning. However, Piaget's biologically readied schemata for initiating the development of human intelligence are an interesting selection from all the reflexes and responses shown by human newborns. They consist of complex patterns of activity such as looking and vocalizing that function in dynamic coregulation with the available reality. For example, even though an infant's repertoire for vocalization is constrained, it opens a whole range of possibilities for responsive interactions with specific others in discrete contexts, patterned in accord with cultural standards. In Piaget's discussion of these biologically readied behavioral organizations, the limitations that they impose on what the infant can know seem secondary to the fact that they enable the infant to engage with the world not in a rigid manner, but in a dynamic way, that is open to modification through the continual interplay of assimilation and accommodation.

The question that needs addressing is how the interplay of assimilation and accommodation is linked to needs, feelings, and goals. Most theorists concerned with early development, including Piaget, credit infants with the ability to distinguish positive and negative valence, to recognize what is satisfying from what is unpleasant (cf. Baldwin, 1902). This is usually tied to the infant's biological heritage, as a necessity for survival. In addition, Piaget assigned a positive valence to activity in the manner of K. Bühler's (1922) *Funktionlust*. Activity is thought to instigate further activity as it feeds back to existing structures. The motivating nature of activity taken together with the kinds of biologically readied behavioral patterns highlighted by Piaget—looking, listening, vocalizing, sucking, and grasping—suggests that the Piagetian infant can be viewed as prepared for intrinsically instigated, directional, and affectively modulated engagement as a true partner with the surrounding world.

Uniformity of Developmental Course

The period of infancy is also portrayed as having an essential similarity across all circumstances that are at least minimally adequate. It is suggested that infant development is strongly canalized (Scarr, 1983), that is, that any induced variation from the expected pattern is quickly corrected by biologically given processes. Evidence of greater stability of individual differences as well as their increasing connection to life's circumstances following the period of infancy is cited to support this view. Interestingly the position that infancy is a well-buffered period is usually taken in regard to intellectual development, but not personality development. Moreover, a uniform definition of an adequate environment is proposed that includes specific family arrangements (e.g., a single main caregiver) characteristic of certain historical times and places. Such views may have a strong ideological component (Okin, 1989).

Piaget's theory is sometimes seen as in line with this buffered view of infancy, because of its emphasis on the generalizable features of human functioning. The notion of homeorhesis, introduced by Piaget (1971) to underline the cohesion of knowledge structures over the course of development highlights the self-regulatory nature of these structures, but it does not deny their particularization due to functioning. It seems to me that uniformity of developmental sequence need not be asserted at the level of constituent schemes for the overall integrity of Piaget's edifice. The constructivist project implies sequential regularity and emergence of qualitatively different organizations from constituent elements, but it does not necessarily require a full complement of constituent elements or their identity in each instance. Both cultural values and infant interests create the texture of actual interactions. Piaget's theory can be expanded to consider strands and variations arising within different contexts of development without giving up the essential frame of structural organization.

My interpretation is that activity, structural organization, a dynamic interaction with the world, and qualitatively distinctive reorganizations are essential to Piaget's theoretical enterprise. Other emphases given in his numerous expositions are not always essential. A number of considerations that have lately taken on considerable importance, as, for example, social and cultural dimensions of experience, were not given prominence by Piaget, but are not thereby incompatible with his overall position. The approach taken by M. Chapman (1988) in his exposition of the Piagetian perspective seems highly desirable: to start revisions from a sympathetic understanding of the theory. Piaget's approach needs elaboration and extension in many areas, but if it contains openings to allow for such extensions, then it is precisely these openings that make it valuable. In my own work, my goal has been to extend the Piagetian approach so as to deliberately give a much more central role to interpersonal activities in early development.

INFANT IN INTERPERSONAL PERSPECTIVE

The Personal Relation

My starting point is the assumption that infant development takes place in relation to Other (Užgiris, 1984, 1989). The formulation of this position by the philosopher Macmurray (1961), who made the personal relation fundamental to human existence, has greatly influenced my thinking. He wrote:

> Thus, human experience is, in principle, shared experience; human life, even in its most individual elements, is a common life; and human behaviour carries always, in its inherent structure, a reference to the personal Other. All this may be summed up by saying that the unit of personal existence is not the individual, but two persons in personal relation, and that we are persons not by individual right, but in virtue of our relation to one another. The personal is constituted by personal relatedness. The unit of the personal is not the "I," but the "You and I." (p. 61)

Macmurray claimed that infants develop as human beings in a personal relation to others. The personal relation is fundamental, and out of this relation both self and other are constructed. For me, this is an essential assumption, because it defines the infant's field of experience as constructed jointly with another person. It means that the personal functioning of an Other—the intentions, judgments, and valuations of others—are part of the reality in which the infant functions. This jointly constructed reality is where infant actions unfold. Although Macmurray spoke of the mother as being the first Other for the infant, his perspective requires only that it be a person caring enough to relate to the infant as a person, not as an object. Most studies of early interactions have focused on infants and their mothers, but it is clear that similar interactions can occur with fathers, siblings, and other persons.

Psychological theorizing about interpersonal development tends to assume that each participant must possess certain capacities to make relating possible. Thus, the infant must have intentionality, or agency, or intersubjectivity first, and only then interpersonal relations can begin; they are made a consequent of individual development. However, if the field of interpersonal activity is thought to be jointly constructed, then the infant does not have to be an equally contributing partner to partake of the experience made possible through interpersonal interaction (Užgiris, 1989).

The Centrality of Communication

A joint field of experience presumes communication between the participants. My assumption is that preverbal communication occurs in infancy and that communication through nonverbal means is very important throughout human development. Its centrality was pointed out by Macmurray (1961):

> In the human infant—and this is the heart of the matter—the impulse to communicate is his sole adaptation to the world into which he is born. Implicit and unconscious it may be, yet it is sufficient to constitute the mother–child relation as the basic form of human existence, as a personal mutuality, as a "You and I" with a common life. For this reason the infant is born a person and not an animal. (p. 60)

Macmurray did not equate communication with language; rather it is "our ability to share our experience with another and so to constitute and participate in a common experience" (1961, p. 60). Affectivity, action contours, and the patterning of exchanges during interaction are a means for communication without explicit symbols.

Considerable research has provided a rich description of the facial expressions, vocal patternings, bodily movements, and postures that serve as meaningful guides to the coordination of action with an Other (e.g., Stern, 1985). This is fundamentally important to my case. I am presuming not only that an adult is able to understand the infant's expressions and to impute meaning to them, thereby helping the infant to construct socially meaningful signals out of originally noncommunicative acts, but that the infant at the outset finds certain aspects of the Other's actions meaningful when they are carried out together with the infant. This does not imply that the infant interprets the Other's actions with the full range of meanings apprehended by adults in that culture. Nor does this imply that the infant's actions have a transparent meaning for the Other. Both the infant and the Other construct meaning out of the conjoining of acts, in which the acts of Other and of the self define each other in the immediate context. This communication with the Other is deemed important not only for constructing interpersonal relations, but for the development of knowledge overall, because all the infant's activities take place in an interpersonally constructed field of action.

Tacit Knowledge in Infancy

The knowledge constructed during infancy is knowledge embedded in action; to borrow a phrase from the philosopher Polanyi (1964), it may be called *tacit knowledge*. Although prevailing in infancy, it is a kind of knowledge that continues to be constructed throughout life. Polanyi used the examples of skills and connoisseurship to discuss its nature. It is knowledge that is typically gained through coparticipation in certain kinds of activities with another who is more knowledgeable or expert. Only some of this kind of knowledge can be symbolized through various symbol systems or captured by formalisms. Often, it is knowledge that is more easily demonstrated than described.

Piaget (1962) explored in considerable detail how symbols are progressively constructed in action during infancy and then reconstituted as mental symbols through reflection to the representational plane, thus creating a strand of continuity between action knowledge and symbolically represented knowledge. More recently, the relations of represented knowledge and knowledge-in-use have been examined through research on procedures (Brown & Weiss, 1987). However, for my case here, I want to emphasize two other aspects of this action-based knowledge. First, symbolization of action-based knowledge is probably never complete or exhaustive. Tacit knowledge is richer than knowledge formulated in reflective thought because it includes the parameters of action coordination, the specifications for a here-and-now embodiment of general schemes. Second, different cultures, traditions, or styles of interpersonal relating may favor the symbolization of some aspects of this tacit knowledge over others. Children's different modes of participation in cultural activities are being examined in the work of Rogoff and her colleagues (Rogoff, 1993; Rogoff, Mistry, Göncü, & Mosier, 1993), showing that there is variation across cultural groups in what is made explicit.

Such tacit knowledge may be a source of a sense of "rightness" about certain actions derived from an implicit standard that may not be easily accessible to reflective thought. Among cultural groups, there may be a shared understanding of how to carry out such interpersonal activities as praising, consoling, approaching, or leaving that is not fully stated in any rules of conduct. Thus, actions carried out in accordance with an explicit set of rules may not have the same degree of "fittedness," because they include different tacit understandings.

Emotion in Communication

It is being increasingly recognized that emotion has an important communicative function. Emotional states permeate the body and are a constituent of interpersonal actions, giving them distinctive contours and patternings. Although emotions can be reflected on and communicated symbolically, they are primarily realized as bodily changes that modulate ongoing activities. Lyon (1994) drew together many sources to support the position that emotion, conceived not as an inner experience, but as a fact of our embodiment and our functioning, serves to regulate interpersonal interactions throughout life. She drew on evidence from cultural history to show how the meaning of bodily processes is socially constructed and went on to discuss the interpersonal synchronization of bodily processes such as breathing that may occur during emotion-laden activities (e.g., chanting or dance).

With respect to infancy, it is generally accepted that even neonates have different arousal states and patterns of bodily organization, but they are not necessarily credited with a range of differentiated emotions. Even so, some range of affective tone permeates their activities and is an aspect of interpersonal coregulation. The communicative aspect of emotion is undoubtedly important, and it has been emphasized in descriptions of mutual regulation with preverbal infants (Trevarthen, 1979). Another aspect of affective interaction is equally important for this discussion. The interpersonal relations in which infants participate have distinctive affective contours that derive from the particular participants as well as from cultural understandings of specific activities. My suggestion is that these contours become known both tacitly and reflectively and thereby permeate the organization of knowledge in general. Being derived from interpersonal relations, they may become constituents in the construction of standards for the good as well as the expected.

SOME RELEVANT PIAGETIAN CONCEPTS

Before presenting a few specific illustrations of the multilayered functioning of infants, I want to discuss a few Piagetian concepts, so as to link my ideas with Piaget's theory. My goal is to proceed in the spirit of extending and elaborating Piagetian theory rather than contradicting it.

Action Scheme

The starting point for my thinking is action; therefore, the main concept that I want to discuss is the action scheme. It is clearly a fundamental concept in Piaget's theory. An action scheme is already a structure, but it is an open structure, subject to differentiation and to coordination into more complex structures. Piaget (1971) defined action schemata as "whatever, in action, can thus be transposed, generalized, or differentiated from one situation to another; in other words, whatever there is in common between various repetitions or superpositions of the same action" (p. 7). In an earlier work dealing with the development of symbolic representation, Piaget (1962) stated that schemes "are systems of relationships susceptible of progressive abstraction and generalization" (p. 99).

For example, we may speak of a grasping scheme. Across instances of grasping actions, the actual movements involved vary, depending on the distance of what is to be grasped, its size, the position of our body, the presence of an instrument, and so forth. However, there is a basic pattern derived from action

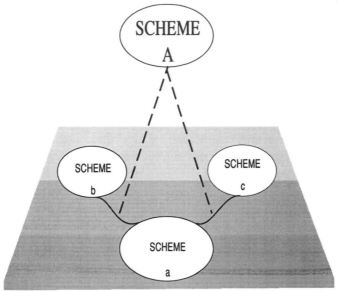

FIG. 2.1.   An illustration of Coordination Scheme A derived from relations between schemes.

that constitutes the meaning of grasping and serves as the organization of symbolic activities of a similar kind, to support such notions as the metaphoric grasping of ideas, or, grasping to different levels of consciousness.

The notion of action scheme grounds the invariant functions of assimilation and accommodation and provides the simplest examples for understanding equilibration in the construction of knowledge. Through the interdependent functions of assimilation and accommodation, the action scheme serves as a kind of standard for what is relevant and what is interesting at any moment in development. What can be assimilated in some manner is relevant and generates value for that part of reality that supports the functioning of the scheme. There must be some assimilatory scheme for meaning to exist; there must be modifiability in the scheme for the meaningful interaction to have long-term importance.

To talk about an individual scheme, however, is really to misrepresent the thrust of Piaget's theory. A scheme makes sense only in coordination with other schemes, as part of a larger structure. Although it is congenial to talk about patterns of action as constituted by a single scheme, it may be more accurate to conceive of schemes as coordinated into subsystems that are integrated into larger systems, in the manner of Koestler's (1967) holons. The stabilized coordinations between action schemes also become schematized and, at higher levels of organization, compose those structures. Figure 2.1 is an attempt to illustrate the derivation of new schemes from the coordinations among existing ones. Assuming that the coordination between Schemes a and b, a and c, and so on have a certain commonality, then that commonality may become Scheme A. The Coordination Scheme A then functions as other schemes, assimilating and accommodating relevant reality.

Although not at great length, Piaget discussed the logic of action in terms of such coordination schemes. For example, consider the scheme of joining. If we differentiate it into concrete actions, it may include acts of taking, putting together, and maintaining the connection that comes to be established. Minimally, it encompasses the coordination of at least three schemes and can be thought to be an integration of those coordinations. It is precisely the integration of those coordinations into the scheme of joining that allows it to be reflected to a symbolic level so that we come to mentally join all sorts of realities. It is these coordination schemes that seem to be central to Piaget's (1970) idea that relations of sequence, of inclusion, of magnitude, and so on, embedded in actions, give a foundation to logic.

Coordination schemes may derive from interpersonal activities as well. For example, relations between actions constituting engagement, modulation of engagement, and disengagement may result in a coordination scheme. As interpersonal activities are carried out jointly, they involve selection from among possibilities through negotiation of a shared goal or of the means to a goal. Thus, the construction of coordination schemes may provide one path for the value dimension permeating interactions to become conserved in knowledge structures.

Interest

The notion of scheme is also linked to Piaget's concept of interest. Although Piaget attributed inherent activity to the schemes on the basis of a need to function, he also introduced the concept of interest to explain the directionality of actions. For example, with respect to visual activity, Piaget (1952) related interest to the functioning of assimilatory schemes as follows: "The subject looks neither at what is too familiar, because he is in a way surfeited with it, nor at what is too new because this does not correspond to anything in his schemata" (p. 68). In a more general vein, Piaget (1952) wrote:

> This interest in novelty, therefore—however paradoxical this assertion may seem—results from assimilation itself. If the new object or phenomenon had no connection with the schemata of assimilation they would not be of interest and that is why, in fact, they arouse nothing in a child who is too young. . . . Whereas, to the extent that they are almost assimilable, they rouse an interest and an attempt at accommodation still greater than if they were assimilable immediately. That is why, the more complex the system of the schemata of assimilation, the greater the interest in novelty in general. New events have the more opportuni-

ties of animating at least one particular schema according as the ensemble of the schemata formed is large. (pp. 276–277)

In his later writings on equilibration, Piaget elaborated the discrepancy notion and proposed several ways of dealing with perturbations (ignoring, distortion, and incomplete assimilation), but did not abandon the idea of a tie between the system of assimilatory structures and interest. A need, including a need to function, is manifest as interest (Piaget, 1985). But because schemes differentiate and change as a result of functioning, interest also depends on previous constructions. My point is to emphasize that those previous activities need to be thought of as carried out in conjunction with others, either directly or indirectly.

Manner of Action

Insofar as coordinations between schemes also become schematized, I want to suggest that certain aspects of activity that may be called the *manner* of carrying out actions are also embedded in such coordinations and may come to be schematized. Activity can be characterized by such aspects as expansiveness, tempo, rhythmicity, synchrony in relation to others, and so on that recur across interactions in different contexts. As Fig. 2.2 shows, the coordination of Scheme a and b, Scheme a and c, and so on, may yield a coordination scheme such as joining. In addition, an action contour in the coordination of Scheme a and e, Scheme c and f, and so on (e.g., pace of action, affective tone), may

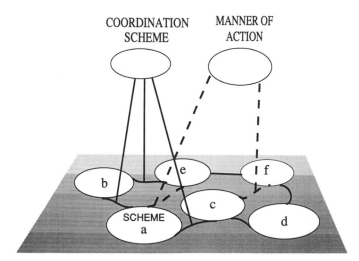

FIG. 2.2.   An illustration of a Manner of Action Scheme as one type of coordination scheme.

result in a coordination scheme for the commonality inherent in those contours that I am referring to here as the manner of action.

It seems possible that schemes pertaining to the manner of acting also generate interests. Carrying out actions in a particular manner comes to be valued and discrepancies from that manner may be noted. This may provide a context for reading Piaget's statement that "values *enrich* action. This may be in terms of force; but more than anything else, it is a functional enrichment in that valued objects and people provide the subject with new goals" (Piaget, 1981, p. 43).

Thus, the notion of interest bridges the relation of the infant's individual and interpersonal existence. Assimilatory schemes organize the acts of the infant; they provide directionality to the infant's behavior, imbuing relevance to aspects of the infant's environment. On the other hand, insofar as the infant is in relation with an Other, the environment that is most accessible to the infant is organized by the intentions, beliefs, and values of the Other. What is available to become of interest to the infant is negotiated with the Other, but what is right for the infant's schemes to maintain interest depends on the structure of the schemes. In the interplay of goals (infant's and Other's) within the interpersonal relation, the roots of satisfaction appear linked to the infant's assimilatory schemes as they develop in the context of a cultural understanding of personal existence.

Interest and Interaction

Piaget's notion of interest was elaborated by Hunt (1980) as the notion of "the match" in his motivational theory for cognitive development. Hunt conceived of intrinsic motivation as tied to discrepancy, with a moderate degree of discrepancy from what is familiar being most motivating of attempts at understanding. However, Hunt explicitly recognized that the familiar was a moving target in the course of development and, therefore, searched for ways to recognize optimal discrepancy. He discussed "the problem of the match" as the challenge faced by caregivers to keep discrepancy within the optimal range for children to remain interested and engaged. The twist that is important to me is the role given by Hunt to communication. Hunt suggested that the way caregivers can solve the problem of the match is to attend to communicative signals indicating interest, boredom, or frustration. Interacting so as to maintain signs of interest was the way to foster infant development. Hunt did not view the communication between infant and caregiver reciprocally and did not take into account how the caregiver's communications regarding the infant's actions may also direct interest and modulate effort and engagement. From an interpersonal perspective, the centrality of communication in personal relations suggests that interest needs to be viewed as formed bidirectionally, in the confluence of activities of both participants.

FIG. 2.3.   The relation of interest to the contour of actions.

Figure 2.3 illustrates my proposals so far. The structure of schemes at some given time is the basis for generating selective interest in activities. Interest has motivational aspects and gives directionality to activity. At the same time, being embodied and organizing the postures, rhythms, and facial expressions of the person, it has a communicative aspect relevant to interpersonal interaction. The communicative aspect also contributes to the manner of activity. Figure 2.3 depicts these two aspects of interest, but not the interplay between the interests of the participants in any interpersonal interaction. The ensuing common activity and its manner would depend on coregulation, relying on communication to negotiate both the directionality and manner of the joint activity.

SOME ILLUSTRATIONS FROM RESEARCH

To illustrate the preceding statements claiming that infants function in relationships with others within particular cultural contexts, and that the dimension of value is entailed in that functioning, I briefly describe some lines of research that seem relevant and lend support to these ideas.

Together With Others

The first line of research pertains to the rather elaborate interpersonal interactions between young infants and their caregivers observed in Western middle-class families (e.g., Stern, 1977). They have been described by numerous investigators as face-to-face engagements that involve interpretation of attentiveness, feelings, needs, and desires of one participant by the other, with ensuing adjustments toward mutual acknowledgment, if not fulfillment. The verbal statements of the adult are the easiest to follow, but they are enveloped by various nonverbal signals; the infant's contributions are all nonverbal. The adult's statements usually refer to the infant's likes, wishes, and intentions, but sometimes also describe their own. Although some see in these statements only pretend conversations, evidence is accumulating to support a significant contribution on the infant's part as well.

In one of our studies (Kruper & Užgiris, 1987) of 3- and 9-month-old infants interacting face-to-face with one of their parents, we found that both mothers and fathers talked about their infants' subjective state, suggested consonant activities, and offered the infant choices in regulating shared activity. They made more comments about their infants' feelings and wishes when interacting with the 3-month-olds than with the older infants. It is possible to interpret this difference as indicating that communication with the younger infants required more effort and the manner for proceeding through disagreements or affirming joint interests was less well-established. The communications of the older infants may have been clearer, requiring less overt deliberation by the parents.

These kinds of interactions have been extensively studied by Papoušek and Papoušek (1991) and their collaborators. They suggest that these interactions reveal the mutual adaptation of the infant and caregiver over the course of evolution so as to facilitate infant development, calling these patterns *intuitive parenting*. My interpretation of their work may not mesh in all respects with theirs, but their observations beautifully document the communicative richness of these early interactions.

They have described how the infant's facial expressions, gestures, and vocalizations provide important information for the caregivers, which is interpreted in consistent ways (Papoušek, Papoušek, & Harris, 1987). Similarly, parents respond to infant communications in ways that are meaningful to the infant. For example, melodic contours and stress patterns of adult vocalizations contain regularities that may help infants organize such communications. Papoušek and Papoušek (1991) reported that while interacting with 2-month-old infants, mothers use distinct melodic contours for different interactive contexts in a similar way across cultures. For example, mothers use rising contours to encourage attention and participation by the infant, falling or bell-shaped contours to acknowledge smiles, pleasant vocalizations or other positive infant acts, and brief, steeply falling contours at a high pitch to discourage fussiness or other unwanted acts. Although the Papoušeks emphasized contextual distinctiveness irrespective of culture, they also reported some cross-cultural differences in degree of melodic expansions and pitch variations. It is just such differences, manifest across contexts, that may be integrated as the manner for carrying out specific acts.

Through such communications, infants construct interpersonally meaningful ways of greeting, playing, teasing, leave-taking, and so forth. This happens in the first year of life and does not depend on verbal aspects of language. Moreover, as Halliday (1975) showed, intonation continues to be relevant to the child even when beginning to use verbal language for communication. In describing intonational patterns, studies usually emphasize the typical patterns characteristic of specific pragmatic functions such as drawing attention to something or questioning a state of affairs. Within interpersonal relationships, characteristics of intonational contours may also come to reflect patterns of relating in the same way as typical intonations reflect conventional communication functions.

Another important fact of the early communication system is affective expression, not only through the face and voice, but also through general bodily action. The possibility of such affective communication is important in two respects. Infants' interests that motivate the pursuit of different activities can be communicated to others and receive either encouragement or opposition. The value orientations of parents will influence their interpretation of infant interests. In turn, parents' interests will influence the opportunities that they give to infants to pursue different activities. For example, Kaye (1979) described how mothers try to maximize or minimize specific emotional states during face-to-face interactions by modulating the way they mirror back infant expressive behaviors. The significant point is that the availability of this nonverbal communication system permits negotiation and mutual regulation toward some and away from other activities. This also implies that certain kinds of coordinations among schemes become more likely in some cultural groups and contribute to the body of tacit knowledge shared by the participants.

In addition, valuations often apply not to activities as such, but to the manner of carrying them out. Action contours such as intensity, redundancy, definitiveness, expressiveness, and so on constitute the manner of carrying out specific activities. Being tied to action, understandings with respect to manner are likely to be negotiated early in life through the nonverbal communication system. They may also be examples of coordinating schemes that do not get completely represented in symbolic thought.

My second illustration pertains to the cultural framing of early interactions. We tend to assume that the dyadic interaction pattern is typical of interactions between young infants and adults. However, this does not seem to be the case the world over. Studies of infancy in other cultures show that face-to-face interaction of the type practiced in middle-class Western families is not present in cultures in which interactions between a young infant and other people are discouraged or in which the baby is typically held outward to face the world together with the caregiver. This does not mean that nonverbal communication does not occur, only that it does not take the same form; and that is the point.

For example, Japanese mothers tend to favor soothing and quieting activities and coordinate more subdued interactions with their infants (Clancy, 1986; Fogel, Toda, & Kawai, 1988). Similarly, Gusii mothers in Kenya structure their interactions around control of the infant's attentiveness and favor nonvocal means to do so (Dixon, Tronick, Keefer, & Brazelton, 1981). My point is that through the nonverbal communication system, the manner of carrying out interpersonal activities begins to be regulated in accord with cultural values and personal inclinations from the earliest months of life.

The manner of interpersonal activities is also related to the structure of early interactions. Ramirez (1993) observed toddler play in the family setting in her native Colombia and in the United States. She observed play activities in families with a 19- to 21-month-old toddler and at least one older sibling when the whole family was present. Among other findings, she observed that the dyadic unit was the preferred organization for play in middle-class U.S. families. When there were two children, mother and father tended to pair off and each play with one of the children. In contrast, in the Colombian families, the most prevalent structure was a pair of active participants with an observer, who at any moment could become active and shift the interaction into a group structure. In such simple organizations of play, we can see both a reflection of cultural values for interpersonal relations, the induction of the infant into such relations, the infant's gaining knowledge of how to organize acts within each kind of interaction structure, and the incorporation of value considerations in the organization of these kinds of understandings. Thus, Ramirez found differences in the two cultures with respect to symmetry or asymmetry in interpersonal relations and encouragement of individuality or group cohesion within the context of play. The point is that although we become capable of these various kinds of human interactions in all cultures, we connect them with somewhat different valuations, depending on the prevailing standard in the culture. At the level of action, we form somewhat different configurations of schemes that may contribute to our feeling of "fittedness" about one manner of interacting compared to another.

Moreover, we do not have to look to faraway cultures to observe differences in the manner and organization of simple interpersonal activities. Heath (1983) documented how different the experiences of infants born into three geographically close communities in the southeastern United States can be. These differences stem not only from differences in the material provisions made for infants in these three communities, but even moreso from conceptions about the place of the infant within the family group, the preference for interpersonal and independent activities, the value placed on scheduling and ordering of life, and the value placed on such types of verbal communications as reporting, planning, entertaining, and so on. The detailed descriptions of family interactions provided by Heath help to explain how such modulations create distinctly textured webs of interpersonal relations within which growth and development are realized.

The Child Apart

The preceding examples illustrate the centrality of communication with others in early human development. Yet it is clear that the child does not spend all the hours of the day in the company of a caregiver, and that the time spent alone varies greatly across cultures. In the United States, observations show that toddlers spend about two thirds of their waking time alone, engaged in what we call playing, although they may be within sight and earshot of a caregiver who intervenes when necessary (e.g., White & Watts, 1973). What is happening when the child seems alone?

My idea is that during the time of acting alone, the child sets goals and attempts to achieve them on her own, but not necessarily out of relation with the Other. This might be considered the time for integration, for the consolidation of structures of knowledge.

Let me take just two examples. Many have observed children to repeat a fortuitously obtained result numerous times in an apparent attempt to understand it. Preyer (1893) observed his child lift and drop an object 119 times in a row. Piaget (1952) also reported numerous instances of his children repeating an action such as flipping up a box or striking an object with a stick in an apparent attempt to understand the effect. In everyday language, we would call this practice, but it is not necessarily the simple practice of a skill. It is the practice of running through patterns of schemes with variation. The importance is that the pattern gets consolidated and can serve as a meaning structure in subsequent activities.

To use the language of equilibration, the repetition of the complex scheme with variation allows the filling in of gaps and the extension of assimilatory possibilities to a greater range of instances. In that sense, it can be viewed as a verification procedure, a checking out by the child that something really works the way it worked the first time and that the procedural knowledge is firm. Being firm, it can also come to be symbolically represented.

However, these repetitions are not carried out without reference to the attitudes of the Other. Although Piaget did not report on them, it is exactly these kinds of consolidations that most often result in referencing looks and invitations to the Other to share in the child's satisfaction with her accomplishment (Cohen, 1987). Within the possibilities of conflict between the knowledge of how something works and the knowledge of whether it is valued or not may begin the differentiation of "that's how it is" and "that's what is good," of cognitive and moral knowledge. In that sense, to the extent that Piaget was more focused on the child working alone rather than in interaction with others, his theory may be said to have been focused more on cognitive knowledge than ethical knowledge.

Another example is of verbal monologues that children who begin to speak conduct when alone. The published collection of Emily's monologues (Nelson,

1989) analyzed from several angles provides an insight into Emily's efforts to consolidate her understandings in language. Although the strings of repetitions contained in those monologues are in some ways more meaningful to us than the action repetitions practiced by children from early infancy, they can be viewed as related. In all these instances, the child works on establishing relations between different schemes or meaning structures through the sorting out of variations that those combinations of schemes accommodate. What is to be noted in these kinds of records is that the patterns worked on are multifaceted, and the Other as the observer or addressee of the monologue is generally evident, making these seemingly individual actions interactive and dialogic in character.

A Caveat

Having written all this, I am concerned that a very rosy picture of early development is constructed. This might be a reflection of our cultural values as much as is the idea of individual self-sufficiency. In our descriptions, mothers are generally caring, interested, and involved with their infants; the infants are responsive and communicative as long as someone takes an interest in them. Yet obviously this is not always true. Stern (1985) pointed out that there is room for pathology during early interactions. Due to her own problems, a mother may not recognize, reflect back, and legitimate certain of her child's interests. Similarly, a child may make it very difficult for the parent to enter the process of communication as a result of some physical impairment such as blindness or a disorder like autism.

Studies of early interactions tend to highlight the positive dimension. However, early interactions include disagreement, frustration, conflict, and other aspects of negativity (Bradley, 1991), which come to be constructed in the same way as the positive aspects of relationships. Moreover, even in normal, healthy relationships, the overall positive tone covers much day-to-day variation. I think this variation is important because without it, there would not be the contrasts for the value dimension to come to the fore. Because there are contrasts between times of sadness and times of happiness, between easy understanding and baffled giving up, and between encouraged initiatives and abruptly denied intentions, the relations of joy, puzzlement, success, and denial can be constructed and provide a foundation for their symbolic elaboration. The child–caregiver relationship is the field for constructing the schemes for carrying out activities with another and for acting in the world when the other is not physically present.

To summarize these ideas, Figure 2.4 illustrates the dimensions of cultural understandings, interests, communications, and interpersonal coregulations in the construction of action schemes of an infant in relation to an Other. It is meant to suggest that cultural practices permeate communication patterns, interests, and schemes of action. However, they permeate them as a dimension of activity and, therefore, can become part of the knowledge structures in their own right. Yet they do not exist as a body of knowledge, a separate layer of context for everyday human activities, but only as a dimension of those activities, embodied in communication and the manner of doing things.

CONCLUSIONS

Because I have been discussing infancy, one can still ask whether all this matters in the long run. Do all these interactions in infancy add up to anything significant later? I do not wish to go over the ground of whether or not early experience matters, but I hope that I have indicated how early experience might matter in ways other than those we usually consider.

Throughout the chapter, I have highlighted the construction of the manner for carrying out actions in the context of interactions during infancy. Later, when children enter school, it becomes evident that the "how" of activities matters a great deal. A child whose narrative style does not fit the one expected in the classroom will have much more accommodating to do than one whose style does (Heath, 1983). Similarly, a child in a group care setting whose mode of

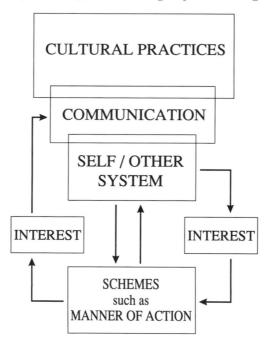

FIG. 2.4.   The paths of relations in the Self/Other system of interactions that include the value dimension.

communication is more conventional and whose understanding of interpersonal routines is more valued is likely to find the care facility a happier place. In this chapter, I have suggested that in addition to forming relations among schemes in the means–ends fashion, the child is also forming relations of the action contour kind, of the manner for engaging in those means–ends patterns. For example, what becomes the complex of actions connected to doing intimacy, imagination, assertion, self-effacement may be what makes for cultural and individual differences (Wierzbicka, 1992). I have suggested that development of this knowledge does not begin when infancy ends; a foundation for it as much as for logic is set in interpersonal action during the infancy years.

In discussing anthropological studies of diverse cultures, Spiro (1990) talked about making the strange familiar and the familiar strange. I find this a helpful metaphor. It seems to me that if different patterns of interaction were totally strange, there would be no way to assimilate them and to understand them for what they are. If our own experience did not provide us contrasts for ways of doing things dispersed along different value dimensions, we would have no way to reflect on the familiar and the desirable. It is the variations experienced in the construction of consolidated structures that allow an intuitive understanding of even those forms of human relations that are not selected out, reflected on, and codified in the culture of one's existence.

What kinds of values do I have in mind? If I have to name one kind, then the conception of values as virtues presented in MacIntyre's (1984) work comes closest to what I think gets played out in early interpersonal interaction. To the extent that the good is specified in a set of virtues explicitly recognized by the adults of a society, to that extent it is more likely to frame the practices of child-rearing; however, the everyday interactions constituting those practices also carry implicit and tacit understandings. Within those practices, the preverbal dialogues of enhancement and suppression, approval and discouragement, and interest and neglect create the field within which the work of constructing understanding takes place. A child comes to understand the world enough to live in it, but also comes to understand it in a manner that makes living within that community of values congenial, as anyone can testify who has had to change such communities.

ACKNOWLEDGMENTS

I am very grateful to members of my research group, especially Fran Hagstrom, Catherine Raeff, Chikako Toma, and Angela Wiley, who provided valuable comments on an earlier version of this chapter. I thank the editors of this volume for many helpful suggestions as well. The technical preparation of the chapter was greatly enhanced by the skill of Kathy Sutton and John Taenzler.

REFERENCES

Als, H. (1979). Social interaction: Dynamic matrix for developing behavior organization. In I. Č. Užgiris (Ed.), *Social interaction and communication during infancy*. New Directions for Child Development, 4. San Francisco: Jossey-Bass.

Baldwin, J. M. (1902). *Social and ethical interpretations in mental development*. New York: MacMillan.

Bowlby, J. (1969). *Attachment and loss: Vol. 1. Attachment*. New York: Basic Books.

Bradley, B. S. (1991). Infancy as paradise. *Human Development, 34,* 35–54.

Brown, T., & Weiss, L. (1987). Structures, procedures, heuristics, and affectivity. *Archives de Psychologie, 55,* 59–94.

Bühler, K. (1922). *Die Geistige Entwicklung des Kindes* [The psychological development of the child]. Jena: Verlag von Gustav Fischer.

Chapman, M. (1988). *Constructive evolution*. New York: Cambridge University Press.

Clancy, P. M. (1986). The acquisition of communicative style in Japanese. In B. B. Schieffelin & E. Ochs (Eds.), *Language socialization across cultures* (pp. 213–250). New York: Cambridge University Press.

Cohen, D. (1987). *The development of play*. New York: New York University Press.

Dixon, S., Tronick, E., Keefer, C., & Brazelton, T. B. (1981). Mother–infant interaction among the Gusii of Kenya. In T. M. Field, A. M. Sostek, P. Vietze, & P. M. Leiderman (Eds.), *Culture and early interactions* (pp. 149–168). Hillsdale, NJ: Lawrence Erlbaum Associates.

Emde, R. N., Gaensbauer, T. J., & Harmon, R. J. (1976). Emotional expression in infancy: A behavioral study. *Psychological Issues, 10*(1, Whole No. 37).

Fogel, A., Toda, S., & Kawai, M. (1988). Mother-infant face-to-face interaction in Japan and the United States. *Developmental Psychology, 24,* 398–406.

Guisinger, S., & Blatt, S. J. (1994). Individuality and relatedness. *American Psychologist, 49,* 104–111.

Halliday, M. A. K. (1975). *Learning how to mean*. London: Edward Arnold.

Heath, S. B. (1983). *Ways with words*. New York: Cambridge University Press.

Hunt, M. McV. (1980). *Early psychological development and experience*. Worcester, MA: Clark University Press.

Kaye, K. (1979). Thickening thin data: The maternal role in developing communication and language. In M. Bullowa (Ed.), *Before speech* (pp. 191–206). Cambridge, UK: Cambridge University Press.

Koestler, A. (1967). *The ghost in the machine*. New York: Macmillan.

Kruper, J. C., & Užgiris, I. Č. (1987). Fathers' and mothers' speech to young infants. *Journal of Psycholinguistic Research, 16,* 597–614.

Lyon, M. L. (1994). Emotion as mediator of somatic and social processes. In W. M. Wentworth & J. Ryan (Eds.), *Social perspectives on emotion* (Vol. II). Greenwich, CT: JAI Press.

MacIntyre, A. (1984). *After virtue*. South Bend, IN: University of Notre Dame Press.

Macmurray, J. (1961). *Persons in relation*. London: Faber & Faber.

Mahler, M. S., Pine, F., & Bergman, A. (1975). *The psychological birth of the human infant*. New York: Basic Books.

McCall, R. B., Eichorn, D. H., & Hogarty, P. S. (1977). Transitions in early development. *Monographs of the Society for Research in Child Development, 42*(3, Serial No. 171).

Nelson, K. (Ed.). (1989). *Narratives from the crib*. Cambridge, MA: Harvard University Press.

Okin, S. M. (1989). *Justice, gender, and the family*. New York: Basic Books.

Papoušek, H., & Papoušek, M. (1991). Innate and cultural guidance of infants' integrative capacities: China, the United States, and Germany. In M. H. Bornstein (Ed.), *Cultural approaches to parenting* (pp. 23–44). Hillsdale, NJ: Lawrence Erlbaum Associates.

Papoušek, M., Papoušek, H., & Harris, J. (1987). The emergence of play in parent–infant interactions. In D. Görlitz & J. F. Wohlwill (Eds.), *Curiosity, imagination, and play* (pp. 214–246). Hillsdale, NJ: Lawrence Erlbaum Associates.

Piaget, J. (1952). *The origins of intelligence* (M. Cook, Trans.). New York: Norton. (Original work published 1936)

Piaget, J. (1962). *Play, dreams and imitation in childhood* (C. Gattegno & F. M. Hodgson, Trans.) New York: Norton. (Original work published 1945)

Piaget, J. (1970). *Genetic epistemology* (E. Duckworth, Trans.). New York: Columbia University Press.

Piaget, J. (1971). *Biology and knowledge* (B. Walsh, Trans.). Chicago: University of Chicago Press. (Original work published 1967)

Piaget, J. (1981). *Intelligence and affectivity: Their relationship during cognitive development* (T. A. Brown & C. E. Kaegi, Trans.). Palo Alto, CA: Annual Review, Inc. (Original work published 1954)

Piaget, J. (1985). *The equilibration of cognitive structures* (T. Brown & K. J. Thampy, Trans.). Chicago: University of Chicago Press. (Original work published 1975)

Polanyi, M. (1964). *Personal knowledge.* New York: Harper Torch.

Preyer, W. (1893). *Mental development in the child* (H. W. Brown, Trans.). New York: Appleton. (Original work published 1882)

Ramirez, M. C. (1993). *Cross-cultural differences in parent-toddler play.* Unpublished doctoral dissertation, Clark University, Worcester, MA.

Richards, M. P. M. (1974). *The integration of a child into a social world.* Cambridge, UK: Cambridge University Press.

Rogoff, B. (1993). Children's guided participation and participatory appropriation in sociocultural activity. In R. H. Wozniak & K. W. Fischer (Eds.), *Development in context* (pp. 121–153). Hillsdale, NJ: Lawrence Erlbaum Associates.

Rogoff, B., Mistry, J., Göncü, A., & Mosier, C. (1993). Guided participation in cultural activity by toddlers and caregivers. *Monographs of the Society for Research in Child Development, 58*(8, Serial No. 236).

Scarr, S. (1983). An evolutionary perspective on infant intelligence. In M. Lewis (Ed.), *Origins of intelligence* (2nd ed., pp. 191–223). New York: Plenum.

Schaffer, H. R. (1984). *The child's entry into a social world.* London: Academic Press.

Spiro, M. E. (1990). On the strange and the familiar in recent anthropological thought. In J. W. Stigler, R. H. Shweder, & G. Herdt (Eds.), *Cultural psychology* (pp. 47–61). New York: Cambridge University Press.

Stern, D. N. (1977). *The first relationship.* Cambridge, MA: Harvard University Press.

Stern, D. N. (1985). *The interpersonal world of the infant.* New York: Basic Books.

Trevarthen, C. (1979). Communication and cooperation in infancy. In M. Bullowa (Ed.), *Before speech* (pp. 321–347). Cambridge, UK: Cambridge University Press.

Trevarthen, C. (1980). The foundations of intersubjectivity. In D. R. Olson (Ed.), *The social foundations of language and thought* (pp. 316–342). New York: Norton.

Užgiris, I. Č. (1984). Imitation in infancy: Its interpersonal aspects. In M. Perlmutter (Ed.), *Minnesota Symposium on Child Psychology* (Vol. 17, pp. 1–32). Hillsdale, NJ: Lawrence Erlbaum Associates.

Užgiris, I. Č. (1989). Infants in relation. In W. Damon (Ed.), *Child development today and tomorrow* (pp. 288–311). San Francisco: Jossey-Bass.

White, B. L., & Watts, J. C. (1973). *Experience and environment* (Vol. 1). Englewood Cliffs, NJ: Prentice-Hall.

Wierzbicka, A. (1992). *Semantics, culture, and cognition.* New York: Oxford University Press.

Youniss, J. (1983). Piaget and the self constituted through relations. In W. F. Overton (Ed.), *The relationship between social and cognitive development* (pp. 201–227). Hillsdale, NJ: Lawrence Erlbaum Associates.

3

Morality and the
Personal Sphere of Actions

Larry P. Nucci
University of Illinois at Chicago

Morality and personal freedom are often thought of as opposing poles in the affairs of human conduct. Freud (1923/1961), for example, saw the process of socialization as involving the formation of an intrapsychic moral control structure that functioned to harness or keep in check the passions and destructive impulses of individuals. Contemporary theorists also tend to portray freedom and morality in oppositional terms. Social constructionists and culture theorists, for example, tend to classify the morality of various societies on a continuum from the individualistic/permissive to the collectivistic/traditional in terms of the degrees of individual freedom and autonomy granted to members relative to the given cultural system of moral rules and obligations (Miller & Bersoff, 1992; Shweder, 1990). In this chapter I explore an alternative thesis: that morality and personal freedom are interdependent and that personal freedom is necessary both for the construction of moral understandings and engagement in moral action. In the process I want to revisit Piaget's (1932) discussion of moral autonomy and offer an expanded interpretation that emphasizes the role of social autonomy in the child's construction of morality.

In *The Moral Judgment of the Child,* Piaget (1932) presented the first research-based argument for the tie between the emergence of personal freedom and the development of mature forms of moral understanding. In particular, Piaget described a parallel development in the growth of morality and autonomy. He claimed morality produces a shift from conceptions of morality in terms of authority-based rules to conceptions of morality in terms of just reciprocity, and this is intertwined with a shift from unilateral respect for authority to a social perspective based on mutual respect and cooperation. Piaget saw this process as being aided by social experiences in which the child interacts with others of similar social power. In the main, these experiences are afforded by peer relations, but they are also supported by adults willing to reduce their power relative to children. Piaget's central concern was the process by which morality moved away from external and unilateral regulation by authority toward autonomous recognition of mutual interpersonal obligations. His emphasis on the shifts in power relations and the increased freedom of the child was in the context of his assumption that cooperation among equals was the social experiential basis for autonomous morality. As he put it, "(Moral) Autonomy . . . appears only with reciprocity, when mutual respect is strong enough to make the individual feel from within the desire to treat others as he himself would wish to be treated" (Piaget, 1932, p. 196). Whereas Piaget emphasized the role of children's autonomy in moral development, he did not examine the development of children's personal freedom per se, nor did he explore the potential contribution that the experience of personal liberty has on the development of moral sentiment. I take up these issues in two ways. First, I argue that children attempt to secure an area of behavioral discretion, a personal domain, as a means of establishing personal boundaries and individual identity that serves as a necessary condition for a morality of mutual respect and cooperation. As Piaget (1932) put it, in his sole reference to the role of individuality in moral development, "It is only by knowing our individual nature with its limitations as well as its resources that we grow capable of coming out of ourselves and collaborating with other individual natures" (p. 393). Second, I contend that the personal freedoms children claim for themselves serve as the source of interpersonal resistances that allow them to extend conceptions of fairness and human welfare to construct an interpersonal equilibrated moral conception of rights.

THE PERSONAL DOMAIN AND FORMATION OF THE INDIVIDUAL

The Personal

The connections between personal freedom and morality are based on the identification of an area of behavior termed the *personal*. The personal refers to the set of actions that the individual considers to be outside of the area of justifiable social regulation. These actions are subject not to considerations of right and wrong, but to preferences and choice. It should be noted that, while allowance for some area of personal choice appears to be culturally universal (J. G. Miller, personal communication, November 12, 1993), the specific content of the personal is culturally variable. These cultural issues are discussed in more detail later. Examples of personal issues within North American culture include the content of one's correspondence and self-expressive creative works, one's recreational activities, one's choice of friends or intimate associates, and actions that focus on the state of one's own body (Nucci, 1981; Nucci, Guerra, & Lee, 1991; Nucci & Herman, 1982; Smetana, Bridgeman, & Turiel, 1983). By their very nature, personal issues are a circumscribed set of actions that define the bounds of individual authority. As such, the identification and maintenance of control over the personal serves to establish the social border between the self and the group. The exercise of choice within the personal permits the construction of what is socially individual or unique about the person, as opposed to one's biologically inherited unique features (i.e., fingerprints, facial image), and serves as the instantiation of oneself as agent rather than scripted by socially inherited roles and contexts. In sum, the personal represents the set of social actions that permit the person to construct both a sense of the self as object, what James (1899) called the "me," and the subjective sense of authorship, or what James referred to as the "I." The "me" that is constructed is at once culturally and contextually situated as well as an existentially singular product of decisions within one's personal sphere.

The Social Origins of the Personal

Thus far I have proposed that an area of personal freedom is necessary for the formation of the social individual which in turn, as Piaget acknowledged, is necessary for the person to engage in relations of reciprocity and cooperation. The view of the self contained in this proposition is compatible with psychological theories offered by writers of diverse perspectives who also see a close link between personal autonomy and the formation of the individual (Baldwin, 1897, 1906; Damon & Hart, 1988; Erikson, 1963, 1968; Kohut, 1978; Mahler, 1979; Selman, 1980), and developmental perspectives, which see strivings for control over a personal sphere of actions present in early childhood and perhaps even in infancy (Mahler, 1979; Stern, 1985). In recent years, however, the view of the self as autonomous has been criticized as reflecting a particular Western cultural construction, in which the self as individual is decontextualized from the social cultural milieu (Cushman, 1991; Sampson, 1985; Shweder & Bourne, 1984). These critiques seem to me to be justified as a counterpoint to romanticizations of the individual as an autochthonous system. (See Smith, 1994, for a comparative discussion of romantic and contemporary views of self.) On the other hand, such critiques themselves risk engagement in oversimplification and stereotyping by dichotomizing cultures into those that recognize autonomous selves and those that do not (Greenfield & Cocking, 1994; Turiel, 1994). For one thing, it is not the case that conceptions of self as autonomous are restricted to Western culture. Although notions of "self" like beliefs about the personal are culturally variable, all observed cultures contain some differentiated view of self, and members of all cultures appear to hold idiosyncratic individual views of themselves as distinct persons with particular interests (Spiro, 1993). The preponderance of evidence is consistent with the alternative hypothesis that Western and non-Western cultures alike contain heterogeneous perspectives on self as both autonomous and interdependent (see Turiel, chap. 5, this volume). Kim and Choi (1994), for example, in their review of various models of individual–group relations described what is referred to as the coexistence mode, in which collectivistic values such as family commitment and interdependence coexist alongside individualistic values such as self-development and personal achievement. This coexistence mode, according to Kim and Choi, appears to fit Indian, Japanese, and Chinese culture better than one-dimensional characterizations of these cultures as collectivistic.

The view of the individual being presented here is consistent with characterizations of self as heterogeneous rather than simply individualistic. The personal that is constructed is always situated and in dialogue with others, with social norms and cultural metaphors (Hermans, Kempen, & van Loon, 1992; Sarbin, 1986). Thus, the particular expression of the personal will be a function of the historical and cultural context. Moreover, the very process by which one becomes individual requires social comparison. If I may borrow again from Piaget (1932), "In order to discover myself as a particular individual, what is needed is continuous comparison, the outcome of opposition, of discussion, and of mutual control" (p. 393). While it is now generally recognized that the self is constructed in social contexts (Damon & Hart, 1988), it is less clear that the individual is societally determined. In contrast with the social constructionists (Cushman, 1991; Shweder & Bourne, 1984), the present argument is that the child establishes personal borders through a process of interpersonal negotiation rather than through a mere reconstruction at an individual level of tacit and overt social messages that define the parameters of the personal. The child, according to this perspective, is active not only in the sense of interpreting input, but actively seeking to establish areas of choice and personal control within which to operate as an individual.

We now have observational evidence that bears on this issue from a study (Nucci & Weber, 1995) of the at-home interactions of 20 mother–child dyads with children between the ages of 3 and 5. These were middle-class U. S. families in which the parenting styles of the mothers fell within what Baumrind (1971) described as authoritative parenting. These mothers had a set of firmly established behavioral expectations, but were flexible in their disciplining of children. Each family was observed during three activity periods throughout the day for 3 days. In addition, mothers tape-recorded interactions with their children during bath and bedtime.

A number of types of social events were observed as a part of the study. What we need to focus on here was the pattern of interactions pertaining to personal issues. Such event sequences were classified by trained coders as personal when the event sequence revolved solely around a personal matter, or mixed when the event entailed significant overlap between a child's personal domain and an existing social convention or the needs of others. The observed patterns of interaction took three forms. The least common of these were sequences in which the mother conveyed an explicit social message that the behavior or issue in question was clearly within the child's jurisdiction. This pattern is illustrated in the following excerpt from a discussion between a mother and her daughter over the girl's hairstyle:

Mother: If you want, we can get your hair cut. It's your choice.
Child: I only want it that long—down to here. [Child points to where she wants her hair cut.]

Exchanges of this type involving direct social messages from the mother made up less than one third of the observed sequences pertaining to social events. More frequently, the mothers indirectly conveyed that an issue was a matter of the child's personal choice as illustrated in the following exchange:

Mother: You need to decide what you want to wear for school today.
Child: [Opens a drawer.] Pants. Pants. Pants.
Mother: Have you decided what to wear today?
Child: I wear these.
Mother: Okay, that's a good choice.
Mother: How would you like your hair today?
Child: Down. [Child stands by the bed, and her mother carefully combs her hair.]

The interaction in the preceding example nicely corresponds to what Shweder, Mahapatra, and Miller (1987) called *tacit communication*. The mother, through a series of offered choices conveyed the idea that dress and hairstyle are matters for the person to decide. The child might accordingly infer that such behavior is personal. In effect, the mothers in both of these examples were transmitting the cultural message that dress may be individualized. Although it is important to recognize that such cultural messages occur, they do not in and of themselves demonstrate that the child merely recapitulates society.

The third common pattern of interaction in personal sequences is resistance from the child and subsequent negotiation and compromise by the adult. In such sequences, adult comments can take either direct or indirect forms. Negotiation took place in roughly one quarter of the events coded as personal, and about half of the events coded as mixed.

Mother: Evan, it's your last day of nursery school. Why don't you wear your nursery sweatshirt?
Child: I don't want to wear that one.
Mother: This is the last day of nursery school, that's why we wear it. You want to wear that one?

Child: Another one.
Mother: Are you going to get it or should I?
Child: I will. First I got to get a shirt.
Mother: [Goes to the child's dresser and starts picking out shirts.] This
one? This one? Do you know which one you have in mind? You have to
decide, because we have to do car pool. Here, this is a new one.
Child: No, it's too big.
Mother: Oh Evan, just wear one, and when you get home, you can pick
whatever you want, and I won't even help you. [Child puts on shirt.]

In this case we see a conflict between a dress convention (wearing a particular shirt on the last day of school) and the child's view that the selection of
which of his articles of clothing he is to wear is a personal choice. The mother
in the scene acknowledged the child's resistance and attempted to negotiate,
finally offering the child a free choice once school was over. Mixed events of
this kind, involving issues such as control over dress or recreation, where the
child's interpretation of an act as personal conflicted with the adult's view of
the same act as conventional or prudent or practical, were associated with child
resistance in the form of choice assertions or privacy statements in roughly
90% of the cases. These responses by children were not simply evidence of a
generalized resistance to adult authority (Brehm & Brehm, 1981; Kuczinski,
Kochanska, Radke-Yarrow, & Girnius Brown, 1987), but a delimited set of
claims to choice over a personal sphere. In contrast with their behavior in the
context of personal or mixed events, children offered resistance to adult authority less than 10% of the time in the context of moral events, and about 25%
of the time in the case of conventional events. As I noted before, parents entered into negotiation with the children about half of the time. These negotiations indicate that the parents also valued their children's claims and contributed to the children's construction of areas of discretion and personal control.
The types of conflicts we witnessed were similar in many respects to issues
identified by adolescent subjects in Smetana's (1989) research as sources of
conflict between themselves and their parents. What is important here is that
children are not simply passively accepting the personal as defined by their
parents, but are engaging in active challenge to authority and asserting a claim
to freedom of action within a personal sphere. These challenges make up a part
of what I referred to earlier as the resistances children offer in their interpersonal negotiations in the construction of their moral conceptions of reciprocity and mutual respect. And, to anticipate my argument a bit, these resistances stemming from claims to freedom in the personal domain comprise the
experiential source of the child's construction of moral conceptions of rights.
    As already stated, the child's construction of the personal is not accom-
plished solely at the individual level, nor determined by the culture, but
through reciprocal interaction between the child and members of society.

Thus, we would expect adult members of the culture to have some understanding of the child's need for freedom. This, indeed, appears to be the case. Smetana and I (Nucci & Smetana, 1994) recently completed a study in which we interviewed mothers from the same community where Weber and I had conducted our observations. The family incomes of the mothers included a wide range (from $10,000 to over $100,000 per year). We asked the mothers about their views of which behaviors children age 4 or age 6 should be allowed to decide for themselves, which behaviors adults should regulate, and what sorts of issues mothers should be willing to negotiate with children. The mothers' spontaneous responses to these questions were interesting in that the items they mentioned as ones children should control and over which they would negotiate closely paralleled the types of issues we had observed. In general, mothers thought young children should have a say in personal areas such as what types and how much food they eat, who they choose to play with, what clothes they wear, and what games they play. When asked to justify why these activities should be left up to the child, mothers gave reasons supportive of the child's emerging autonomy, agency, and personal competence.

The fact that both of these studies were conducted within the United States limits their generalizability, and cross-cultural research must be conducted before we can make definitive statements about children's early experiences in the development of their understandings of the personal realm. To examine other cultural settings, we have begun research of this type in Brazil (Nucci, Camino, & Sapiro, 1993). The first of these studies was conducted in the northeastern coastal city of Natal. This region of Brazil has been characterized as a collectivistic culture in comparison with the United States and Europe (Triandis, Bontempo, Villareal, Asai, & Lucca, 1988). In the study we interviewed 240 children and adolescents from four social classes and three ages (6–8, 10–12, and 14–16 years of age) about which matters children should be able to control themselves and which should be regulated by parents or the social group. The items used in the study were ones selected by the Brazilian researchers in the project as ones that fit the theoretical definitions of the moral, conventional, and personal categories. We found that Brazilian children differentiate among moral, conventional, and personal issues. However, we also found social class differences in the age at which the majority of children consistently identified a set of issues as personal. Middle-class children tended to claim an area of behavioral discretion at an earlier age than did lower class children. By adolescence (age 14–16), however, there were no social class differences in children's judgments of items as ones that should be up to the children to control, nor were there class differences in justifications given for why an action should be a matter of the child's discretion. By adolescence, across social classes, the majority of subjects justified control over personal issues in terms of personal rights, and the need for personal privacy. There were no age or class differences in children's evaluations of moral or conventional issues.

The children saw these actions as within the legitimate sphere of adult and societal regulation.

In a second study, we interviewed 120 Brazilian mothers about the same issues we had interviewed mothers of young children in the United States about. Half of the mothers were from northeastern Brazil. The other half of the sample was from a large industrial city in the southern region of the country. This area of Brazil is culturally similar in many respects to the United States and western Europe. The population of the city where we conducted our research is mostly European in origin, and the middle- and upper middle-class are well off by Brazilian standards. As with the mothers in our U.S. study, the Brazilian mothers identified areas of children's' personal discretion. There were, however, regional and social class differences in their tendencies to offer choice to children. These differences occurred in reference to young children, with the lower class and northeastern mothers less likely to identify behaviors as ones young children should have control over. Southern Brazilian and middle-class mothers of young children from both regions, on the other hand, responded in ways similar to U.S. middle-class mothers. Brazilian mothers of adolescents, irrespective of region or social class, consistently identified personal, but not conventional or moral issues as actions the children should control. They also tended to use reasons similar to those of their U.S. counterparts, which expressed a desire for their child to establish uniqueness, autonomy, competence, and agency. Interestingly, Brazilian mothers from all of the groups, including lower class mothers of young children, responded affirmatively to the question of whether it was important for a child to develop a sense of individuality. Indeed, language referring to individual autonomy was spontaneously employed during the interviews by the Brazilian mothers irrespective of region or class. That is, the Brazilian mothers expressed essentially the same concerns in this regard as did the U.S. sample in the Nucci and Smetana (1994) study.

In sum, these Brazilian data demonstrate that children across cultures construct understandings about personal issues, and that parental beliefs about children's personal choice are not confined to mothers from "individualistic" cultures. Across social classes and geographic regions, the Brazilian mothers expressed beliefs that children require areas of personal discretion for their personal growth. The research also shows that there are culture and class differences in the age at which the personal is fully accorded to children. These differences appear to stem from cultural assumptions about the nature of children's needs and capacities. As demonstrated in other research (Wainryb, 1991), the informational assumptions that parents have about the nature of children, such as whether children benefit from corporal punishment, have a powerful impact on how they treat their children. Such variations in informational assumptions about children notwithstanding, we found in our study of Brazilian mothers that even the mothers from the more traditional regions of Brazil valued the eventual emergence of individuality and agency in adolescence. Observational studies would need to be conducted to determine the pattern of interactions associated with children's construction of the personal in these Brazilian contexts. An issue of particular interest would be whether and in what ways children's resistance to parental control over personal issues manifests itself, and how it is dealt with by adults. A recent study by Yau and Smetana (1994) has provided evidence that adolescent–parent conflicts occur over personal issues even in non-Western societies in which parent–child relations have been characterized as "harmonious" or conflict free (Baumrind, 1973). In their study, Yau and Smetana (1994) found that Chinese adolescent–parent relations also contain conflict (although less so than in the United States), and that conflicts are over the same types of issues as experienced by their U.S. counterparts. Moreover, the adolescents in that study positioned their arguments in terms of exercising personal jurisdiction.

THE PERSONAL AND THE MORAL

Having discussed some of the features of the personal, let us turn to direct consideration of the role of personal freedom in moral development. The general theoretical context for this discussion is what has been termed the *domain approach* to social cognitive development (Turiel & Davidson, 1986; Turiel, Killen, & Helwig, 1987). This view of social development holds that children construct social concepts within discrete conceptual and developmental systems that are generated out of qualitatively differing aspects of their social interactions (Turiel, 1978). These domains correspond to what Piaget (1985) referred to as partial systems or subsystems with respect to the mind as a totality. Each partial system forms an internally equilibrated structure that in certain contexts may interact with other systems requiring interdomain equilibration or coordination. Within this theoretical framework a distinction is drawn, on the one hand, between morality (concepts of nonarbitrary and unavoidable features of social relations pertaining to matters of human welfare, and fairness), and social convention (concepts of contextually dependent and consensually agreed-on social rules), and, on the other hand, between the personal (Nucci, 1981) and morality and convention. It is important to keep in mind that what is being referred to as conceptual domains are dynamic, interactive systems of psychological equilibration (Piaget, 1985), and not static information-processing templates. Thus, changes in one system have ramifications for the way in which issues are dealt with or understood within other conceptual systems. The arguments that follow concerning the relations between personal freedom and morality are based on assumptions about the ways in which such systems of social understanding may interact and influence one another in the course of development and in contextualized decisions. I begin by looking more carefully at the functional relationship between the personal and the moral in terms of one's ability or propensity to engage in moral reciprocity, and then at the specific contributions the personal may have for the construction of moral concepts.

Personal Freedom and the Capacity for Moral Reciprocity

As already noted, Piaget (1932) assumed that a degree of individuality was a necessary precondition for interpersonal morality. His assumption, of course, was based on the notion that *interpersonal* requires a *personal*. In addition, I have proposed that the personal is not a cultural invention, but a psychological necessity for the establishment of the social self. Although there is little research that bears directly on this issue, a wealth of clinical data have demonstrated that disruption in the formation of personal boundaries damages individual psychological health (Kernberg, 1975; Kohut, 1978; Mahler, 1979; Masterson, 1981), and suggests that there are basic psychological limits to the extent to which others (including society) can impinge on the private lives of individuals. In fact, contemporary anthropology has moved away from romanticisms about the "group mind" or collective consciousness of so-called primitive peoples (Shweder, 1979a, 1979b) and has instead focused attention on cultural influences in individuation (Crapanzano, 1990) and on the definition of personhood (Shweder & LeVine, 1984).

If our assumptions about the linkage between personal freedom and morality are correct, then we should see evidence of disruptions in the expression of moral reciprocity among individuals with pathological experiences in their formation of areas of personal freedom. Because psychopathology, within broad limits, has to be culturally contextualized, I would like to suggest that an ideal group of people with whom to explore this hypothesis would be Western adolescents and young adults diagnosed as having borderline personality disorders. This is a complex and controversial area within clinical psychology, and I do not mean to reduce this form of psychological disorder simply to an issue of personal autonomy. I also note that some of the broader connections between moral development and borderline personality are being explored by Noam (1993). However, I do want to draw attention to the possible connections between the experiences of these adolescents in the formation of their personal domain and their treatment of themselves and others as a way of exploring the more general thesis under discussion.

I begin with reference to a clinical case study of a young woman who will be referred to by the pseudonym "Linda." Linda entered therapy after having been hospitalized for major depression, bulimia, and suicidal thoughts. [Linda was a client of Maria Santiago Nucci. Linda voluntarily consented to allow her case to be employed for research purposes. Quotations attributed to Linda are from an interview conducted by Dr. Santiago Nucci with Linda as a part of her research. The interview occurred after Linda was no longer a client of Dr. Santiago Nucci. The interview was not part of a therapy session. The interview has been made available to Linda for her own use.] Her parents were well off financially. Her father was a corporate executive, and both parents were concerned about social propriety, and had a strong desire that their daughter, Linda, conform to social class standards. Linda's mother, whom we call "Cathy," displayed particular concern that Linda not only illustrate the social ideal for a woman of her class, but that Linda in some ways be a perfect younger expression of Cathy. Thus, Linda's mother attempted throughout Linda's life to control Linda's behavior in some of the very areas that middle-class children and mothers identify as part of the child's personal domain. One such area was that of control over dress. As a young girl, Linda wanted to dress in rough and tumble clothes and not always wear a dress. Her mother, however, always insisted that Linda dress like a "young lady." Interviewed at age 20, Linda had this to say:

> Even now, like at Easter, when I went to Church, my Mom was real concerned with what I was going to wear. And I finally just said, "Look, I'm going to wear what I am going to wear, Mom." I didn't wear anything outrageous, a skirt and a blouse. But here I am 20 years old, and it was such a concern about what I was going to wear.

The importance of Linda's dress to illustrate the needs of the mother came out later in the interview:

> Even now, when we go shopping, she tries to buy things for me that she would wear. And I think, "My God, I've been living with you for 20 years and you know I am not going to wear that." [The interviewer asks: Why do you think she does that?] I think she still has this idea of who I am eventually going to be. Like I am just going through a phase, and I'll snap out of it, and I'll turn out to be Cathy number two.

The needs of Linda's mother to illustrate herself through her daughter came out in the mother's attempts to control Linda in other personal spheres including Linda's eating (from childhood her mother expressed concerns that the already thin Linda not eat too much and gain weight), her personal friendships, and her recreation activities. Although each of these areas is a normal source of adolescent–parent tension (Smetana, 1989), the degree of control and intrusion exerted by Linda's parents was atypical. As a result, Linda engaged first in overt rebellion: "Well, I'd just throw things up in her face. I felt like . . . I just wanted her to know who I am, not who she wants me to be."

In the end, this young woman of seemingly privileged circumstances responded to her situation through acts of self-destruction, which, interestingly, included an eating disorder. Linda's inability to negotiate a middle ground with her mother led not only to difficulty in establishing a sense of self-ownership and identity, but to a bipolar rather than reciprocal set of relations with others. As she put it, "I tend to put people in black and white categories." When asked to describe herself, she first described herself as fair, and then went on to say:

> I am either completely unselfish and go out of the way to be nice to people, I'm like the supernice person, I'm nice to everyone, like the non-English speaking people where I work—I go out of my way to make them feel like I like them and stuff, and then, all of a sudden, I'll get upset about something, and I'll hate everyone, and no one cares about me, and I'll be mean and totally selfish and unfair.

Linda's morality as expressed in her own statements is not without evidence of empathy or caring, or a sense of human welfare, but it is nonreciprocal, egocentric, and ultimately infantile. Linda is a highly intelligent young woman from a privileged background who seemingly has everything. Yet, the velvet prison of her childhood has left her locked within her "self" and its needs for expression. Of course, Linda's personal relations with her mother need to be seen within the broader sociopolitical context of the role of women in contemporary U.S. society. Linda was aware of these connections, and stated that her individual experience reflected some of the more general pressures on women in terms of what it means to be feminine. Within that social context, however, Linda's problems were very much personal and tied to her inability to establish boundaries between herself and her mother's intrusive authority. In Piaget's conception of autonomy, Linda would need to experience a life space in which her needs for personal freedom would be met in the context of a dialogue with the separate legitimate needs of others. Selman and Schultz (1990) worked on a therapeutic approach for people like Linda that uses friendship as the context for self-exploration. The key to friendship, of course, involves cooperation, reciprocity, and the freedom to be oneself.

The Personal and the Construction of Rights and Moral Obligations

As we have seen, the establishment of a personal sphere would appear to be a prerequisite for engagement in the forms of interpersonal reciprocity central to Piaget's conception of autonomous morality. I turn now to consideration of the specific contribution of the personal to the construction of morality itself, and in particular, I develop the view that the personal is necessary for the construction of concepts of rights. Whereas moral structures of reciprocity require that rights and protections granted oneself be extended to others, moral conceptions of justice and beneficence do not in and of themselves provide us with the means to identify personal rights and freedoms. The linking of personal concepts with rights claims is consistent with philosophical perspectives that ground the notion of rights in the establishment and maintenance of personal agency (Dworkin, 1977; Gewirth, 1978, 1982). For example, Gewirth (1978) argued that "agents value their freedom or voluntariness as a necessary good as long as the possibility remains of purposive action—that is, of action that is able to fulfill and maintain at least those purposes required for the continuation of agency" (p. 53). Later he added: "Since the agent regards as necessary goods the freedom and well-being that constitute the generic features of his successful action, he logically must also hold that he has rights to these generic features, and he implicitly makes a corresponding rights claim" (p. 63).

Personal concepts serve to identify freedom as a necessary good for maintaining agency and uniqueness. The content of the personal domain is the content of the individual's identified freedoms. This specific content will be influenced by cultural norms and reflect individual idiosyncrasies. Thus, no claim is being made for a universal collection of specific personal rights. Moreover, many of the specific actions people consider personal are trivial in nature, and would not in and of themselves comprise core values. For example, one can hardly imagine anyone claiming a moral right to have green hair. However, these specifics can be seen as manifestations of broader core requirements for establishing personal boundaries for the self as object and related requirements (for personal agency, continuity, and uniqueness) for establishing a sense of self as subject (Damon & Hart, 1988). These basic elements are one's body, and claims to freedom of expression, communication, and association. These generic claims are obviously canalized by culture, and variations in the degree and form that these freedoms take in turn establish the observed cultural variations in moral content.

The personal provides the source and the conceptual justification for the individual's claims to freedom. Such claims to personal liberty do not in and of themselves constitute a moral conception of rights. Personal concepts provide the basic datum (i.e., the psychological necessity of the personal sphere) requisite to extend the moral conceptions of justice and beneficence to include a moral conception of rights. In terms of the interdomain interactions, one would not expect a tight structural relation between the personal and the moral. On the other hand one can assume that developmental changes in personal concepts influence structural changes in moral understanding.

As has been repeatedly demonstrated in a large number of studies conducted since 1980, very young children display concepts of morality differentiated in terms of objective, universalistic, and categorical criteria. These early childhood expressions of fairness and human welfare are best thought of, however, as a set of intuitive understandings or inferences drawn from social interactions involving moral acts rather than as fully elaborated formal conceptualizations of moral judgment (Shweder, Turiel, & Much, 1981). In research on age-related changes within the moral domain, Davidson, Turiel, and Black (1983) found that up to about age 6 moral judgment is primarily regulated by concerns for maintaining welfare and avoiding harm and is limited to directly accessible acts. Not until about age 10 do children develop concepts of fairness and consistently regulate competing welfare claims with concerns for just reciprocity, and not until about age 12 do moral concepts of fairness consistently go beyond direct reciprocity and involve coordination of concerns for equality with considerations of equitable welfare (Damon, 1977).

The thesis here is that personal concepts inform the construction of morality by extending conceptions of harm and welfare to include the psychological requirements of personal freedom. In young children this forms the basis of an intuitive moral sense of rights wherein children understand infringement of their personal freedom as harmful or unfair. A working hypothesis is that only later in middle childhood do they incorporate these intuitions about liberty within a moral framework regulated by just reciprocity. Paradoxically, then, the child's early intuitions about moral claims to liberty without a conception of moral equality based on just reciprocity make her moral system unstable in that she appears to understand moral conceptions of harm and welfare and yet acts out of self-interest. I offer this interpretation of the instabilities in the young child's moral system as an alternative to the classic Piagetian view of moral egocentrism. It is not just that children act out of self-interest because of an inability to see the needs of others; it is that they see their own self-interests as morally legitimate and in the absence of moral reversibility cannot coordinate their own moral claims with those of others. This instability in a child's moral framework, occasioned in part by extending issues of harm to include constraints on personal freedom, is amplified by instabilities in the child's underlying conceptions of the personal, which provide the basis for her claims to freedom in the first place. Conceptions of the personal undergo development structured by underlying changes in the child's conceptions of self and personal identity. A synopsis of the five levels of understanding about personal issues is presented in Table 3.1. (More extensive discussion of these levels with examples of subject responses can be found in Nucci, 1977, and Nucci & Lee, 1993.) As shown in Table 3.1, it is not until late childhood or early adolescence that the child structures concepts of the personal with a consolidated understanding of self as subject, and only at this and later points in development can we say that moral concepts of rights are truly based on a view of persons as agents.

In our developmental study of children's concepts of the personal, we have seen that the young child bases her intuitive sense of rights and liberty on a physicalistic sense of self. This is not to say that the child has no conceptions of interiorized feelings or intentions (recent work on children's theories of mind have provided ample evidence that children have such conceptions); the claim is rather that the primary and most stable elements of the child's conception of self are directly apprehensible. It is not until late childhood or in some cases early adolescence that the child conceptualizes the personal in psychological rather than physical or behavioral characteristics of the self. It also seems that it is only after children conceptualize the personal in these psychological terms that they enter the final phase of individuation, for only then do

TABLE 3.1

Description of Major Changes in Conceptions of Personal Issues

1. *Establishing concrete self/other distinctions.* The individual conceptualizes the personal domain as an observable body and an equally concrete realm of things and activities. The individual sees control over personal affairs as extending and enforcing one's sense of uniqueness, self-mastery, and personal identity by establishing observable difference between the self and others and by differentiating what is "mine" from what is "yours."

2. *Establishing a behavior style and concern about group opinion.* The individual extends the conception of the person to include the notion of personality, defined as a set of characteristic behaviors. The view of the group as mere "other" shifts to a view of the group as evaluator and comparer of individual personal qualities. Control over personal actions is seen as establishing a behavior style or personality while protecting the self from negative public labels.

3. *Establishing the self as an individual defined in terms of a unique set of ideas or values.* The individual begins to define the self in terms of internal cognitive processes. Control over personal matters is conceived as establishing oneself as an individual. Loss of control over the personal domain of actions is viewed as risking absorption by the group: to change one's ideas and values is seen as giving up one's distinguishing psychological features.

4. *Coordinating the self esteem.* The individual views control over events within the personal domain as essential to coordinating all aspects of the self into an internally consistent whole. Consciousness is understood as having depth. At the center of consciousness the individual has an immutable essence around which the self system is constructed. Control over the personal is seen as a means of coordinating one's actions with this essence and as a mechanism for probing aspects of the personal system.

5. *Transforming the labile self.* Instead of viewing the self as an essence the individual comes to view the self as labile, as a constantly evolving product of one's personal decisions. The individual sees control over actions within the personal domain as essential if decisions serving to create oneself are to follow the individual's subjectively valued course.

they view their personal sphere as fully beyond the legitimate intrusion of parents. Until about age 10, children seem to hold two conflicting views of parental authority with regard to their personal domains. On the one hand, children assert that they ought to have authority over issues they consider personal, for example, choice of friends, hair length, and privacy of conversations (Tisak, 1986). On the other hand, they simultaneously maintain that their parents (and no one else) have the right to override and determine things for the child. Children maintain this view even when they view parents' reasons as whimsical (e.g., the parent simply dislikes the friend and forbids him or her to play with the child). When asked to explain why the parent has the right to override a child's decision in the personal area, children provide justifications consistent with an underlying conception of the self as physical rather than intrasubjective. They offer statements like the following comments (taken from Nucci, 1977), in which a 10-year-old boy explained his claim that a child's parents "can tell him what to do because they own him."

Question: Do they have a right to sell him or give him away?
Answer: Yes, because, like I said, they own him.
Question: Can they do anything they want with him?

Answer: No. They can't hurt him or anything, because well, they don't own him exactly. It's like he's a library book on loan from God.

In effect before about age 10, children view their personal domain as shared with parents as if they were cosigners on a loan for a piece of property. This view of the parent–child relationship ends when children begin to conceive of the personal domain as an aspect of an internal self knowable only to the individual. It should be noted here that the cross-cultural applicability of this developmental progression toward an interiorized self has been questioned (Shweder & Bourne, 1984). I am not in a position to claim that all children in all cultures will necessarily construct the same conceptualization of self. I would like to mention, however, that there is considerable data indicating that conceptions of an interiorized subjective self or ego are maintained among individuals across a wide range of cultures including members of groups, such as Theravada Buddists, whose central religious tenets deny the existence of the individual ego or soul (Spiro, 1993). In his account of these findings, Spiro (1993) argued that individuals' own subjective cognitive and emotional experiences may lead them to construct conceptions that are at variance with "official" cultural or religious explanations. (See Turiel, chap. 5, this volume, for a more extensive discussion of this research.) Our data from studies with lower class children and their mothers in northeastern Brazil also provide evidence that the developmental changes I have described have a significant degree of cross-cultural applicability. As I stated before, our data show that lower class northeastern Brazilian children from early adolescence onward treat issues of friendship choice, privacy of communication, hairstyle, and privacy of one's diary as personal and beyond legitimate parental regulation. Interestingly, the mothers we interviewed held that young children should not be given much freedom because they do not have the internal intellectual tools to handle personal choices. According to these Brazilian mothers, however, in late childhood or adolescence, children become individuals with distinct interior lives and decision-making capabilities and must be given freedom as people.

The emergence in late childhood of a conception of the personal as fundamentally divorced from parental ownership (as opposed to parental influence) has important implications for interpersonal relations, because it marks an end to conceptions of a fundamental relationship (that between parent and child) in which intimacy (the permeation of personal boundaries) is confused with possession. These developmental changes in conceptions of personal issues are also likely to have two primary influences on the development of moral reasoning. First, the development of an understanding of self as fundamentally rooted in consciousness provides depth to conceptions of rights by articulating a psychological need for liberty. A child's moral system now has impinging on it claims for freedom of action that are clearly differentiated from issues of physical harm and even go beyond the child's psychological pain of injustice or hurt feelings. The child begins to understand that one's self depends on the unique features of one's internal makeup and accordingly, begins to structure the intuitions about liberty just referred to.

Second, these developmental changes in concepts of the personal may affect moral understanding more generally by encouraging the child to view others as subjects. When one conceives agency as connected to freedom of choice and privacy of ideas, one cannot readily reduce personhood to "thingness," or resolution of interpersonal conflicts to pragmatics devoid of moral implications. As noted earlier, however, these hypothesized influences of personal concepts on the moral system, as well as others we might extrapolate, should be interpreted not as determinants of moral development but as important sources of information that can extend the types of interpersonal dealings handled with moral reasoning.

CONCLUSION

In this chapter I have tried to illustrate how the child's development of concepts of personal freedom interacts with and serves the development of moral understanding. In the process I hoped to expand Piaget's discussion of autonomous morality to more explicitly include the role of personal liberty in the construction of moral reciprocity and conceptions of rights. The research and theory I have reviewed suggests that formation of the personal and the individual's claims to freedom are necessary for the individual to engage as an individual in the discourse (both public and internal) that leads to moral reciprocity, mutual respect, and cooperation. Moral discourse transforms individual claims to freedom into mutually shared moral obligations. Without such mutuality, as Piaget correctly pointed out in his discussion of the relation between egocentrism and heteronomous morality, personal claims to freedom can also serve as the source of narcissistic or exploitative orientations. On the other hand, in the absence of claims to freedom emerging from the personal, there can be no moral conception of rights. Thus, morality and personal freedom are interdependent rather than oppositional features of human development.

It should be self-evident from what was just stated that beyond the most abstract categories we cannot anticipate the content of such discourse. Nor can we anticipate with certainty whether the claims of individuals will be viewed as touching on mutual transpersonal concerns. It is the historically situated generation of individual claims to freedom reflecting ahistorical basic psychological needs that both stimulates moral discourse and provides the potential for critique of the status quo. Thus, moral development from this modified Piagetian perspective is seen as universal, yet plural; individual, yet social. This view of morality has less in common with the classical Kantian view of autonomous morality, than it does with Habermas' (1991) attempts to account for a postconventional morality through idealized forms of discourse. Ultimately, it also recognizes that although individual moral understandings reflect inherent and unavoidable features of human interaction and individual psychological requirements, the morality of human rights in its most mature and principled forms will always be the product of collective efforts.

ACKNOWLEDGMENTS

This chapter extends the line of argument set out in Nucci and Lee (1993). I wish to express my gratitude to several people in addition to the editors who commented on drafts of the chapter. Their feedback led to several important changes in the manuscript. Thanks are due to Constance Kamii, David Hansen, Joseph Kahne, Joan G. Miller, Judith Smetana, Theodore R. Sarbin, and Theresa Thorkildsen.

REFERENCES

Baldwin, J. M. (1897). *Social and ethical interpretations in mental development.* New York: Macmillan.
Baldwin, J. M. (1906). *Thought and things* (Vol. 1). London: Swan Sonnenschen.
Baumrind, D. (1971) Current patterns of parental authority. *Developmental Psychology Monographs, 4*(1, Part 2).
Baumrind, D. (1973) The development of instrumental competence through socialization. In A. D. Pick (Ed.), *Minnesota Symposium on Child Psychology* (Vol. 7). Minneapolis: University of Minnesota Press.
Brehm, S. S., & Brehm, J. W. (1981). *Psychological reaction: A theory of freedom and control.* New York: Academic Press.
Crapanzano, V. (1990). On self characterization. In J. W. Stigler, R. A. Shweder, & G. Herdt (Eds.), *Cultural psychology: Essays on comparative human development* (pp. 401–426). Cambridge, MA: Cambridge University Press.
Cushman, P. (1991). Ideology obscured: Political uses of the self in Daniel Stern's infant. *American Psychologist, 46,* 206–220.
Damon, W. (1977). *The social world of the child.* San Francisco: Jossey-Bass.
Damon, W., & Hart, W. (1988). *Self understanding in childhood and adolescence.* Cambridge, MA: Cambridge University Press.
Davidson, P., Turiel, E., & Black, A. (1983). The effect of stimulus familiarity on the use of criteria and justifications in children's social reasoning. *British Journal of Developmental Psychology, 1,* 46–65.
Dworkin, R. (1977). *Taking rights seriously.* Cambridge, MA: Harvard University Press.
Erikson, E. (1963). *Childhood and society.* New York: Norton.
Erikson, E. (1968). *Identity, youth, and crisis.* New York: Norton.
Freud, S. (1961). *The ego and the id: Standard edition* (Vol. 19). London: Hogarth Press. (Original work published 1923)
Gewirth, A. (1978). *Reason and morality.* Chicago: University of Chicago Press.

Gewirth, A. (1982). *Human rights: Essays on justification and application.* Chicago: University of Chicago Press.

Greenfield, P. M., & Cocking, R. R. (Eds.). (1994). *Cross-cultural roots of minority child development.* Hillsdale, NJ: Lawrence Erlbaum Associates.

Habermas, J. (1991). *Moral consciousness and communicative action.* Cambridge, MA: MIT Press.

Hermans, H., Kempen, H., & van Loon, R. (1992). The dialogical self: Beyond individualism and rationalism. *American Psychologist, 47,* 23–34.

James, W. (1899). *The principles of psychology.* London: Macmillan.

Kernberg, O. F. (1975). *Borderline conditions and pathological narcissism.* New York: Aronson.

Kim, U., & Choi, S. (1994). Individualism, collectivism, and child development: A Korean perspective. In P. M. Greenfield & R. R. Cocking (Eds.), *Cross-cultural roots of minority child development* (pp. 227–258). Hillsdale, NJ: Lawrence Erlbaum Associates.

Kohut, H. (1978). *The search for the self: Selected writings 1950–1978.* New York: International University Press.

Kuczinski, L., Kochanska, G., Radke-Yarrow, M., & Girnius Brown, O. (1987). A developmental interpretation of young children's non-compliance. *Developmental Psychology, 23*(6), 799–806.

Mahler, M. S. (1979). *The selected papers of Margaret S. Mahler* (Vol. 1 & 2). New York: Aronson.

Masterson, J. (1981). *The narcissistic and borderline disorders.* New York: Brunner/Mazel.

Miller, J., & Bersoff, D. M. (1992). Culture and moral judgment: How are conflicts between justice and interpersonal responsibilities resolved? *Journal of Personality and Social Psychology, 62,* 541–554.

Noam, G. (1993). "Normative vulnerabilities" of self and their transformations in moral action. In G. Noam (Ed.), *The moral self* (pp. 209–238). Cambridge, MA: MIT Press.

Nucci, L. (1977). *Social development: Personal, conventional, and moral concepts.* Unpublished doctoral dissertation, University of California, Santa Cruz.

Nucci, L. (1981). Conceptions of personal issues: A domain distinct from moral or societal concepts. *Child Development, 52,* 114–121.

Nucci, L., Camino, C., & Sapiro, C. (1993, July). *Mothers' and children's concepts of areas of children's personal autonomy and social regulation in the U.S. and Brazil.* Symposium paper presented at the biennial meetings of the International Society for the Study of Behavioral Development, Recife, Brazil.

Nucci, L., Guerra, N., & Lee, J. Y. (1991). Adolescent judgments of the personal, prudential, and normative aspects of drug usage. *Developmental Psychology, 27,* 841–848.

Nucci, L., & Herman, S. (1982). Behavioral disordered children's conceptions of moral, conventional, and personal issues. *Journal of Abnormal Child Psychology, 10,* 411–426.

Nucci, L., & Lee, J. Y. (1993). Morality and personal autonomy. In G. Noam & T. Wren (Eds.), *The moral self* (pp. 123–148). Cambridge, MA: MIT Press.

Nucci, L., & Smetana, J. G. (1994) Mothers' conceptions of young children's personal domain. Unpublished manuscript, College of Education, University of Illinois, Chicago.

Nucci, L., & Weber, E. K. (1995). Social interactions in the home and the development of young children's conceptions within the personal domain. *Child Development, 66.*

Piaget, J. (1932). *The moral judgment of the child.* New York: The Free Press.

Piaget, J. (1985). *The equilibration of cognitive structures.* Chicago: University of Chicago Press.

Sampson, E. E. (1985). The decentralization of identity: Toward a revised concept of personal and social order. *American Psychologist, 40,* 1203–1212.

Sarbin, T. R. (1986). *Narrative psychology: The storied nature of human conduct.* New York: Praeger.

Selman, R. (1980). *The growth of interpersonal understanding: Developmental and clinical analyses.* New York: Academic Press.

Selman, R., & Schultz, L. H. (1990). *Making a friend in youth: Developmental theory and pair therapy.* Chicago: University of Chicago Press.

Shweder, R. A. (1979a). Rethinking culture and personality theory Part I: A critical examination of two classical postulates. *Ethos, 7,* 255–278.

Shweder, R. A. (1979b). Rethinking culture and personality theory Part II: A critical examination of two classical postulates. *Ethos, 7,* 279–311.

Shweder, R. A. (1990). In defense of moral realism: Reply to Gabennesch. *Child Development, 61,* 2060–2067.

Shweder, R. A., & Bourne, E. J. (1984). Does the concept of the person vary cross-culturally? In R. A. Shweder & R. A. LeVine (Eds.), *Culture theory: Essays on mind, self, and emotion* (pp. 158–199). New York: Cambridge University Press.

Shweder, R. A., & LeVine, R. (Eds.). (1984). *Culture theory: Essays on mind, self, and emotion.* New York: Cambridge University Press.

Shweder, R., Mahapatra, M., & Miller, J. (1987). Culture and moral development. In J. Kagan & S. Lamb (Eds.), *The emergence of morality in young children* (pp. 1–83). Chicago: University of Chicago Press.

Shweder, R. A., Turiel, E., & Much, N. (1981). The moral intutions of the child. In J. H. Flavell & L. Ross (Eds.), *Social cognitive development: Frontiers and possible futures* (pp. 288–305). New York: Cambridge University Press.

Smetana, J. (1989). Adolescents' and parents' reasoning about actual family conflict. *Child Development, 60,* 1052–1067.

Smetana, J. G., Bridgeman, D., & Turiel, E. (1983). Differentiation of domains and prosocial behavior. In D. Bridgeman (Ed.), *The nature of prosocial development: Interdisciplinary theories and strategies* (pp. 163–183). New York: Academic Press.

Smith, M. B. (1994). Selfhood at risk. *American Psychologist, 49,* 405–411.

Spiro, M. (1993). Is the Western conception of the self "peculiar" within the context of the world's cultures? *Ethos, 21,* 107–153.

Stern, D. (1985). *The interpersonal world of the infant: A view from psychoanalysis and developmental psychology.* New York: Basic Books.

Tisak, M. (1986). Child's conception of parental authority. *Child Development, 57,* 166–176.

Triandis, H., Bontempo, R., Villareal, M., Asai, M., & Lucca, N. (1988). Individualism and collectivism: Cross cultural perspectives on self-ingroup relationships. *Journal of Personality and Social Psychology, 59,* 1006–1020.

Turiel, E. (1978). The development of concepts of social structure: Social convention. In J. Glick & K. A. Clarke-Stewart (Eds.), *The development of social understanding* (pp. 25–108). New York: Gardner Press.

Turiel, E. (1994). Morality, authoritarianism, and personal agency in cultural contexts. In R. J. Sternberg & P. Ruzgis (Eds.), *Intelligence and personality* (pp. 271–299). Cambridge, UK: Cambridge University Press.

Turiel, E., & Davidson, P. (1986). Heterogeneity, inconsistency, and asynchrony in the development of cognitive structures. In I. Levin (Ed.), *Stage and structure: Reopening the debate* (pp. 108–143). Norwood, NJ: Ablex.

Turiel, E., Killen, M., & Helwig, C. (1987). Morality: Its structure, functions, and vagaries. In J. Kagan & S. Lamb (Eds.), *The emergence of morality in young children* (pp. 155–243). Chicago: University of Chicago Press.

Wainryb, C. (1991). Understanding differences in moral judgments: The role of informational assumptions. *Child Development, 62,* 840–851.

Yau, J., & Smetana, J. G. (1994). *Adolescent–parent conflict among Chinese adolescents in Hong Kong.* Unpublished manuscript, University of Hong Kong.

4

The Gendered Family and the Development of a Sense of Justice

Susan Moller Okin
Stanford University

Increasingly, psychologists and others are looking at the family as an important site for moral development. When do people begin to develop a sense of right and wrong, of justice and injustice? When do we form the basic foundations of our moral selves? Much recent research suggests that this happens very early in life. Damon, in *The Moral Child* (1988), wrote: "Most scholars believe . . . that the potential for moral-emotional reactions is present at birth" (p. 13). There are "many indications," he said, "that enduring aspects of character are indeed formed early" (p. 7). And, he related, "By the age of four or five, children can be interviewed about their views on moral standards like sharing and fairness" (p. 35). Accompanying these conclusions is an increasing focus on relationships and particularly families as an important part of the environment in which moral development takes place (e.g., Cowan & Cowan, 1992; Damon, 1988). What is often missing, however, is sustained attention to the moral structure and practices of families themselves. I argue here that so long as families are crucial formative environments of early childhood, they must themselves be regulated by moral principles—including those of justice or fairness. Simple as this principle would appear to be, it is quite unusual in the context of Western political thought.

Throughout much of our tradition of political thought, an anomaly exists concerning children's moral development. Many of the principal writers in the tradition insist on what modern research has confirmed—that early childhood is a crucial period for moral development. Most also recognize explicitly that moral development takes place largely within families. Yet at the same time,

61

they do not address the morality of relations and behavior within families. They pay very little attention to whether families themselves are structured to be conducive to healthy moral development. Nor do they pay much attention to whether their account of the nature and education of women—whom they assume will play a central role in childrearing—renders them suited to the important role of moral educator. In particular, they have often either not questioned—or, indeed, have explicitly supported—hierarchical relations within families (including those between their adult members as well as those between adults and children). They have done this even when they have advocated far greater equality among citizens in the public sphere. Thus, although concerned with moral development, these writers have bifurcated public life from family life to such an extent that they have had no trouble reconciling inegalitarian, sometimes even admittedly unjust relations within families with a more just, even egalitarian, social structure outside the family. Because this anomaly persists right up into the present, it needs to be explored. After I do this, I look at some of the respects in which various current types of family involve injustice, and consider the actual or likely effects of this on the moral development of children growing up in such families. I then discuss the kinds of family forms that might be most conducive to healthy moral development in children and the public policies that might be likely to foster them.

THE TRADITION: FROM PLATO TO MILL

The earliest major figures in the Western tradition, Plato and Aristotle, placed enormous stress on the influence of very early childhood environment for both moral and intellectual development. Concerned that future citizens be brought up with virtuous habits "from [their] very youth," Aristotle wrote that "the legislator should make the education of the young his chief and foremost concern" (trans. 1946, *Politics* VIII, 1, 1337a). Although the fact is usually overlooked, in his discussion of the best state, he took up more space discussing this subject—including the most minute details of family life—than everything else put together. Unlike Plato, with his proposal for communal living, Aristotle consistently regarded the household as the best environment for young children, because he thought that people take better care of those persons and things to which they are personally attached. The attachment between child and parents is pivotal in his account of moral development, because the child forms good habits in part through following the example of those to whom he is deeply attached.

Whom did he envisage doing the day-to-day early child care, though? Because Aristotle thought male citizens should be very intensely engaged in political speech and action, and also wanted to ensure that "very little of [children's] time is passed in the company of slaves" (*Politics*, VII, 17, 1136a), there seems little doubt that he envisaged mothers as the principal agents of early development; however this involves him in the kind of difficulties I outlined earlier. For, unlike his best state, where those admitted to citizenship are basically each other's equals, Aristotle's household was very much a hierarchical institution. He assumed that women and slaves are intended by nature to serve the various needs of free men, and that the type and extent of goodness and rationality in which they share varies accordingly. Women's rationality, he concluded, befitting her position as one who is permanently ruled by her superior husband, is "without authority." Women's virtues, different from the "human virtues" that free men can attain, are relative to the needs of these men. Thus Aristotle, although perceptive in recognizing the importance of early character development, did not explain how virtue can be learned from a primary parent who is not herself capable of fully human rationality or virtue (see Okin, in press; Sherman, 1989, for further discussion). Neither did he explain how the virtues required in one who is to live as an equal citizen among his fellows can be learned within a context of hierarchy and subordination, justified by allegedly natural differences.

Aristotle has had enormous influence in the history of political and ethical thought. Of particularly strong and long-lived influence has been the distinction he drew between the political realm, which needed to be regulated by the kind of justice that applies among those who are basically equal, and the realm of the household, with its distinctly aristocratic version of justice—with the husband as permanent ruler, on the basis of his natural superiority. This political–domestic dichotomy, in various forms, has pervaded Western political philosophy.

Most political thought of the medieval period justified or advocated hierarchies in the various realms of life, inside and outside the household. However, once the formal political equality of male citizens began to be espoused again in the 17th and 18th centuries, the problem that we saw in Aristotle—how to raise just citizens in an unjust family—resurfaced in a somewhat altered form. Kant, and to some extent Rousseau, tried to resolve the incongruence between the types of family and the types of state they preferred by turning to male tutors or public education as the prime influences in moral development. In Hegel's philosophy, the problem is present in full-blown form. The family is fundamental to moral development, according to Hegel. For it is within the family that citizens first experience, albeit on the level of feeling, the unity or sense of belonging to a greater whole that they will later experience, on the level of reason, in the state. Women have the significant role of guarding the family's divine law and household gods; their moral influence in the family is supposedly great. However, when Hegel speaks of women's nature and capacities, it is difficult to see how this could be so, for he typecasts them as placid and passive, vague and subjective, in contrast to men; indeed, he sums this up by saying: "Men correspond to animals, while women correspond to plants" (Hegel,

1821/1952, p. 263). We must ask what kind of influence such women could have on the early moral development of the children who were to be the next generation of citizens.

This is, as I have pointed out, Aristotle's problem in a somewhat altered form. For in the last few centuries, although the families they envisage are still not congruent with the types of state the theorists are concerned to legitimize, instead of being frankly acknowledged as hierarchical, families are presented as based in feelings—love, generosity, and altruism. Thus the claim, whether explicit or implicit, is that families do not *need* to be just, for they are governed by moral virtues nobler than justice. Rousseau and Hume were prime exponents of this myth, which has been resurrected in recent years by communitarian Sandel (1982).

The first major political theorist and moral philosopher to confront the anomaly we have been examining here was John Stuart Mill. At the time Mill wrote of this, in the third quarter of the 19th century, women had no political rights, and coverture deprived married women of most legal rights, as well. Mill challenged all of this. In *The Subjection of Women* (1869/1984), he took an impassioned stand against the position that justice within the family is irrelevant to the development of just citizens. He argued that the inequality of women within the family is deeply subversive of justice in the wider social and political world, because it undermines the moral potential of men. (He also thought it bad for women, of course.) Making marriage a relationship of equals, by contrast, would transform this central part of daily life from "a school of despotism" (pp. 294–295) into "a school of moral cultivation" (p. 293). Mill discussed, in the strongest of terms, the noxious effects of growing up in a family not regulated by justice. He advised the reader to consider "all the selfish propensities, the self-worship, the unjust self-preference," that are nourished in a boy growing up in a household in which "by the mere fact of being born a male he is by right the superior of all and every one of an entire half of the human race." "What must be the effect on his character, of this lesson?" (p. 324) Mill asked. He concluded that the example of a marital structure "contradictory to the first principles of social justice" must have such "a perverting influence" (p. 325) that it is hard even to envisage all the good effects of changing it. All other attempts to educate people to respect and practice justice, Mill claimed, will be superficial "as long as the citadel of the enemy is not attacked" (p. 325). His hopes for a reformed, more egalitarian version of the family were as strong as his despair at families in their contemporary form. "The family," he said "justly constituted, would be the real school of the virtues of freedom" (p. 295), primary among which was justice. Mill both saw clearly and had the courage to confront what so many other political philosophers either could not see, rationalized, or hid from.

Mill's feminism, however, was much stronger in its more abstract formulations than when applied to matters of practical life. Unfortunately, he thought that the formal legal equality of husbands and wives would suffice to make families just. In spite of his own recognition that earnings affect power in a marriage, and that domestic responsibilities constrain women's opportunities, he was not willing to question the traditional division of labor between the sexes. In fact, he asserted that until a woman had fulfilled her obligation to care for her husband and children, she should not undertake anything else. He thought married women should be able to earn a living, but that they should not, normally, do so. Clearly, though, however equal the legal rights of husbands and wives, this stance largely undermined Mill's insistence on the importance of marital equality for a just society. Absent any special provision for the vast majority of wives of his time, whom Mill's prescription would leave economically dependent on their husbands, it largely undermined his insistence on marital justice as the necessary foundation for social justice.

Therefore, as we have seen, those political theorists of the past who have perceived the family as an important locus of moral development have rarely acknowledged the need for congruence between the family and the wider social order, suggesting that families themselves ought to be just. Even when they have, as with Mill, they have been unwilling to push hard on the traditional division of labor within the family in the name of justice or equality (Okin, 1989).

FAMILIES AND RAWLS' THEORY OF JUSTICE

Contemporary theorists of justice, with few exceptions, have paid scant attention to the question of moral development—of how people are to become just. Strange though it may seem, it is far less often acknowledged in recent than in past theories that families are important for instilling a sense of justice in the young. Among major contemporary theorists of justice, Rawls alone treats the family as the first school of moral development. Concerned with the stability in practice of the just or "well-ordered" society that he created in theory, he argued that this will be assured only if its members continue to develop a sense of justice. Families play a crucial role in the stages by which this sense of justice is acquired. The love of parents for their children, which comes to be reciprocated, is important in Rawls' (1971) account of the child's development of a sense of self-worth. Both by loving the child and by becoming worthy objects of his or her admiration, parents "arouse in him a sense of his own value and the desire to become the sort of person that they are" (p. 465). Good early moral development, Rawls argued, depends on love, trust, affection, example, and guidance.

This account of parental love and children's desire to emulate their parents as important aspects of moral development seems highly plausible. It was developed further in an interesting recent philosophical work on moral development, *Living Morally,* by Thomas (1989).

Later in the developmental process, Rawls (1971) looked again to the family, which he described in gendered terms, as "a small association, normally characterized by a definite hierarchy, in which each member has different rights and duties" (p. 467). He looked to it as the first of many associations in which we learn to think about issues from the different points of view of others—a capacity that he regarded as an essential part of a sense of justice. All this would seem to require that families themselves be just. At times, indeed, Rawls seemed to endorse this view. He included the family in "the basic structure of society" (p. 490), to which his principles of justice applied. However, he also assumed, without further discussion, that the family, in some (unspecified) form, is a just institution. This assumption is stated but then discussed no further, and thus stands in marked contrast with Rawls' lengthy discussions of other institutions of the basic structure, such as government and the economy, to which he applied his principles of justice, arguing that certain forms of them are just and others not. By contrast, the absence of this sort of discussion of families seems to indicate some ambivalence on his part about the need for families to be just.

In Rawls' more recent writings, the ambivalence displays itself in the form of a more blatant inconsistency. In his new book, *Political Liberalism* (1993), despite his somewhat puzzling assertion that "the nature of the family" is part of the basic structure (in *Theory*, he more clearly, if controversially, said that "the monogamous family" is part of the basic structure), he stated on a number of other occasions that his theory is about political justice, as distinguished from the virtues appropriate to other roles and relations in life. What roles and relations? He specified the associational, the personal, and the familial. He wrote, for example, that "the political is distinct . . . from the personal and the familial, which are affectional, . . . in ways the political is not" (Rawls, 1993, p. 137). In a sense, we have come full circle, not only back to Hegel with his reliance on feelings as the grounding of morality in families, but even back to Aristotle and his association of justice "proper" only with the political, which is understood to exclude families.

BEYOND THE TRADITION: BRINGING JUSTICE TO FAMILIES

The problem with such thinking, as I and many other feminists see it, is that the family is a social institution that defies the attempt to draw a sharp line between the political and the nonpolitical. Families are clearly political in important ways: They involve relations of power and dependency; they play a crucial role in making us the persons we become; they are very much shaped and influenced by laws and other decisions that come out of the political system, narrowly defined; and their shape and distribution of responsibility in turn affect who has more and who has less opportunity and power in the world of public and economic life (see Okin, 1989, for arguments to back up these points). Although political in these ways, families are for the most part comparatively private relationships, in which things both good and bad are frequently hidden from public view. Families are often characterized by affection, but sometimes they are not, and very much not. Sometimes they are characterized by naked power and vulnerability. To think that we can rely on affection and altruism as the virtues governing relations within families is to be blind to what goes on within many actual families.

Thus, although I strongly endorse the general idea that families can be a very important foundation for moral development, I question both the assumption that families are just, and the political–nonpolitical dichotomy that suggests that justice may not even be an appropriate standard by which to judge behavior and the distribution of benefits and burdens within them. Families need to be just, both because of the adverse material effects of injustice in families, especially for many women and children, and also because (as Mill saw so clearly) living in an unjust family can have negative effects on the moral development of the next generation. Surely, unless the first formative example of adult interaction children usually experience—that between their parents—is one of justice and reciprocity, rather than one of domination and manipulation or of one-sided altruism and self-sacrifice, and unless they themselves are treated with love, concern, and respect, they are likely to be considerably hindered in becoming persons guided by a sense of justice in their lives. Their moral development is likely to be extremely stunted.

This, however, requires that children have families that provide them not only with what they need on a day-to-day basis, but with a morally healthy environment in which they can develop a sense of justice. Many children in our current society have neither. Of course, in a just or well-ordered society, such as the hypothetical society Rawls wrote about, many of the problems that now afflict families and lead in some cases to children's having very little or no family support at all would be alleviated. Homelessness and dire poverty, for example, presumably have no place in Rawls' just society. Perhaps drug and alcohol addiction would be rare, there, too, for the conditions of hopelessness that breed it would not exist. However, illness, accident, serious personal conflict, and death cannot be eradicated (although they may be reduced) by justice, and these are some of the factors that disrupt family life most of all.

Even for the great majority of children who do have families of one kind or another, there is presently no guarantee that they are just, or in other respects morally healthy families. Rawls, as I have noted, assumed at times that the family, in some form, is just. However, he did not discuss what that form might be, or whether or how actual families might be encouraged or enabled to conform with it. We must ask: Are typical contemporary families in the United States just families? Obviously, there are various forms of injustice that can occur in families and can affect the "moral environment" in which a child develops. One child can be arbitrarily favored over others, for example. The aspect of family injustice I confine myself to here is gender injustice. In *Justice, Gender, and the Family* (Okin, 1989), I argue at some length that typically, heterosexual couple families in our society are unjust in their distributions of at least some benefits and burdens such as work, power, leisure, access to resources, and other important goods. Different forms of gender injustice occur in different types of families, but a great deal of it has to do with the basic fact that women still do a great deal more unpaid family work than men do.

PATTERNS OF INJUSTICE IN EXISTING FAMILIES

Let us look briefly at the different patterns of injustice that exist in different types of family (for further discussion, see Okin, 1989). In single-female-headed households, which are still growing in number, women do all of the unpaid work except what children can contribute. As well as being far more likely to be economically poor, such families—and especially the mothers in them—are more likely than others to suffer from "time poverty."

In heterosexual couple households in which the woman either does not hold a paid job or works half time or less, her assuming the vast majority of the unpaid work does not lead to her being overworked. Except during the early years of childrearing, when such women and men work about equal numbers of hours, full-time housewives on average work about 14 hours a week less than their husbands. Such a division of labor, however, can lead to a diminishment of self-worth, in a society in which worth is often associated with one's paycheck. More importantly, it leads to the woman's economic dependence, which may not be a problem if the relationship is good, but can place her in great jeopardy if it is not. She can then be vulnerable to psychological, physical, or sexual abuse, and is in danger of sudden impoverishment in the event of separation or divorce—as one formerly middle-class divorced woman put it, "one man's affection away from welfare."

In heterosexual couple households in which the woman works for pay full time or close to it, a different form of injustice is found. Many studies have found that the average wage-working wife does twice as much of the unpaid family work—and an even greater percentage of both the dirty work and the unpredictable or unscheduled work—than her male partner. This situation often leads to chronic tiredness and lack of leisure, as well as diminishing the time and energy that such women—aptly called "drudge wives" by Bergmann (1986)—have to devote to their paid work. It should be pointed out that gay and lesbian couples, especially the latter, are considerably less likely to practice either the traditional or the inequitable dual-career division of labor than are heterosexuals (Blumstein & Schwartz, 1983). This seems to suggest that

these divisions have more to do with gender than with anything such as efficiency, despite the claims of some economists.

I return to these family types, their different versions of gender injustice,
and what might be done about them, toward the end of the chapter. First, however, I look at some of the specific patterns of gender injustice, from the more
extreme to the less extreme, that occur in families and consider the effects they
have or might be expected to have on the moral development of the children
growing up in the various types of families. I first briefly consider one of the
most extreme types of family injustice, physical abuse, and then turn to two
pieces of research I have recently come across: one on women's and girls' perceptions of their own situations in very traditional families, and the other on
the division of labor between adolescents of both genders in different kinds of
heterosexual families.

Accurate statistics on family violence are hard to come by for obvious reasons: A great deal of it goes unreported. A national survey done in 1976 estimated that between 1.8 and 5.7 million women in the United States are beaten
each year in their homes. More recently, *The New York Times* (Olmstead,
1993) cited figures of at least 2 million serious domestic beatings of women
each year, and between 2,000 and 4,000 cases per year of women murdered
by their male partners or former partners. Often, child abuse goes along with
wife abuse. Not only are these figures shocking, they certainly present a challenge to those who think the positive feelings experienced in families can be
relied on to regulate behavior within them. They are even more troubling when
we acknowledge that the propensity for family violence is frequently passed
down from one generation to the next. Although it is not clear what all the
mechanisms of transmission are, research indicates that "individuals who are
exposed to frequent conflict and physical aggression in their childhood families are more likely to be involved in violent family relationships later in life"
(Kalmuss & Seltzer, 1989, p. 345). In addition, there is evidence that children
who grow up in high-conflict, although nonviolent families are likely to learn
abusive and manipulative forms of family interaction and may become physically abusive to their own families later in life.

Now let us turn to two pieces of research having to do with other forms of
family injustice. First, consider a recent study done in Israel by Wainryb and
Turiel (1994; see also Turiel, chap. 5, this volume) of women's and girls' perceptions of gender inequality in traditional hierarchical families. The families
studied were Druze Arabs, but the results might well apply to patriarchal religious households more generally, including those in some subcultures in our
own society. Wainryb and Turiel found that the Druze wives and daughters regarded as legitimate the power of fathers and husbands over many aspects of
the women's own lives, such as whether they could get a job or even a driver's
license. However, at the same time, they did not regard this as fair. They saw
no way of resisting the male power because of the sanctions—including being

beaten, thrown out of the house, or divorced—that disobedience might invoke. This acceptance of male dominance as inevitable resulted in what may seem to us to be a clear inconsistency in the answers many of the women and girls gave. Whereas almost 80% of them judged that it was unfair for a husband to dictate his wife's choices, at the same time 93% of them said that the wife should acquiesce. What we see, it seems, is the learned acceptance of injustice, enforced by male power. Such a family seems very like a Hobbesian state with father as Leviathan: His commands have to be obeyed not because of any intrinsic quality, such as justice, but simply because he who makes them has the power to enforce them. Such authoritarian environments are surely not suitable moral training grounds for citizens of either sex.

Finally, let us turn to a less extreme, although still significant and very widespread form of family injustice and its likely effect on children: the unjust division of labor between the adults in heterosexual households. A study by Benin and Edwards (1990) shows that the unequal division of work between mothers and fathers is not only reflected, but magnified, in unequal divisions of work assumed by adolescent children of both sexes. On the one hand, in the households they studied in which there was a traditional gendered division of labor, in which fathers were wage workers and mothers were housewives, the adolescent girls and boys studied did approximately the same amount of household work, although what they did was divided along gendered lines—for example, girls washed dishes, boys mowed lawns. By contrast, in households in which mothers and fathers both worked full time for pay but, as we know, the mothers averaged twice as much unpaid family work as the fathers, the amount of work done by adolescents varied widely by sex. The girls in these households did, on average, 25% more than the girls in the traditional households, whereas the boys did only one third as much as the traditional household boys. This means that the girls in these households did almost four times as much household work as their brothers. Because (as the mother of two adolescents) I find it difficult to imagine that the extra work done by the girls was purely voluntary, I think we have to assume that the boys adopted the pattern of family injustice established by their own fathers and, like them, avoided as much household work as they could. It seems that the daughters allowed themselves to be pushed, at a young age, into an even more exaggerated version of the "drudge wife" model established by their mothers. Unfortunately, because they were using already collected time-use data, the researchers were not able to interview the adolescents (or their parents) about their perceptions of the fairness or unfairness of this situation. However, surely we need to ask if such a family environment is a good place to develop a sense of justice. Weren't these boys, rather, learning quite early in life to have a sense of entitlement, and these girls to have a sense of being obliged to do more than their fair share of the work— purely on account of their sex?

HOW CAN WE HAVE MORE JUST FAMILIES?

It seems that, although few households in the United States are as overtly patriarchal as those of the Druze Arabs, serious inequalities still persist in many. Families typically provide, for the children growing up in them, far less just or fair models of interaction than they might. Women, including mothers, are doing far more wage work than they were 20 years ago, and although men are doing somewhat more childcare and other family work than they were then, their contributions are nowhere near enough to even things out. In their longitudinal study entitled *When Partners Become Parents,* Cowan and Cowan (1992) concluded that "behind the ideology of the egalitarian couple lies a much more traditional reality" (p. 116). They showed that, before becoming parents, couples envisage a far more egalitarian parenting relationship than actually evolves, even very soon after the birth of their first child. They presented a number of interesting findings: that very few men even consider cutting down on their paid work after the baby is born; that whether mothers go back to work or stay home with the baby, they are often conflicted about their decisions; that mothers who return to wage work before their children are 18 months old are less likely to be depressed than those who do not; and, perhaps most significant of all, that the division of labor in the family is by far the greatest cause of conflict between new parents.

Cowan and Cowan thus confirmed Hochschild's (Hochschild with Machung, 1989) conclusion, in *The Second Shift,* that women are getting the short end of the "stalled revolution." Cowan and Cowan (1992) wrote, "Their work roles have changed but their family roles have not. Well-intentioned and confused husbands feel guilty, while their overburdened wives feel angry. . . . It is not simply that men's and women's roles are unequal that seems to be causing distress for couples, but rather that they are so clearly discrepant from what both spouses expected them to be" (p. 26).

This is all very discouraging, but there is a bright spot in the Cowans' conclusions: The minority of fathers who do a substantial amount of day-to-day child care have higher self-esteem, as do their wives, than those in families in which mothers do almost all of the child care. Moreover, again confirming Hochschild's findings, they found that both members of these sharing couples are happier and more satisfied with their marriage. Thus, such an arrangement seems to benefit all, because children are also positively affected by their parents' good relationship, and presumably will benefit in their development from living in a family that is likely to be both amicable and fair.

Thus we know both that couples tend to plan for far more egalitarian parenting and other family work after the birth of a child than actually happens, and that in the rather rare cases in which couples do share paid and unpaid work more equitably, their relationship, and presumably their child, benefits.

What, then, prevents the vast majority of couples from arranging their lives this way? As suggested already, in at least some cases, it seems that men, not realizing that there might be benefits even to themselves in sharing more of the unpaid family work, simply get away with doing as little of it as they can. Then, once the division of labor is established, they can increasingly use their greater earning power as a rationale for not doing more at home. It seems, though, that there are also pressures coming from their parents as well as their friends on fathers who wish to participate equally in raising their children. However, the biggest practical obstacles are undoubtedly the structure and expectations of wage work, which have evolved with the expectation that "workers" had wives at home. It appears that this expectation will not be relinquished without a long struggle. Now, of course, "workers," far more often than not, do not have wives at home, and often are wives and mothers, too. In order to accommodate this change, the hours of work should have been decreasing, over the last 20 years, and its flexibility should have been increasing.

The decrease in hours has not occurred. Instead, the hours of work expected in many jobs have been rising, and the stagnation of real wages has driven some who previously held one job into two or more, or overtime, if available. As an article in *The New York Times* (Uchitelle, 1993) explained, manufacturers, deterred from hiring new workers by the rising costs of recruiting, training, and (especially) benefits, are increasingly turning to overtime rather than creating new jobs when demand for their products rises. The average factory worker was then working 4.3 hours of overtime every week, and the average work week in manufacturing was at its longest since 1966. This certainly does not help those parents who are trying to share paid work and child care more or less equally between them. In academia and the law, to take two examples from the professions, the years when a person's productivity is most crucial—the pretenure or prepartnership years—coincide with the time when he or she is most likely to become a parent. (This already makes things tough enough.) In addition, the level of productivity demanded of these young professionals (the number of publications and billable hours, respectively) has been rising over the past few decades, rather than declining to accommodate the needs of modern parenting. Schor's *The Overworked American* (1991) documents the facts of and the reasons behind the increasing hours many are working.

As far as flexibility is concerned, we now have available legally mandated family leave, at least for those workers who are employed in large-scale enterprises. This is a good start. However, it is, unlike such leave in some European countries, unpaid leave, rendering it less than helpful to single-parent families, or indeed to any family that is tightly dependent on its wages for week-to-week living. In other respects, there has not been nearly enough of an increase in flexibility for workers.

Utopian as it may sound, when U.S. workers are in worldwide competition for jobs, I am convinced there is little chance that we can achieve a much more equitable sharing of work within families until employers are required to rec-ognize and provide for the fact that those who work for them are people with lives, relationships, and personal responsibilities, as well as workers. The facts of life are such that usually, for a lengthy period, workers are parents of chil-dren who need care, and they are often the only active parents of such chil-dren. Often, they are also children of elderly parents who need care. At least from time to time, they are likely to be responsible for sick or disabled people who need care. The costs of such care have stayed off the social agenda for so long because of the age-old expectation that women provide it free of charge. The fact that women often paid a high price for caring for others was long ignored, but is not being ignored as much any longer. Such recognition and provision will require a shorter standard working day, flex time, and paid fam-ily leave, as well as government-subsidized high-quality day care. When it is asked "How can we afford such luxuries?" it must be answered, "How can we not afford them?" For the costs are indeed high: stressed-out families, women and children living in poverty at unprecedented rates, some women whose work training and experience at work are stagnating because of the difficulties of combining wage work and child care, and many children growing up with-out adequate care. Many families are coping with more demands than they have the capacity to tackle, and the next generation of citizens is suffering by consequence.

CONCLUSIONS

Obviously, not all of the country's problems are caused by inequities within families and the failure of the world of wage work to take heed of contempo-rary family realities. However, these are serious problems, and they often ex-acerbate others, such as class-based inequality. Social justice between the sexes has not been achieved, and is unlikely to be achieved, by formal legal equality alone. One reason for this is that so much of the way society is structured is a result of a history in which women were subordinated and in which it was as-sumed that they exchanged sexual and domestic services, including the so-cially crucial task of child care, for economic security in the form of depen-dence on men. But the world has changed. Many women are not prepared to make this kind of exchange, with its incipient risks, and prefer to stay in the workforce—despite the difficulties of doing so—throughout the years of rais-ing children. Many of those who do still make the exchange find themselves unexpectedly vulnerable, in the event of marital conflict, separation, or divorce. Many women—especially African American women—do not have a choice at all, because so many of the Black men of their age cohort are unemployed, in prison, or the victims of accidental death or murder.

No matter how formally equal women are, as long as they disproportionately bear the responsibility for domestic work, raising children, and caring for the sick, disabled, and elderly—and as long as this work is unpaid or underpaid—they will remain systematically socially disadvantaged. Thus those dependent on them will suffer, and the family, where so much of women's work is done, will retain its character as an unjust social institution. No matter how wonderful the most fortunate and well-adjusted families may be, as long as there are systematic injustices pervading the various types of "typical families" in our society, we continue to lack a sound foundation for the moral development of the next generation.

REFERENCES

Aristotle (1946). *Politics* (E. Barker, Ed. & Trans.). Oxford: Oxford University Press.

Benin, M. H., & Edwards, D. A. (1990). Adolescents' chores: The difference between dual- and single-earner families. *Journal of Marriage and the Family, 52,* 361–373.

Bergmann, B. R. (1986). *The economic emergence of women.* New York: Basic Books.

Blumstein, P., & Schwartz, P. (1983). *American couples.* New York: Morrow.

Cowan, C. P., & Cowan, P. A. (1992). *When partners become parents: The big life change for couples.* New York: Basic Books.

Damon, W. (1988). *The moral child: Nurturing children's natural moral growth.* New York: The Free Press.

Hegel, G. W. F. (1952). *The philosophy of right* (T. M. Knox, Trans.). Oxford, UK: Clarendon. (Original work published 1821)

Hochschild, A., with Machung, A. (1989). *The second shift: Working parents and the revolution at home.* New York: Viking.

Kalmuss, D., & Seltzer, J. A. (1989). A framework for studying socialization over the life cycle: The case of family violence. *Journal of Family Issues, 10,* 339–358.

Mill, J. S. (1984). *The subjection of women.* In J. M. Robson (Ed.), *Collected works* (XXI). Toronto: University of Toronto Press. (Original work published 1869)

Okin, S. M. (1989). *Justice, gender, and the family.* New York: Basic Books.

Okin, S. M. (in press). Feminism, moral development, and the virtues. In R. Crisp (Ed.), *How should one live?* New York: Oxford University Press.

Olmstead, L. (1993, May 18). When passion explodes into a deadly rage. *The New York Times,* pp. A1, B4.

Rawls, J. (1971). *A theory of justice.* Cambridge, MA: Harvard University Press.

Rawls, J. (1993). *Political liberalism.* New York: Columbia University Press.

Sandel, M. J. (1982). *Liberalism and the limits of justice.* Cambridge, UK: Cambridge University Press.

Schor, J. B. (1991). *The overworked American.* New York: Basic Books.

Sherman, N. (1989). *The fabric of character: Aristotle's theory of virtue.* New York: Oxford University Press.

Thomas, L. (1989). *Living morally: A psychology of moral character.* Philadelphia: Temple University Press.

Uchitelle, L. (1993, May 16). Fewer jobs filled as factories rely on overtime pay. *The New York Times,* pp. A1, A18.

Wainryb, C., & Turiel, E. (1994). Dominance, subordinance, and personal entitlements in cultural contexts. *Child Development, 65,* 1701–1722.

5

Equality and Hierarchy: Conflict in Values

Elliot Turiel
University of California at Berkeley

The term *values* is usually highly valued. It refers to the good and desirable, especially when linked to the realm of morality. Values and morality are also associated with one of the highly valued concepts in late 20th-century social scientific thought, that of culture. Without denying their clearly positive aspects, this chapter is based on the proposition that values and cultures are dynamic and multifaceted phenomena that can have nonpositive features as well. Values perceived as positive by some people can have negative implications for others. Moreover, a set of values can have both positive and negative implications for the same persons. I consider how values—and social judgments— might embody positive and negative components, whose coexistence can produce changes in social practices and cultural configurations. The idea that value clashes can result in transformations in cultural practices presupposes that values are connected to individuals' social reasoning, that argumentation and rational discourse occur among members of a culture, and that cultural practices or ideologies are interpreted and reflected on by individuals. Viewing culture in conjunction with judgments, reflection, and social discourse implies that diversity is an important component within cultures, as well as between them.

I propose that cultures are not adequately characterized as cohesive or homogeneous, but rather as dynamic and multifaceted, in many instances entailing struggles and disputes among people furthering different values. Varying interests and goals among members of a culture, especially when they hold different roles and status in the social hierarchy, can produce conflict and tensions to go along with sources of cooperation and harmony. Whereas cultures are often portrayed through analyses of social institutions and public ideology as reflecting a cohesive social orientation, I present analyses of individuals' moral, social, and personal concepts that show that within cultures there is heterogeneity in social orientations and diversity in people's judgments and actions.

CULTURAL ANALYSES: DIFFERENCES AND UNITY

An influential figure in the contemporary valuing of culture is the anthropologist Geertz—especially through his volume on *The Interpretation of Cultures* (1973). It was there that Geertz highlighted the idea that culture is necessary for human adaptation and survival with the assertion that without culture people would be "unworkable monstrosities with very few useful instincts, fewer recognizable sentiments, and no intellect; mental basket cases" (p. 49). In this view, culture is formative of what makes humans human: emotions and thought. The influence of this kind of value placed on culture is seen in calls for the establishment of a "new" discipline of cultural psychology to override the traditional subdisciplines (including developmental) of psychology (Bruner, 1990; Shweder, 1990; Shweder & Sullivan, 1993). In these views, culture does not solely provide a background or context for the emergence of emotions and the intellect. Rather, particular kinds of emotions and concepts stem from the culture. For instance, Geertz (1984) also asserted that concepts of self and persons:

> vary from one group to the next, and often quite sharply. The Western conception of the person as a bounded, unique and more or less integrated motivational and cognitive universe, a dynamic center of awareness, emotion, judgment, and action organized into a distinctive whole and set contrastively both against other such wholes and against its social and natural background is . . . a rather peculiar idea within the context of the world's cultures. (p. 126)

These assertions, along with the idea that without culture people would be unworkable monstrosities, well summarize central features of certain approaches to cultural psychology. Concepts of self, persons, self–other relations (Markus & Kitayama, 1991), morality (Shweder, Mahapatra, & Miller, 1987), and much more (Sampson, 1977), are framed by cultural orientations, and cultural orientations vary from each other. Cultural orientations, in these views, are coherent and homogeneous, with definable organizing principles. At the most general level, cultural orientations can be distinguished as individualistic and collectivistic (Triandis, 1989, 1990). Individualistic cultures cohere around personal goals, and people are oriented to self-sufficiency, independence, and resistance to social pressures for conformity or obedience to authority. In accord with the focus on personal goals, the morality of individualists revolves around personal rights and justice. By contrast, collectivistic cultures (most often these are non-Western, traditional, and hierarchical) are organized around shared goals, with interdependence and social harmony. No clear distinction is made between persons and their roles or status in social order, so that concepts of autonomy, personal agency, and individual entitlements are minimal. The morality of collectivistics is based on fulfilling duties and adhering to the requirements of social roles.

Such distinctions between cultures and, particularly, Geertz's assertions about concepts of self, prompted another anthropologist, Spiro (1993), to entitle an essay "Is the Western conception of the self 'peculiar' within the context of the world cultures?" In contrast with approaches that locate diversity only in differences between cultures, Spiro maintained that concepts of self (as well as many other social concepts) vary across individuals within the same society, as well as across societies. Spiro argued that in most cultures there is a mixture of conceptions of self and that cultural ideologies or normative cultural conceptions do not necessarily translate into individuals' conceptions or experiences of self and others:

> A typology of self and/or its cultural conception which consists of only two types, a Western and non-Western, even if conceived as ideal types, is much too restrictive. Surely, some non-Western selves, at least, are as different from one another as each, in turn, is different from any Western self. In short, in my view . . . there is much more differentiation, individuation, and autonomy in the putative non-Western self, and much more dependence and interdependence in the putative Western self, than these binary opposite types allow. (p. 117)

Research reviewed by Spiro shows that people in non-Western cultures do account for personal goals and that self-interest can be a motive for many of their actions. Before considering the evidence reviewed by Spiro, as well as other research in non-Western cultures, I consider issues deemed central to social and moral orientations in Western societies—especially in the United States, which is regarded by proponents of homogeneous cultural orientations as one of the most clearly defined of the individualistic cultures (Hogan, 1975; Sampson, 1977; Triandis, 1990). I consider concepts of equality and rights, which are closely linked to the idea of individualism. The values of equality and rights are part of the ideology prominent in the United States, as often espoused in public pronouncements and embodied in important documents like the Constitution. However, differences among groups of people, such as social class, ethnic, and racial groups, suggest that social hierarchies, inequalities, and serious restrictions of freedoms and rights are also part of the culture. My main focus is on relationships between men and women, which are among the closest of social relationships. Gender relationships often entail conflicts over equality, rights, freedoms, personal entitlements, social hierarchy, and questions of dominance and subordination (Hochschild, 1989; McKinnon, 1993; Okin, 1989). These types of conflicts suggest that the culture cannot be adequately characterized only as a shared system of values.

EQUALITY AND HIERARCHY:
CONTRADICTIONS IN VALUES

It has been documented that inequalities between men and women exist in many spheres of life. Unequal treatment of women is reflected in their underrepresentation in the political system, positions of power and influence in business and the professions, and fewer opportunities for paid work. Moreover, in many fields, women are paid substantially less than men for similar work, even when their qualifications are the same. According to Okin (1989), these apparent injustices in the distribution of benefits (and burdens) have been overlooked by most Western moral theorists since Aristotle, who instead have assumed that relationships between men and women, largely taken to be governed within the family, are collectivistic (my term) and therefore beyond concerns with justice and individual rights. A collectivistic orientation is attributed to the family by moral theorists in that it is assumed that distinctions between people are unbounded, self-interest is not given priority over the interest of others, and relationships are based on affection and altruism. Some of these moral theorists have also explicitly stated that interdependence in the family occurs in the context of a hierarchical order in which men are in dominant positions (see Okin, 1989, for further details on moral theorists' views of the family). Western moral theorists have thus not solely presented individualistic ideas because they attribute interdependence and harmony to the family. Spiro (1993) reminded us that several prominent Western theorists (e.g., William James, George Herbert Mead, Erik Erikson, Isaiah Berlin) have gone beyond individualism to include interdependence, connectedness, and sociability in their analyses of self.

Okin maintained that, in spite of the assumptions made by some moral theorists (not those who accept gender-based hierarchy), inequalities and injustice are very much part of gender relationships in families, such that the interests of men are given priority over those of women. By tradition, in Western cultures, men have been in positions of dominance, with greater decision-making power, access to work, control over finances, and less economic vulnerability in cases of divorce (Blood & Wolfe, 1960; Blumstein & Schwartz, 1983). Traditionally, women have done the work at home, which is regarded to have lower perceived status and esteem (Nussbaum, 1992). Women also have not been given equal opportunities in education or work outside the home. Moreover, in extreme cases women are subjected to the power of men in other ways, including physical and sexual abuse, which is overwhelmingly abuse of females by males (Okin, 1989).

The traditional forms of inequality between husbands and wives are exemplified in the following statements of a man (a plastic surgeon) expressing his expectations of his wife (who works as a part-time receptionist) in an interview reported by Blumstein and Schwartz (1983):

> I don't mind her having a part-time job, but she doesn't have time for a full-time job. . . . I am the breadwinner, she is the homemaker, and that is what we signed up for twenty years ago. . . . We do not make decisions around her work. My work supports us and we put that first. It is her responsibility to do her work well just as it is my responsibility to do my work well. . . . She takes care of our sons and I take care of everyone. It is part of her responsibility not to let her work interfere with her job at home. I don't mind her working as long as dinner is ready on time and the house is neat and clean. I think we deserve that and so far it has worked out well. (p. 119)

In this man's view of the family, there are clearly defined roles and associated responsibilities. His roles are superordinate (she takes care of our sons, I take care of everyone). It is also evident that he considers himself the main decision maker; he does make "concessions" (I don't mind her having a part-time job; I don't mind her working as long as dinner is ready on time) to some of her wishes as long as his desires and expectations are met.

These traditional arrangements have changed in recent years. The number of women who work outside the home has increased substantially since the 1950s; for example, among married women with children from 6 to 17 years of age, 28% worked in 1950 and 68% worked in 1986 (see Hochschild, 1989, for further details). In spite of these changes, inequalities still exist and gender relationships are largely hierarchical. One of the primary indicators of these types of inequalities is that working women do much more of the unpaid work in the home and child care than their husbands (Okin, chap. 4, this volume). Indeed, women have much less leisure time than their husbands and do twice as much of the work in the home. Gender hierarchy also affects the lives of children and adolescents (as noted by Okin) because in families with both parents working full time, girls do more of the household work than boys.

Several survey studies of dual-career families document a common pattern in which women are expected to do more of the undesired tasks, and men have entitlements such as greater time for leisure activities (see Hochschild, 1989, for a review). Researching some of the same questions as explored in the surveys with intensive interviews of 50 couples and observations in several homes, Hochschild (1989) found that husbands and wives are often in conflict and struggle over the distribution of work in the home and over whether and to what extent women should work outside the home. She did find that not all the couples in her sample held the same viewpoints regarding marital roles. Some of the participants in the study accepted traditionally defined gender roles of men with greater power and women with greater responsibility in the home, even if the women were working outside the home. Among those accepting the traditional views of gender differences, the men regarded their wives as being in subordinate roles, and women accepted their subordinate positions. For instance, one man stated, "I feel the man should be the head of the house. He should have the final say. I don't think he should have the only say; my father was the head but a lot of times my mother got her way. But I feel like this is my role in life, and I don't see any reason to want to change it" (Hochschild, 1989, p. 59). This man's wife, who worked only because her income was needed, had views consistent with those of her husband: "I don't want to be equal with Frank. I don't want to be equal in work. I want to be feminine. I want to have frilly things. I don't want to do what my husband's doing. Let him do it. Maybe that's it—I want to be taken care of" (Hochschild, 1989, pp. 64–65).

However, other women in the study believed they should have equal power and responsibilities to their husbands. Often, this was combined with the idea that the man's identity should be tied more closely to work and the woman's identity should be tied to both work and home. More often than not, serious conflicts and disputes arose between husbands and wives over decisions regarding paid work and the distribution of work in the home. In many cases, the wives raised concerns with fairness (e.g., a "50/50" sharing of work in the home), whereas the husbands were concerned with the nature and closeness of the relationship, and sometimes complained that they were not attaining enough nurturance and care from their wives. Hochschild, for instance, reported that in one family experiencing conflict the wife wished that her husband be "considerate of her needs" and honor "her ideal of sharing and equity" (p. 49). By contrast, her husband felt that adequate communication between them was the important factor and that fairness was an impersonal and abstract concept that should not bear on their relationship.

Therefore, real families exist as a complex set of interrelationships with a variety of values, combinations of harmony and conflict, autonomy and interdependence, and tensions between concerns with equality and with hierarchical relationships of dominance and subordination. Furthermore, families differ from each other, and the dynamics of families are not static over time. Although conflicts within families are not new (Skolnick, 1991), their nature and sources have shifted over the years with the increased number of women engaging in paid work outside the home. Moreover, transitions in families produce changes in the nature of relationships. For instance, when couples become parents their relationships often change because of conflicts over the division of labor and modes of childrearing (Cowan & Cowan, 1992). One persistent feature across many families and across time is tied to conflicts over equality and fairness.

Conflicts produced by the structure of dominance and subordination in male–female relationships extend beyond the family. For instance, in the 1990s there has been increased concern with gender issues in hierarchical relationships outside the family (an area of public and legal concern is sexual harassment in the workplace). This provides good examples within the United States of conflicts between extant hierarchical orderings and individual rights, a kind of conflict that reveals different value systems in operation. An interesting example to consider is the debate about pornography and freedom of speech, which has revolved around dominance and subordination in gender relationships (McKinnon, 1993). Highly controversial challenges to freedom of speech through proposed censorship of pornography have been based on the idea that harmful consequences ensue from pornography, along with the idea that pornography causes a subordination of women resulting in further inequality and diminished political power for women (McKinnon, 1993). These propositions led to the adoption of an ordinance in Indianapolis, Indiana that outlawed all pornography (although this law was eventually ruled unconstitutional by a Court of Appeals), as well as a statute in Canada that was upheld by Canada's Supreme Court. McKinnon and others argue that freedom of speech needs to be restricted, in part, because pornography causes violence against women (i.e., viewing pornography leads men to rape and physically assault women). However, their arguments (and the Court's ruling regarding the statute in Canada) are also that pornography directly contributes to the subordination of women and their lack of political power. In fact, McKinnon (1993) maintained that the U.S. Constitution's First Amendment rights to free speech in the case of pornography (and some other speech acts) are in conflict with protections of equality in the Fourteenth Amendment.

The debates are over restrictions of freedom of speech (although most acknowledge speech can be legitimately restricted in some situations), and whether pornography causes rape, physical assault, and the subordination of women (see Dworkin, 1991, 1993). McKinnon maintained that free speech serves to support social dominance and inequality by allowing depictions of the physical and sexual subordination of women by men. Although it is accepted that rape and physical assaults against women occur, it has not been shown that this is caused by pornography (Dworkin, 1993). Similarly, it is unclear that inequality and subordination are consequences of pornography. However, it is the backdrop of inequality and relationships of dominance and subordination that give the argument any plausibility and allowed Canada's Supreme Court to uphold the censorship of pornography on the grounds of gender equality. Indeed, one of the difficulties in arguing that pornography should be banned because it promotes the subordination of women is that many other forms of speech do so to at least as great an extent and impact many more people than does pornography. As put by Dworkin (1993): "No doubt mass culture is in various ways an obstacle to sexual equality, but the most popular forms of that culture—the view of women presented in soap operas and commercials, for example—are much greater obstacles to that equality than the dirty films watched by a small minority" (p. 36). Dworkin's examples demonstrate that even if one does not accept the idea that pornography is causally linked to gender inequality, conflicts between social hierarchy and equality are present in many realms of public discourse.

VALUES AND CONTEXTUAL VARIATIONS

From the perspective of characterizations of Western culture as egalitarian and individualistic, it may be surprising that issues of inequality, roles, and social hierarchy are so prevalent in fundamental interpersonal relationships and in the structure of society. From the perspective of the research evidence, however, it should not be surprising that people struggle with seemingly opposing concepts like fairness, equality, rights, and dominance and subordination. These juxtapositions of seemingly different social orientations are consistent with many studies showing that judgments and behaviors differ in accordance with contextual variations and that such variations are associated with different domains of the individual's social reasoning.

A few brief examples can serve to illustrate the point. (For more extensive discussions see Turiel, 1994, and Turiel & Wainryb, 1994. For discussion of relevant literature from social psychology see Ross & Nisbett, 1991, and Ross & Ward, chap. 6, this volume.) First, there is substantial evidence that Americans do not always endorse individual freedoms, liberties, or rights, including rights to free speech. In fact, the challenges by some feminists to pornography as protected free speech are not isolated instances. In addition to the many challenges to free speech regarding pornography on the part of conservative religious leaders and politicians (see Dworkin, 1991), the American public frequently does not agree that many other types of freedom of speech should always be allowed. This is evidenced by a number of large-scale public opinion surveys conducted by sociologists and political scientists (e.g., McClosky & Brill, 1983; Stouffer, 1955) assessing attitudes toward freedom of speech, as well as freedoms of press, assembly, religion, and rights to privacy, dissent, and divergent lifestyles. These surveys have consistently revealed that freedoms, liberties, and rights are not always upheld by Americans. In some contexts (e.g., when put in the abstract), freedoms and rights are endorsed (see also Helwig, 1995a, 1995b), whereas in other contexts (e.g., when in conflict with other moral or social concerns) the same freedoms and rights are not upheld.

Contextual variations are also evident in people's social behaviors. For instance, it has been demonstrated that people obey authority in some experimental conditions and defy authority in other conditions (Milgram, 1974), conform with the judgments of a group in some situations and disagree in other situations (Asch, 1956), and that individuals are influenced by groups in decisions as to whether to help someone in distress (Latenée & Darley, 1970). Studies (Haney, Banks, & Zimbardo, 1973) have also shown that Americans readily adhere to designated roles requiring them to behave in harmful ways toward others (i.e., when subjects are assigned roles of guards in a simulated prison). The findings of this body of research demonstrate not only that behaviors vary by context, but also that people's orientations to a given situation are more complex than that expected from dichotomous categories like individualism and collectivism or independence and interdependence.

As an example, when encountered with situations in which a person is in distress, an individual is more likely to intervene to help others if he or she is alone rather than in the presence of others who do not intervene (Latenée & Darley, 1970). Thus, when alone, people act independently, taking personal initiative, but they do so in the service of interdependence (i.e., to further the welfare of others). When they are in the presence of others, people are influenced by the group in that they fail to intervene; in that case, one form of interdependence is at the expense of interdependence in the form of the welfare of those in distress. (For additional examples of the weaving of independence and interdependence in various situations, see Turiel & Wainryb, 1994; Wainryb & Turiel, 1995.)

Contextual variations in judgments and behaviors are partly a function of how individuals construe social situations (see Ross & Ward, chap. 6, this volume, and Turiel & Wainryb, 1994). This proposition is consistent with Asch's (1952, 1956) interpretation of his research findings in the "conformity" studies. In those studies, subjects were asked to judge the length of lines in group settings; the other participants were confederates of the experimenter who at specified times gave incorrect judgments. As opposed to simply interpreting the results as instances of social influences of the group on individuals, Asch's interactional analyses focused on subjects' judgments about the context, including the actions of others and the contradictions between their own and others' perceptions. To state it briefly, because the judgments about the lengths of the lines were unambiguous and subjects could see no apparent reasons for the (incorrect) judgments made by all the others in the group, they were led to question their own perceptions and give credence to the group (see Asch, 1956, for more details of this interpretation and supporting evidence). Subsequent research (Ross, Bierbrauer, & Hoffman, 1976) supported this interpretation by showing that when subjects can attribute a particular motivation to the actions of people in the group (e.g., attaining a material payoff) they conform much less than when the reasons for the group's actions are unspecified.

Social situations, then, are interpreted by individuals and their interpretations take into account the features of contexts. The contextual variations evident in social attitudes and behaviors indicate that general social orientations do not hold for people in Western cultures, because greater cross-situational consistency than that found would be expected. The contextual variations, nevertheless, are linked to systematic judgments held by individuals. In part, contextual variations occur because individuals interpret different aspects of social situations from the perspective of distinctly different domains of social reasoning (Turiel, 1983). These domains include concepts about morality (justice, rights, and welfare), social conventions (coordinations of social interactions in social systems), and psychological and personal attributes (including personal agency, autonomy, and jurisdiction; see Nucci, chap. 3, this volume). These domains of social judgment interact with features of social situations, resulting in variations in behaviors, as well as in conflicts within and between individuals. Conflicts and variations are especially evident in the context of gender relationships, where there is an intersection of moral concerns (with fairness, harm, and equality), issues of personal entitlements, and social structural arrangements of hierarchy.

PERSONAL AGENCY AND HIERARCHY: JUXTAPOSITION OF VALUES

Considering again the conflicts between men and women in the family, workplace, and society at large, it is possible to point to several elements that reflect individualistic concerns. These are that women struggle with and assert concerns with rights, equity, and their personal preferences. Furthermore, in these conflicts men further their interests and assert their personal entitlements. The other side of the coin, however, is that these "individualistic" concerns are linked to collectivistic ones. The gender conflicts occur in the context of hierarchical social arrangements, which entail relationships of interdependence and include specified roles and duties (for husbands and wives).

It could be said that this mixture of social orientations exists because we are actually referring to two divergent cultures (or subcultures) defined by the orientations of men and women. That is, men's orientation to social relationships differs from that of women in ways analogous to differences between cultures. (This proposition would be consistent with the idea that a mixture of social orientations exists because the United States is a multicultural society.) Gilligan (1982) and her colleagues (Gilligan, Ward, & Taylor, 1988; Gilligan & Wiggins, 1987), portrayed women's concepts of morality and self as different from those of men in ways that are strikingly similar to the distinctions drawn between collectivistic and individualistic cultures. Gilligan maintained that there are two moral orientations, one reflecting an ethic of care and the other an ethic of justice, which are strictly (see earlier Gilligan) or loosely (see later Gilligan) associated with gender. In Gilligan's formulation, the two moral orientations extend beyond care and justice because they encompass concepts of self and the nature of relationships with others.

The ethic of care associated with females is linked to concepts of self as unbounded and attached to social networks. The ethic of justice associated with males is linked to concepts of self as autonomous, individuated, and separated from social networks. The rather different orientations to self in social relationships entail corresponding divergences in morality. A morality of care, based on attachments to others, "arises from conflicting responsibilities rather than from competing rights and requires for its resolution a mode of thinking that is contextual and narrative rather than formal and abstract" (Gilligan, 1982, p. 19). A morality of justice, based on separateness, "ties moral development to the understanding of rights and rules" (p. 19). Moral decisions made through the (usually male) lens of justice are based on logical justification and quantification ("he abstracts the moral problem from the interpersonal situation, finding in logic of fairness an objective way to decide who will win the dispute," p. 32), whereas moral decisions made through the (usually female) lens of care are based on social relationships (a "construction of the dilemma to a network of connection, a web of relationships that is sustained by a process of communication," p. 32).

One of Gilligan's claims is that justice and fairness are emphasized in most explanations of moral development because it is mainly male psychologists, with their better understanding of male than female psychology, studying mainly males, who put forth theories of moral development. The idea that theories of justice are due to constructions by males may be overdrawn. We have seen, for instance, that the arena of justice, fairness, and rights is not restricted to males. First, several female scholars (from various fields, including psychology, anthropology, sociology, and political science) studying women's roles in the family and society have been concerned with the ways women are denied rights, justice, and equality. Approaches to moral problems, especially among those addressing women's roles, do not neatly divide into differences between female and male scholars (see Mednick, 1989; Okin, 1989; Pollitt, 1992; Stack, 1990).[1] Second, in certain contexts (especially in the family) wo-

---

[1]Concerns with justice and rights on the part of females can be seen in social scientific analyses and journalistic accounts. In her essay in this volume and in her book *Justice, Gender, and the Family,* Okin (1989) asserted that "the distinction between an ethic of justice and an ethic of care has been overdrawn. The best theorizing about justice, I argue, has integral to it notions of care and empathy, of thinking of the interests and well-being of others who may be very different from ourselves" (p. 15). As another example, Hochschild (1989) discussed inequalities due to divorce as follows: "Patriarchy has not disappeared; it has changed form. In the old form, women were forced to obey an overbearing husband in the privacy of an unjust marriage. In the new form, the working single mother is economically abandoned by her former husband and ignored by a patriarchal society at large" (p. 25).

On the journalistic side, Pollitt, writing in *The Nation* (December 28, 1992) critiqued gender distinctions of the type proposed by Gilligan and other social scientists for ignoring the role of economics and issues of justice in women's lives. Pollitt believed that some social scientists "cannot say that the differences between men and women are the result of their relative economic posi-

men appear to be more concerned with justice, rights, and equality. In studies of conflicts between married couples over the division of labor in the home and child care (Cowan & Cowan, 1992; Hochschild, 1989) it was found that many women focused on fairness, justice, and rights. In those contexts, it is often the women who believe that it is necessary that their husbands share work equally (even in the quantitative sense of "50/50"), and that their husbands be more concerned with the fairness of their contributions to the household. Sometimes fairness was linked to care, in the sense that fair treatment was seen by the woman as a manifestation of love. It was often the man who justified existing arrangements on the basis of role responsibilities in the family (Blumstein & Schwartz, 1983), thought that fairness was an impersonal, abstract concept, and asserted that communication and nuturance were central in the relationship (e.g., Hochschild, 1989).

Proposed dichotomies in social orientations based on gender or culture share the idea that groups can be divided into people maintaining different global, homogeneous types of reasoning and behavior. However, the propositions that the dichotomy is based on gender or culture pose conceptual problems for each other. The proposition of gender differences in orientations to self and morality implies that within a culture there is a mixture of care and interdependence, and justice and independence. It could be argued that females and males constitute separate cultures, thus preserving the idea that social orientations differ by culture, which in turn would negate the idea that Western cultures are mainly individualistic. (It could be further argued that cultural analysts have restricted themselves to males, who are individualistic, in their characterizations of Western cultures.) Describing females and males as constituting separate cultures, however, is also unsatisfactory (and certainly dilutes the concept of culture) because it ignores all the experiences and social structural features shared by them (especially in the family), as well as the sustained nature of social relationships among females and males.

Perhaps recognizing that the idea of differences in orientation is a challenge to the proposition of cultural divergence, Miller and Bersoff (1995) argued that the distinction between a morality of care and a morality of justice is a cultural

---

tions because to say that would be to move the whole discussion out of the realm of psychology and feel-good cultural pride and into the realm of a tough political struggle over the distribution of resources and justice and money" (p. 806). Pollitt argued that the discussion should be moved to the realm of justice: "No one asks that other oppressed groups win their freedom by claiming to be extra-good. . . . For blacks and other social minorities, it is enough to want to earn a living, exercise one's talent, get a fair hearing in a public forum. Only for women is simple justice an insufficient argument" (p. 807).

In another journalistic account, Bumiller (1990), writing about the plight of women in India, summarized the situation for the future of India with reference to the central role for justice: "In the end, the country's three biggest challenges—maintaining democracy, secularism, and national unity—cannot be accomplished without justice, including justice for women" (p. 289).

and not a gender difference. Miller and Bersoff maintained that the "individualism" of U.S. culture impacts on females, and that females and males from the same culture will have more commonalties than people of the same gender in different cultures (although they do not account for the reasons interdependence has been attributed to a large segment of Western culture). In their view, females and males in non-Western cultures have an unbounded conception of self and hold concepts of interdependence in social networks.

However, the multiple orientations to self and morality thus far considered are not restricted to Western cultures. For instance, Spiro (1993) reviewed research showing that individuation and autonomy are part of non-Western conceptions of self—especially when researchers investigate individuals' conceptions of self and persons rather than relying on an examination of a set of cultural symbols of a group. Individuals' experiences of thoughts, desires, and intentions of persons (self and others) can result in conceptions that differ from public pronouncements or doctrines constituting part of the cultural symbols. One example of how the two differ comes from Spiro's research of Buddhism in Burma. Although one of the central doctrines of Theravada Buddhism is that there is no soul, ego, or transcendental self, Spiro (1993) found that these ideas are not upheld by the Burmese he studied. Instead, "they strongly believe in the very ego or soul that this doctrine denies . . . because they themselves experience a subjective sense of self, the culturally normative concept does not correspond to their personal experience" (p. 119). Moreover, the Burmese believe that the self or ego has continuity with its reincarnations.

Spiro also provided ethnographic evidence of conceptions of a bounded self with self-interested goals and concerns with personal entitlements among the Balinese, South Asians (Indians, Pakistanis, Nepalese), and Japanese—that is, members of cultures often cited as maintaining interdependent, unbounded conceptions of self. For instance, studies show that in their work, northern Japanese villagers are motivated not so much by group goals as individual goals of power, self-esteem, and pride (see Spiro, 1993). It has also been reported that village women act both in accord with the interests of others, their roles in the family, and "self-serving personal desire." The Japanese villagers seem to recognize a discrepancy between the cultural ideology of interdependence and how individuals actually function because they believe that people are fundamentally individually centered and nonsocial. Spiro cited several other ethnographers working in other non-Western cultures who report discrepancies between public presentations (in terms of the cultural ideology of interdependence) and individual representations or conceptions of selves as including separation, distinctions of persons, and concerns with self-interest.

In addition to discrepancies between individual conceptions and cultural ideologies (or cultural symbols), it may be the case that different, and sometimes contradictory, social orientations are embedded in particular cultural practices and social structural arrangements. The structure of hierarchical arrangements, particularly in gender relationships (as well as relationships between members of different classes and castes), is a case in point. Usually, the focus is on specified duties and roles in hierarchical relationships, without considering the other side of the coin of dominance and subordination—which is the possibility that personal entitlements are accorded to those in positions of power. It is generally acknowledged that in many societies around the world, especially in traditional ones, relationships between men and women are organized hierarchically. It is also often asserted that in such traditional, hierarchically structured societies, personal agency, self-interest, and personal entitlements are minimal because concepts of self and social relationships are based on shared goals and interdependence (the ideas of unbounded self and nondifferentiation of self and other).

However, in traditional cultures with gender-based hierarchical arrangements it is not always the case that the interests of women are furthered or that in these regards there is always harmony and interdependence. (For a discussion of how influencing cultural changes in positive ways requires shifts in attitudes toward groups lacking power, such as women, see Cabral, 1973.) Recent journalistic accounts document several ways in which both the emotional and physical well-being of women are adversely affected by their subordinate positions and lack of power. In many countries, women's work is difficult and oppressive, they are more vulnerable to poverty than their male counterparts, and they often experience physical and sexual abuse (Nussbaum, 1992; Okin, in press). For instance, it has been reported that in India, marital conflicts often lead to large numbers of women being maimed or killed by their husbands and in-laws (often referred to as "bride burning") who want larger dowries than those provided by the wife's family. According to an article in *The New York Times,* there is a statistical association between small dowry payments and wife beatings (Rao, 1994). Furthermore, many abortions occur to prevent the birth of females (Bumiller, 1990; Lastreto & Winnans, 1989). As put by a psychologist (Suman Nangia) from India: "Violence to women in India is an accepted form of life. There is a line of violence from the day they are born to the day they die" (Angelis, 1993).

In African countries, as another example, the AIDS epidemic is impacting severely on women in part because infected men and men who are at risk for AIDS demand that their wives engage in sexual relations with them (Perlez, 1990, 1991). Also, female circumcision is a social practice considered by some as harmful to women and a result of male dominance (Walker & Parnar, 1993). Dr. Henriette Koyate, a gynecologist and secretary general of the Senegalese National Committee on Traditional Practices, attributes the practice to "the desire and need of men to control the sexuality of the woman" (Walker & Parnar, 1993, p. 299). Another Senegalese woman, the political organizer Awa Thian, explained why the practice of female circumcision still exists:

> I think the answer is contained in the questions "Why is it that everywhere women are dominated? Why is it that on all five continents one finds a quasi-identical situation, different only in its form? Why is it that women always end up doing the domestic jobs?" You can go wherever you want—to America, France, India—and everywhere you will find women in the middle of doing domestic chores. . . . Another thing is that women on all five continents are subordinate to men. (Walker & Parnar, 1993, pp. 284–285)

It is important to note that in the context of women's movements protesting female circumcision, there are many African women who do support the practice because it is a cultural tradition.

Aside from violence and other forms of physical harm inflicted on women, it appears that domestic situations in non-Western countries have interesting parallels to the situations in Western countries depicted by Hochschild, Okin, and others. Consider the following description by Bumiller (1990), an American correspondent who spent time living in a farming village (Khajuron) in northern India:

> I spent my working hours in long interviews, sometimes two hours at a time, with what eventually amounted to twenty-five women from the highest to the lowest castes. By the end of the year, I came to two unqualified conclusions. First, both men and women struggled in the village, but the women because of their gender, struggled and suffered twice as much as the men. Second, the women of Khajuron had one of two lots in life, defined entirely by caste. If a woman belonged to one of the upper or middle castes, she was virtually a hostage, confined within the walls of her home to isolation and demanding housework, which her husband did not consider work. Many men said their wives did "nothing" all day, even though most women never stopped working at physically exhausting household chores. If a woman belonged to the lower castes, she was free to leave her house, usually to work at seasonal labor in the fields for less than fifty cents a day. She was of course expected to handle all housework and child care as well. (p. 79)

If the interests of people in subordinate positions are restricted, it raises the question of whether, in turn, the interests of people in dominant positions are furthered. It may be not only that restrictions on the interests of some (e.g., females) come with benefits to others (e.g., males), but also that those in dominant positions are believed to have autonomy and legitimacy in asserting their personal prerogatives and entitlements. In such a case, the values of hierarchy and particular duties would be positive for some but negative for others. As already noted, analyses drawing dichotomies in cultural orientations have focused mainly on judgments as to whether socially prescribed duties and role obligations need to be maintained (e.g., Shweder et al., 1987). Virtually no attention has been given to the dynamics of relationships between persons in dominant and subordinate positions. A fuller understanding of duties and roles within social hierarchies requires study of how people conceptualize self and morality with regard to those in dominant and subordinate positions. It may be that those in dominant positions are accorded personal autonomy and independence. It may also be that, in certain respects, those in subordinate positions regard their roles to entail injustices.

In order to directly examine how people in a traditional culture think about personal agency and fairness in gender relationships, studies (Wainryb & Turiel, 1994) were conducted among Arab Druze villagers residing in northern Israel (for details of the Druze as a traditional hierarchical culture see Turiel & Wainryb, 1994). The research examined the ways the Druze make judgments about decision making in everyday activities (e.g., choices of occupational and educational activities, household tasks, leisure activities). In one study, judgments were elicited from adolescent and adult males in reaction to situations presenting decision-making conflicts between husband or fathers and wives, sons, or daughters. In one set of situations, the person in a dominant position objected to the choices of activities on the part of a person in a subordinate position (e.g., a husband objects to his wife's decision to take a job). In another set, the person in a subordinate position objected to the dominant person's choices (e.g., a wife objects to her husband's decision to change jobs).

The results of this study clearly show that concepts of persons as autonomous, independent, and entitled to make personal choices are part of the orientation to social relationships of males in this non-Western setting. Alongside such concepts of personal autonomy, the males maintain concepts of interdependence in that particular roles in the hierarchy dictate how individuals act. However, the expectations of independence and interdependence between persons are neither equal nor reciprocal. One way of characterizing the results is to say that most of the participants in the study thought that males should make decisions for themselves and for their wives and daughters. When a husband or father objects to the choices of a wife or daughter, they should not engage in the activity. In turn, a man is free to choose his activities even if his wife, daughter, or son object. It was also thought that sons should be able to make their own decisions over objections from their fathers.

The inequality in decision making is based on different ways of conceptualizing interdependence and independence in relationships (as ascertained by interviews eliciting subjects' reasons for their judgments about decision making). In the context of a man who objects to the activities of his wife or daughter, the relationships were conceptualized as hierarchical, and it was thought that role obligations, responsibilities, and competencies dictated what people should do. In the context of a wife or daughter who objects to the activities of husband or father (as well as a father who objects to a son's activities), the relationships were conceptualized as ones of independence, and it was thought that personal choices and entitlements dictated what people should do. It appears, then, that persons are conceptualized as autonomous, independent, and as legitimately making personal choices. People are also conceptualized as part of a social network in which their independence and personal jurisdiction are subordinated to others and the requirements of their role. For certain types of actions within the family, males are viewed in terms of independence, autonomy, and separation, whereas women are regarded as dependent on their role in the system and connected to the responsibilities of those in the role of husband or father.

The findings of this study lend support to propositions put forth by Nucci (chap. 3, this volume) regarding the realm of the personal. Nucci proposed that a personal sphere with a sense of boundaries between self and others is a necessary component of moral and social development. The research with the Druze provides empirical verification for Nucci's propositions because concepts of personal autonomy were found to be present in a setting where the role of the individual is de-emphasized in public discourse. Moreover, the study showed connections of the personal realm to concepts of social relationships within a hierarchical system. The research with the Druze also shows that it is not only people in dominant positions who form concepts of personal autonomy. In another study (also reported in Wainryb & Turiel, 1994) it was found that in some respects Druze females (children, adolescents, and adults) think about decision-making conflicts in ways similar to that of males. They, too, judged that wives and daughters are bound by role obligations and should not act contrary to the man's wishes, whereas a husband or father is an autonomous agent with realms of personal jurisdiction. Unlike the male subjects, however, female subjects often justified their judgments about how women should act on pragmatic grounds; that is, women might very well suffer negative consequences like physical violence, abandonment, or divorce if they did not acquiesce to the man's wishes. Furthermore, the majority (78%) of the Druze females thought that it was unfair for a husband or father to interfere with the choices of activities on the part of a wife or daughter. Girls and women in a traditional culture, therefore, believe that people in dominant positions have decision-making authority because of their power to inflict serious negative consequences on those in subordinate positions, and they evaluate the situation as unjust. In this respect, we see an opposition between men and women within the family. Such opposition is by no means complete or even primary. Along with females' pragmatic concerns and the perceived injustice of the situation, there is an acceptance of the legitimacy of the hierarchical arrangements and associated roles and responsibilities. People in subordinate positions take multiple stances in relation to the social structure and prevailing ideology. Although Druze women accept the status distinctions and the autonomy of males, they are also aware of the power held over them by men. This complex juxtaposition of different orientations to power, coercion, and dominance is likely to make for tension within individuals and in social relationships.

THE ACQUISITION OF SOCIAL JUDGMENTS

Constructing a description of traditional, hierarchically organized cultures, such as the Druze, as collectivistic, as maintaining primarily concepts of interdependent and unbounded selves and a morality of duties in the social order can serve to obscure central features of relationships with elements of dominance and subordination in which some people enjoy personal entitlements drawn from their status and relative power. In part, gender relationships among people in some traditional cultures entail connectedness toward the aim of individuation. That is, roles and duties in the social order serve to prescribe activities of interdependence that also permit people in dominant positions to assert their individuality and independence. As we have seen from the research with the Druze, this is not a straightforward matter of people in dominant positions asserting their wills over those subordinate to them, who lack the power to resist (although that is part of it). Both males and females accept the idea that males have realms of personal jurisdiction, entitlements, and independence. Males and females also, at the same time, conceptualize social relationships to entail elements of interdependence, including the necessity of moral duties and obligations. Yet females, at least, juxtapose a morality of duty with a conflicting morality of justice and rights (i.e., that duties in hierarchical relationships can produce injustices).

The embedded quality of individuation in connectedness, as an example, illustrates that the heterogeneity in people's thinking about the social world is not solely a matter of serially applying different judgments to different situations (although that occurs as well). Particular judgments cannot simply be matched with particular social contexts or situations. If, indeed, different types of judgments can be embedded in social contexts, then it becomes extremely difficult to attempt to identify an ideology or orientation that would be acquired by members of the culture. The complexity of heterogeneity and embeddedness indicates that social values can be in conflict, and that they can produce conflicts among people—even those in close relationships.

There are various facets to the intersection of values in gender relationships within the context of more or less hierarchical social structures. In more strict hierarchies (such as in traditional cultures) values of duties and interdependence may have positive connotations for those in dominant positions and negative ones for those in subordinate positions. As we have seen, values of duties and interdependence can secure the ends of attaining power, independence, self-interest, and the achievement of personal prerogatives for those in dominant positions. In turn, those in subordinate positions are, because of roles and duties associated with the hierarchical structure, subject to unfair treatment, denial of rights, and coercion through the ever-present threat of denial of material goods or abandonment in the family, physical harm, and, in extreme cases, loss of life. Several examples of real consequences to women were mentioned earlier: lack of decision-making power, unequal work and leisure time, sexual abuse, "bride burning," increased susceptibility to disease, and female circumcision (which some consider a form of sexual mutilation). These potential value conflicts, however, are not solely between males and females. Perhaps to as great an extent, there is a conflict for those in subordinate positions between the value they place on duties and roles in the hierarchy and the negative facets of relationships of dominance and subordination. Consequently, there are points of shared values and points of value conflicts between them.

A corresponding set of positive and negative value connotations exists in gender relationships within the context of less strict hierarchies (such as in Western cultures). Consider the distinction drawn by Gilligan (1982) between an orientation to interdependence, responsibility, and networks of relationships on the one hand, and independence, autonomy, and rights on the other hand. In Gilligan's formulation, the orientation to interdependence and relationships represents positive values, because it is proposed as women's primary means of attaining moral ends. However, commentators also taking a feminist perspective (e.g., Abu-Lughod, 1991; Okin, 1989; Pollitt, 1992) have maintained that insofar as women are primarily oriented to interdependence and connection (they also argue that often women have other moral concerns), it can have negative consequences in their lives by stereotyping them into traditionally accepted roles that serve to distance women from aspects of society (e.g., the workplace, politics, struggles for rights, equality, and justice). It is also argued that concerns solely with interdependence would serve to perpetuate a system that directs women to be caretakers and nurturing, whereas men can be the beneficiaries of caretaking and still maintain their independence and "rights" (Pollitt, 1992). The underlying message in the feminist critiques of proposed gender distinctions in morality is that interdependence is a two-sided value for women because it can conflict with justice and rights. Through Hochschild's (1989) work we have already seen that for men values of justice and equality can conflict with the value they place on hierarchy and interdependence in family relationships (where they sometimes give priority to hierarchy and interdependence in the relationship between husbands and wives).

The coexistence of values, with their positive and negative connotations, appears to be a source of social conflict. Insofar as males accept a degree of hierarchy in gender relationships, values placed on interdependence are likely to be less than totally reciprocal and linked to inequalities. A potential tension exists between their concepts of interdependence within hierarchy and their concepts of fairness and equality. Similarly, there is potential tension between women's concerns with fairness, equality, personal entitlements, and values placed on interdependence or their roles in a hierarchical system. Moreover, there are potential tensions between males and females involving differences in perspectives on fairness, equality, interdependence, and dependence of an unequal kind (often females are dependent on males for their livelihood).

These types of conflicts, it can be speculated, may constitute sources of change within individuals and societies. One indication that value conflicts can be a source of change is the existence of indigenous groups in several non-Western cultures addressing the problems faced by persons in subordinate positions (especially women, but also people in lower social classes and castes). Women's movements and political parties devoted to the rights of women and those of the untouchable castes are active in India (Bumiller, 1990; Fineman, 1990). Groups and organizations devoted to furthering the rights of women and protecting their physical welfare (e.g., from wife beating) are active in several Middle Eastern and African countries. Organizations also exist in several African countries (e.g., Nigeria, Sudan, The Gambia, Senegal) devoted to protecting the health of women, particularly with regard to female circumcision (Walker & Parnar, 1993). The existence of such groups suggests that changes can be stimulated, from within cultures, through those who highlight one side or another of the tensions between values or different moral and social concepts maintained.

Whether conflicts between diverse moral, social, and personal concepts, within individuals, between people, and at the cultural or societal level are sources of change for individuals and cultures is an open question. However, there is substantial evidence that the concepts held by individuals are not isomorphic with cultural ideologies, or orientations described by social scientists, or even ideas embedded in public documents and official pronouncements. This evidence fails to support the proposition that social and moral development in individuals is a process of cultural reproduction. As already noted, Spiro (1993) provided several examples from non-Western cultures of how individuals maintain social and personal concepts that differ from central forms of cultural ideology, such as symbols, linguistic categories, and religious doctrines (e.g., the studies of Buddhism in Burma already mentioned).

Several other examples relevant to issues pertaining to women's roles, social class differences, and personal rights serve to illustrate the point. In a non-Western setting, the anthropologist Abu-Lughod (1993) studied Bedouin women in Egypt by living with families for long periods and gathering women's stories and conversations around several themes pertaining to their roles in the culture. The stories and conversations with women are in the backdrop of a cultural ideology that emphasizes patriarchy and patrilineality, particularly marriage arrangements and submission of women to men's wishes and commands. Living among Bedouin women and listening to their stories and conversations about their life experiences provided Abu-Lughod views from the perspective of girls and women not necessarily in complete accord with cultural ideology. She was able to determine that there are differences and disagreements among group members, conflicts between people, efforts to alter existing practices, and struggles between wives and husbands and parents and children. As examples, women protest, resist, and even subvert arranged marriages when they are not to their satisfaction. Women who wish to marry some-one different from the person chosen by the parents sometimes attempt to find ways to thwart parental dictates. Married women find some of their husbands' demands unacceptable. Typical means used to control and even dominate husbands are through the wife's connections to her parents and, at a later age, to grown sons. Girls do persist in their efforts at pursuing chosen activities, particularly with regard to schooling. These and several other examples show that the cultural ideology among the Bedouins often does not correspond to individuals' perspectives and behaviors. (See also Mernissi, 1994, for reflections on her upbringing in a harem in Morocco of the 1940s.)

Another example of opposition between individual perspectives and aspects of the social context comes from Willis' (1977) ethnographic analyses of British working-class youth in school settings. Willis documented continual clashes between many working-class youth and the dominant cultural values and ideology, insofar as they are represented by teachers, administrators, and even middle-class students. The working-class adolescents oppose and defy authority, criticize the demeanor of teachers, reject many of their values, and often fail to adhere to their rules. Moreover, working-class adolescents are critical of and feel superior to other students who are perceived to be part of mainstream culture and who behave and think in ways conforming to mainstream cultural ideology. Here, too, there is a mixture of individuation and connection. The working-class youth studied by Willis continually displayed behavior that was independent and rebellious relative to school authorities, other students, and cultural symbols. Their independence, however, also was linked to cohesiveness among working-class adolescents or what Willis referred to as the counterculture group. The combination of opposition and connection was evident in the youths' relationships with their parents. Whereas parents sometimes opposed their children's conflicts with school authorities, for instance, they also were in conflict with the perceived values and ideology of school authorities, thereby connecting with their children.

Willis' descriptions show that conflicts are ubiquitous in relationships between certain groups of youth and institutionalized authority. It is also evident that sharp discrepancies exist in social orientations among people in society. These discrepancies include "independence between parents and kids" (Willis, 1977, p. 73). The attitudes of Americans toward civil liberties and rights, as assessed by the public opinion surveys discussed earlier, provide an additional example demonstrating that the contents of culturally significant public documents and symbols are not necessarily reproduced in the beliefs of individuals. Two facets of the findings from the surveys are relevant. One is the discrepancy between public documents (e.g., the U.S. Constitution, with its Bill of Rights) or associated public pronouncements and the attitudes of the majority of individuals, who do not believe freedom (to speech, press, religion, assembly) should be allowed in many contexts. In this regard, it is interesting that, as a national survey has shown, the majority of Americans believe that people should not be allowed to make statements critical of the Constitution. Evidently, a good deal of interpretation and assimilation is done by laypersons.

That interpretations are made by laypersons is further documented by a second facet of the survey findings—namely, that the general population sometimes thinks about issues of freedoms and rights differently from several groups of public leaders. In addition to national cross-section random samples (of 2,931 adults), McClosky and Brill (1983) included samples (2,987 adults) of community leaders in various fields and occupations. Those identified as public leaders worked in government, universities, and the press; they also were lawyers, judges, police, school administrators and teachers, and leaders in business and unions. There were commonalities and differences in findings from the two types of samples. For the most part, both groups agreed in endorsing freedoms, liberties, and rights when put in the abstract or when they were not in conflict with other social considerations. In many cases, although not all, results differed between the two groups when the freedoms or rights were placed in conflict with other moral and social considerations. In the conflict situations, the public leaders frequently endorsed freedoms and rights to a greater extent than the general public. Moreover, leaders from the legal professions responded differently (more often endorsing the freedoms and rights) from the other groups of public leaders. It should be noted, however, that all groups generally endorsed freedoms and rights to a lesser extent when in conflict with other considerations than when put in the abstract or when they did not involve strong conflicts.

These findings have implications both for cultural and developmental analyses. With regard to culture, we see once again diversity among groups within the society. The findings have developmental implications because the attitudes of people in the general population do not always correspond with those who would most publicly communicate a cultural orientation. In a similar vein, a number of studies have found significant discrepancies between parental attitudes toward various areas of values (including political attitudes) and those of their children (see Turiel, Killen, & Helwig, 1987, for a summary). There is comparable evidence, presented by Hochschild (1989), of differences between parents and children in attitudes toward hierarchy or equality in gender relationships. Hochschild found that men who share the work at home with their wives were not any more likely than men who did not share in the housework to have had fathers who also shared in the housework or to have had mothers who worked outside the home. Nor was it the case that the men who shared the work were trained by their parents to do chores at home to a greater extent than those who did not share the work. If anything, men who shared in child care viewed their fathers as negative role models who were not sufficiently involved in child care. Hochschild also cited several other studies showing little relationship between a man's upbringing and the amount of work he did at home as an adult.

CONCLUSIONS: INTERACTION, DIVERSITY, AND CONTEXTUAL VARIATIONS

Evidence of discrepancies between individuals' judgments or behaviors and cultural ideologies or symbols, between laypersons and public leaders, and between parents and their offspring, are consistent with the proposition that individuals interpret and reflect on social interactions and cultural practices. The evidence supports an interactional view of the individual and social practices, which in turn requires a dynamic concept of culture. Indeed, several anthropologists recognize that people interpret social practices, engage in rational discourse about them, and that individuals do not solely reproduce culture (Abu-Lughod, 1991, 1993; Appadurai, 1988; Strauss, 1992). As Abu-Lughod (1993) put it, "others live as we perceive ourselves living—not as automatons programmed according to 'cultural' rules or acting out of social roles, but as people going through life wondering what they should do, making mistakes, being opinionated, vacillating" (p. 27). A similar message came from Strauss (1992): "The social order is not a master programmer in any simple straightforward way" (pp. 1–2).

Along with the idea that individuals do not solely reproduce culture, these anthropologists maintain that cultures ought not be characterized as homogeneous, coherent, or timeless (Abu-Lughod, 1993). According to Strauss (1992), cultural understandings include "conflicts, contradiction, ambiguity, and change" (p. 1). Even though cultures may sometimes have dominant ideologies, "rarely, if ever, does the public realm of culture present a single, clearly-defined, well-integrated reality" (p. 11). Social life, including that in traditional societies, is sufficiently complicated and contested that knowing what people are exposed to publicly is insufficient for an understanding of how they think about social interactions and practices. Appadurai (1988) argued that the attribution of "nativeness" to groups in remote parts of the world has served to characterize those peoples as "confined by what they know, feel, and believe," and as "prisoners of their mode of thought" (p. 37). Appadurai suggested that "natives" are a construction of the "anthropological imagination."

It is noteworthy that Geertz, in recent statements, appeared to recognize a way of approaching the concept of culture different from his previous positions. He believes there is a virtual crisis in the field (Geertz, 1994):

> Descriptive reports of "organic" societies governed by "integrated" cultures, settled shapes, and solidified structures "real as seashells," grow unpersuasive. Stark "great divide" contrasts between "modern" and "premodern" societies, the one individualistic, rational, and free of tradition, the other collectivistic, intuitive, and mired in it, look increasingly mythical, summary, and simple-minded. (p. 3)

A conception of culture accounting for conflicts, contradictions, and change, and allowing for interpretations, reflection, and critique on the part of individuals is suggested by several analyses in this volume. Okin's perspective on

justice and injustices in the family makes clear that this primary social institution is complex and multifaceted, with several areas of conflict. Conflicts and
negotiations in the family are due not only to divergent interests and goals
among its members, but also to a structure that combines close attachments
with social hierarchy and power relations. Similarly, the realm of the personal,
as presented by Nucci, results in efforts at negotiations with others and adaptations to the social structure with regard to autonomy, freedom, and morality.
Such negotiations among members of cultures are other sources of conflict
and contradiction. The analyses, provided by Ross and Ward, of social construal and "biased" perceptions of situations and other persons dramatically
show that variations in social judgments occur between individuals and for the
same person from one situation to another. The research of Ross and Ward
demonstrates that it does not take differences between cultures to create diversity and difficult-to-resolve conflicts or differences in perspectives.

Several research trends provide a basis for understanding variability in
thoughts and actions. One of these is findings (Mischel, 1968, 1969) of situational variability in behaviors (rather than consistency in personality traits).
Another is the contextual variation observed in the types of social psychological experiments discussed already. Those studies have yielded findings
indicating that there is variability in behaviors and judgments associated with
different social situations. As another example, research on domain specificity
has provided evidence of systematic variations in people's social reasoning—
variations that contribute to observed contextual variations.

If, therefore, we take seriously social contexts, situational variability, domain specificity, and social interactions as sources of individual and societal
change, we are led to variations within cultures, a breakdown of dichotomies
in orientations to self or morality, and a focus on similarities and differences
among cultures. I have considered how situational variability, context dependence, and domain specificity all reflect heterogeneity within cultures, as well
as individuals' interpretations of social events and social relationships. These
features also reflect individuals' engagement in the social world, such that conflicts, argumentation, and negotiations, along with agreement and harmony,
are part of social life (Habermas, 1984). Some common areas of conflict, negotiation, dispute, and harmony appear in different cultures, despite differences in their ideologies. Relationships tied to social hierarchies (social class
or gender) seem to be one of those areas. Gender relationships do differ according to culture. In many traditional cultures, role distinctions between
women and men are drawn more sharply, with associated inequalities, than in
many Western cultures. Nevertheless, there are similarities in the concerns,
struggles, and ways power and role distinctions serve to benefit one group over
the other. Social hierarchies produce inequalities, opportunities for the assertion of personal entitlements, and contexts for judgments about welfare, justice, and rights. Social structural arrangements and experiences within the

parameters of those arrangements influence people's judgments. When people interact with each other, they can generate shared understandings, construct ideas novel to them, and often enough, produce points of conflict.

REFERENCES

Abu-Lughod, L. (1991). Writing against culture. In R. E. Fox (Ed.), *Recapturing anthropology: Working in the present* (pp. 137–162). Santa Fe, NM: School of American Research Press.

Abu-Lughod, L. (1993). *Writing women's worlds: Bedouin stories.* Berkeley: University of California Press.

Angelis, T. (1993, November). Yoke of oppression weighs on women. *APA Monitor,* p. 41.

Appadurai, A. (1988). Putting hierarchy in its place. *Cultural Anthropology, 3,* 36–49.

Asch, S. E. (1952). *Social psychology.* Englewood Cliffs, NJ: Prentice-Hall.

Asch, S. E. (1956). Studies of independence and conformity: A minority of one against a unanimous majority. *Psychological Monographs, 70*(9).

Blood, R. O., & Wolfe, D. M. (1960). *Husbands and wives: The dynamics of married living.* Glencoe, IL: The Free Press.

Blumstein, P., & Schwartz, P. (1983). *American couples.* New York: Morrow.

Bruner, J. (1990). *Acts of meaning.* Cambridge, MA: Harvard University Press.

Bumiller, E. (1990). *May you be the mother of a hundred sons. A journey among the women of India.* New York: Fawcetts Columbine.

Cabral, A. (1973). Return to the source: Selected speeches. *Monthly Review Press,* 39–56.

Cowan, C. P., & Cowan, P. A. (1992). *When partners become parents: The big life change for couples.* New York: Basic Books.

Dworkin, R. (1991, August 15). Liberty and pornography. *New York Review of Books,* pp. 12–15.

Dworkin, R. (1993, October 21). Women and pornography. *New York Review of Books,* pp. 36–42.

Fineman, M. (1990, May 14). Death of a martyr shakes the land of untouchables. *Los Angeles Times,* p. 1.

Geertz, C. (1973). *The interpretation of cultures.* New York: Basic Books.

Geertz, C. (1984). From the natives' point of view: On the nature of anthropological understanding. In R. A. Shweder & R. A. Levine (Eds.), *Culture theory* (pp. 123–136). Cambridge, UK: Cambridge University Press.

Geertz, C. (1994, April 7). Life on the edge. *New York Review of Books,* pp. 3–4.

Gilligan, C. (1982). *In a different voice: Psychological theory and women's development.* Cambridge, MA: Harvard University Press.

Gilligan, C., Ward, J., & Taylor, J. (Eds.). (1988). *Mapping the moral domain: A contribution of women's thinking to psychological theory and education.* Cambridge, MA: Harvard University Press.

Gilligan, C., & Wiggins, G. (1987). The origins of morality in early childhood relationships. In J. Kagan & S. Lamb (Eds.), *The emergence of morality in young children* (pp. 277–305). Chicago: University of Chicago Press.

Habermas, J. (1984). *Moral consciousness and communicative action.* Cambridge, MA: MIT Press.

Haney, C., Banks, C., & Zimbardo, P. (1973). Interpersonal dynamics in a simulated prison. *International Journal of Criminology and Penology, 1,* 69–97.

Helwig, C. C. (1995a). Adolescents' and young adults' conceptions of civil liberties: Freedom of speech and religion. *Child Development, 66,* 152–166.

Helwig, C. C. (1995b). Social context in social cognition: Psychological harm and civil liberties.

In M. Killen & D. Hart (Eds.), *Morality in everyday life: Developmental perspectives* (pp. 166–200). Cambridge, UK: Cambridge University Press.

Hochschild, A. (1989). *The second shift.* New York: Avon.

Hogan, R. (1975). Theoretical egocentrism and the problem of compliance. *American Psychologist, 30,* 533–539.

Lastreto, N., & Winnans, W. (1989, July 2). The high price of marriage in India: Burning brides. *San Francisco Chronicle,* pp. 10–13.

Latanée, B., & Darley, J. M. (1970). *The unresponsive bystander: Why doesn't he help?* New York: Appleton-Crofts.

Markus, H., & Kitayama, S. (1991). Culture and self: Implications for cognition, emotion, and motivation. *Psychological Review, 98,* 224–253.

McClosky, M., & Brill, A. (1983). *Dimensions of tolerance: What Americans believe about civil liberties.* New York: Russell Sage.

McKinnon, C. A. (1993). *Only words.* Cambridge, MA: Harvard University Press.

Mednick, M. T. (1989). On the politics of psychological constructs: Stop the bandwagon, I want to get off. *American Psychologist, 44,* 1118–1123.

Mernissi, F. (1994). *Dreams of trespass: Tales of a harem girlhood.* Reading, MA: Addison-Wesley.

Milgram, S. (1974). *Obedience to authority.* New York: Harper & Row.

Miller, J. G., & Bersoff, D. M. (1995). Development in the context of everyday family relationships: Culture, interpersonal morality, and adaptation. In M. Killen & D. Hart (Eds.), *Morality in everyday life: Developmental perspectives* (pp. 259–283). Cambridge, UK: Cambridge University Press.

Mischel, W. (1968). *Personality and assessment.* Stanford, CA: Stanford University Press.

Mischel, W. (1969). Continuity and change in personality. *American Psychologist, 24,* 1012–1018.

Nussbaum, M. (1992, October 8). Justice for women. *New York Review of Books,* pp. 43–48.

Okin, S. M. (1989). *Justice, gender, and the family.* New York: Basic Books.

Okin, S. M. (in press). Gender inequality and cultural differences. In M. Nussbaum & J. Glover (Eds.), *Human capabilities: Women, men, and equality.* Oxford, UK: Oxford University Press.

Perlez, J. (1990, October 28). Toll of AIDS on Uganda's women puts their roles and rights in question. *The New York Times,* p. 11.

Perlez, J. (1991, February 24). Uganda's women: Children, drudgery, and pain. *The New York Times,* p. 10.

Pollitt, K. (1992, December 28). Are women really superior to men? *The Nation,* pp. 799–807.

Rao, V. (1994, January 16). [Letter to the editor]. *The New York Times,* p. 16.

Ross, L., Bierbrauer, G., & Hoffman, S. (1976). The role of attributional processes in conformity and dissent: Revisiting the Asch situation. *American Psychologist, 31,* 148–157.

Ross, L., & Nisbett, R. M. (1991). *The person and the situation: Perspectives on social psychology.* Philadelphia: Temple University Press.

Sampson, E. E. (1977). Psychology and the American ideal. *Journal of Personality and Social Psychology, 35,* 767–782.

Shweder, R. A. (1990). Cultural psychology—What is it? In J. W. Stigler, R. A. Shweder, & G. Herdt (Eds.), *Cultural psychology: Essays on comparative human development* (pp. 1–43). Cambridge, UK: Cambridge University Press.

Shweder, R. A., Mahapatra, M., & Miller, J. G. (1987). Culture and moral development. In J. Kagan & S. Lamb (Eds.), *The emergence of morality in young children* (pp. 1–83). Chicago: University of Chicago Press.

Shweder, R. A., & Sullivan, M. A. (1993). Cultural psychology: Who needs it? *Annual Review of Psychology, 44,* 497–527.

Skolnick, A. (1991). *Embattled paradise: The American family in an age of uncertainty.* New York: Basic Books.

Spiro, M. (1993). Is the Western conception of the self "peculiar" within the context of the world cultures? *Ethos, 21,* 107–153.

Stack, C. (1990). Different voices, different visions: Race, gender, and moral reasoning. In R. Ginsburg & A. Tsing (Eds.), *The negotiation of gender in American culture* (pp. 19–27). Boston: Beacon Press.

Stouffer, S. (1955). *Communism, conformity, and civil liberties.* New York: Doubleday.

Strauss, C. (1992). Models and motives. In R. G. D'Andrade & C. Strauss (Eds.), *Human motives and cultural models* (pp. 1–20). Cambridge, UK: Cambridge University Press.

Triandis, H. C. (1989). The self and social behavior in differing cultural contexts. *Psychological Review, 96,* 506–520.

Triandis, H. C. (1990). Cross-cultural studies of individualism and collectivism. In J. J. Berman (Ed.), *Nebraska Symposium on Motivation: 1989, Vol. 37. Cross-cultural perspectives* (pp. 41–133). Lincoln: University of Nebraska Press.

Turiel, E. (1983). *The development of social knowledge: Morality and convention.* Cambridge, UK: Cambridge University Press.

Turiel, E. (1994). Morality, authoritarianism, and personal agency in cultural contexts. In R. J. Sternberg & P. Ruzgis (Eds.), *Personality and intelligence* (pp. 271–299). Cambridge, UK: Cambridge University Press.

Turiel, E., Killen, M., & Helwig, C. C. (1987). Morality: Its structure, functions and vagaries. In J. Kagan & S. Lamb (Eds.), *The emergence of morality in young children* (pp. 155–244). Chicago: University of Chicago Press.

Turiel, E., & Wainryb, C. (1994). Social reasoning and the varieties of social experience in cultural contexts. In H. W. Reese (Ed.), *Advances in child development and behavior* (Vol. 25, pp. 289–326). New York: Academic Press.

Wainryb, C., & Turiel, E. (1994). Dominance, subordination, and concepts of personal entitlements in cultural contexts. *Child Development, 65,* 1701–1722.

Wainryb, C., & Turiel, E. (1995). Diversity in social development: Between or within cultures.In M. Killen & D. Hart (Eds.), *Morality in everyday life: Developmental perspectives* (pp. 283–316). Cambridge, UK: Cambridge University Press.

Walker, A., & Parnar, P. (1993). *Warrior marks: Female genital mutilation and the sexual blinding of women.* New York: Harcourt Brace.

Willis, P. (1977). *Learning to labor: How working class kids get working class jobs.* New York: Columbia University Press.

6

Naive Realism in Everyday Life: Implications for Social Conflict and Misunderstanding

Lee Ross
Andrew Ward
Stanford University

One of social psychology's most enduring contributions has been to highlight the importance of subjective interpretation. Long before the intellectual community began to struggle with the implications of hermeneutics and deconstructionism, Asch's (1952) classic text reminded us of the need to pay attention to the individual's subjective understanding of events and cautioned us that apparent differences in judgment about particular social objects might actually reflect differences in the way those objects of judgments are being perceived or construed by different actors. Indeed, in a slightly earlier and less celebrated text, Krech and Crutchfield (1948) challenged the prevailing objectivist traditions of the day with the following, decidedly postmodern contention: "There are no impartial 'facts.' Data do not have a logic of their own that results in the same perceptions and cognitions for all people. Data are perceived and interpreted in terms of the individual perceiver's own needs, own connotations, own personality, own previously formed cognitive patterns" (p. 94).

Both Asch's and Krech and Crutchfield's arguments, in turn, owed an obvious (and clearly acknowledged) debt to an earlier psychological tradition—to Lewin's (1935) field theory, which emphasized the organizing role in perception played by specific current goals, and to Thomas and Znaniecki's (1918) even earlier exhortation to attend to the actor's "definition of the situation."

We shall not pause here to review the classic empirical demonstrations and conceptual analyses that Asch and others offered in hoisting the subjectivist banner (see Griffin & Ross, 1991; Ross & Nisbett, 1991). Nor shall we review the work of other pioneers who helped to launch the cognitive revolution in the social and personality areas—pioneers like Ichheiser (1949), whose analyses of the cognitive processes and biases underlying stereotyping and prejudice remain fresh today, or Kelly (1955), whose clinical account of interpersonal problems and misunderstandings so clearly anticipated the central concerns of this chapter. Nor, at least for the moment, shall we discuss the seminal work of Piaget, whose discussion of early developmental limitations, and later adult mastery, in social perspective taking provides the most obvious stimulus for our present undertaking (see Inhelder & Piaget, 1958; Piaget, 1926, 1928; see also Flavell, 1963, 1985). Instead, we begin our discussion of the subjectivist tradition by distinguishing between two separate assertions: The first assertion is simply that differences in subjective interpretation or construal *matter,* that they have a profound impact in the conduct of everyday social affairs. The second assertion is that social perceivers characteristically make *insufficient allowance* for such impact in the inferences and predictions they make about others.

CONSTRUAL AND SOCIAL INFERENCE

The Impact of Construal

It is appropriate, perhaps, to begin by noting that the fate of attempts to understand, predict, or control behavior in the political arena often hinges not on success in recognizing or invoking differences in ethical values, but rather on success in understanding, predicting, or controlling the way in which the relevant issues are construed. In the 1930s, Roosevelt and his New Deal lieutenants recognized that the proposed new program of intergeneration income transfer, which we now know as the social security system, would face substantial opposition if it were presented as an income equalization scheme with connotations of "welfare" or "socialism." Instead, the plan was portrayed as a combination of personal pension and insurance. The image put forward was one of a steadily accumulating nest egg to be tapped in one's golden years—with immediate benefits to be available if unanticipated misfortune struck—notwithstanding the fact that there really was no such gradually accumulating account, either individual or collective, only the government's promise to keep the social security system solvent enough to meet financial obligations as they arose. There was no explicit acknowledgment that the early beneficiaries would receive many times what they ever contributed, nor that subsequent generations of workers would be obliged to pay much more and to receive a much less generous return on their investment.

Today, of course, debate about the social security system is becoming increasingly heated, and critics are offering images and construals that are far less positive—that is, a "gift" to (often well-off) retirees by tax-burdened (often not-so-well-off) younger workers, or even as a "pyramid scheme" bound to collapse when not enough new "suckers" can be persuaded to pour fresh money into the system. A more mundane view of the system, of course, might be that the federal government essentially is collecting taxes from current wage earners and providing benefits to retired or disabled workers (and, after the workers' deaths, to their dependents) in fulfillment of the same kind of social contract to be found in virtually every industrialized country in the world. The system will not collapse unless the government itself goes bankrupt, but over the long haul total government expenditures of all sorts, including the required social security payouts, will have to be balanced (or nearly so) by the total government revenues collected from all sources.

Our point, again, is simply that such differences in construals, whether the product of political manipulation or the result of more spontaneous processes, *matter* in determining political behavior. At times, they even can be determinative of policy. More often, they serve to justify policies that are dictated by the standard combination of necessity, ideology, and special interests, but that clash with broadly held personal, political, or ethical values. The political battle to manipulate construals and thereby win support or marshal opposition to particular policies goes on constantly. Thus, depending on the views and interests of those controlling the media, we hear references to "illegal aliens" versus "undocumented workers," to "terrorists" versus "freedom fighters," to "surgical" strikes and "police" actions versus bombings and invasions, or the "right to life" versus the "right to choose." As George Orwell (1949) warned us so chillingly in *1984,* those who have the capacity to control language and media images—those who control the way in which objects of political consideration are subjectively construed—enjoy the power to control political attitudes and behavior. Indeed, the manipulation of labels and language can be used effectively to disengage normal mechanisms of moral evaluation, that is, to promote and justify individual or collective actions that might otherwise be constrained by moral or ethical standards (see Bandura, 1990).

The psychological literature contains many studies showing that proponents and opponents of particular policies, such as capital punishment, liberalized abortion rights, or military intervention in service of U.S. interests construe those policies and the facts and concerns that give rise to them quite differently (e.g., Doob & Roberts, 1984; Lord, Desforges, Fein, Pugh, & Lepper, 1994). Furthermore, several investigators have shown that manipulations in the way problems or decisions are framed (Tversky & Kahneman, 1981, 1986), or manipulations making particular schemas and knowledge structures more or less salient can significantly influence the respondents' choices (Gilovich, 1981; Higgins, Rholes, & Jones, 1977; Read, 1984, 1987; Spellman & Holyoak, 1992). We restrict ourselves here to an account of one such study recently conducted in our laboratory—a study that manipulated the way subjects construed and subsequently played what is perhaps the best known and most widely researched of all strategic "games."

The Wall Street/Community Game. This simple experiment (Ross & Samuels, 1993) essentially pitted the determinative power of a construal manipulation against the predictive power of subjects' reputation for cooperativeness or uncooperativeness. The experiment had two separate phases. In the first phase, dormitory advisors on the Stanford University campus were asked to nominate male undergraduates living in their dorm who they thought especially likely to "cooperate," or especially likely to "defect" (i.e., not cooperate) in playing the so-called Prisoner's Dilemma Game (Rapoport, 1960; see also Dawes, 1991). More specifically, after hearing a detailed account of the specific payoff resulting from each combination of cooperation and/or defection by the two players on each round of the game,[1] the dorm advisors were asked to estimate the probability that their particular nominees would choose to cooperate rather than defect on the first trial of the game. In the second phase of the study, the two types of nominees—that is, those designated "most likely to cooperate" and those designated "most likely to defect"—were recruited and given an opportunity to play the game in question. We were thus able to see whether each nominee in fact opted, on the first round of the game and then on six subsequent rounds, to cooperate or to defect.

The construal manipulation was a very simple one. As the experimenter explained the nature of the game and the payoff matrix it provided, he explicitly labeled it, on two separate occasions, either as the *Wall Street Game* or the *Community Game*. In every other respect, the subjects in the two experimental conditions were treated identically. The investigators' concern, of course, was the impact of this difference in labels (and, presumably, of the differing construals or associations evoked by such labels) on subjects' play—especially their choice of moves on the very first trial, when there was no history of cooperation or defection on previous trials to influence the subjects' expectations and responses. Three questions were to be answered: First, how much difference would the labeling manipulation make for the two kinds of players? Second, how would the influence of the label compare with the influence of the players' nomination status as most likely to cooperate versus most likely to defect? Third, how would these two influences compare to the estimates made by the nominators (who, it should be emphasized, knew whether

---

[1] The "payoff matrix" characterizing this game guarantees that on any given round each player, regardless of the response chosen by his or her partner, receives a more positive payoff for choosing Response D (defection) than Response C (cooperation). At the same time, however, the players both jointly fare less well when they mutually opt for Response D than when they mutually opt for Response C. Hence the "dilemma," which is called the *Prisoner's Dilemma* because it resembles the quandry faced by a pair of criminal suspects, each of whom must decide whether to cooperate with his partner by remaining silent or to defect (by confessing and implicating his partner) under circumstances in which each suspect, regardless of the other's decision, improves his situation by defecting, but in which joint cooperation or mutual silence yields both suspects a better fate than mutual defection.

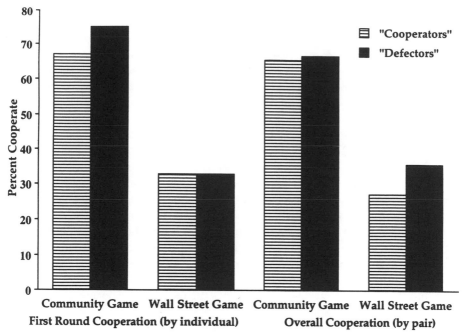

FIG. 6.1.　Percentage of cooperation by nominated "cooperators" versus "defectors" in the first round and over all seven rounds in *Community Game* versus *Wall Street Game*.

the game their nominees were to play would bear the *Wall Street* or the *Community* label).

The results of the study were simple and dramatic (see Fig. 6.1). The construal manipulation exerted a large and significant impact on subjects' play. Only about one third of players elected to cooperate on Trial 1 of the *Wall Street Game,* whereas more than two thirds elected to cooperate on Trial 1 of the *Community Game.* These differences, moreover, persisted on subsequent trials. The label attached to the game through the experimenter's two casual references—now buttressed by the tendency for initial mutual cooperation to encourage further cooperation and for initial defection by either player to produce subsequent defection by both players—induced subjects in the *Community Game* to cooperate more than twice as much (and to earn considerably more money than those in the *Wall Street Game*).

Nomination status or reputation, by contrast, exerted virtually no impact on play. Players nominated as most likely to cooperate versus most likely to defect showed similarly low levels of first trial cooperation in the *Wall Street Game,* and similarly high levels of first trial cooperation in the *Community Game.* Moreover, this pattern persisted throughout the subsequent trials of the game, despite the fact that the dyads always consisted of two subjects with the same most likely to cooperate or most likely to defect status. These findings can be expressed somewhat differently and perhaps more dramatically: A Prisoner's Dilemma game participant would be twice as likely to receive initial and sustained cooperation from a player whose reputation led him to be nominated as most likely to defect but who happened to be playing the *Community Game* as he would from a player who was nominated as most likely to cooperate but who happened to be playing the *Wall Street Game.*

Further research will be required to determine exactly why the particular label attached to the game exerted so large an effect—that is, to what extent the label influenced subjects directly (i.e., determined the way subjects felt they ought to play) and to what extent it influenced them indirectly (i.e., by changing their expectations about how the other player would choose to play, or even by altering their beliefs about how the other player would expect them to play). But the power of the label—that is to say, its impact on the way the game was construed by the players, what they felt it was about, and what kinds of real-world situations and associations came to mind as they made their choices—seems indisputable. The manipulation of construal by the experimenter mattered, and it mattered deeply.

What also seems to be beyond question is the fact that the dorm counselors who made the nominations and furnished the probability estimates drastically underestimated the impact of the game label on the subjects' construal and play (and, incidentally, they also drastically overestimated the predictive value of the impressions they had formed about the subjects' personality traits and reputations after having observed them in other situations). Indeed, even when they were explicitly asked to offer a second set of predictions and likelihood estimates, this time with the other label suggested as a hypothetical alternative, the nominators continued to feel that the nominees' previously revealed personality or character would be a far more powerful predictor than the label attached to the game. In short, the nominators failed to recognize the importance of the participants' construal of the situation or game to which those individuals would be responding. This finding thus serves to reintroduce our second assertion about the significance of subjective representation or construal. That is, we argue that in seeking to understand, predict, and control each other's behavior and in attempting to make inferences about each other on the basis of such behavior, social perceivers characteristically fail to make adequate allowance for the variability and/or impact of subjective construal. It is to this second, more subtle assertion that we now turn our attention.

Insufficient Allowance
for Construal Differences

Failure to recognize the importance of intersubjective differences in construal can play havoc in a number of judgment and decision-making contexts. In the context of interpersonal prediction, for example, failure to make sufficient allowance for the possibility that the situation facing the actor actually will be quite different from the way we presently are construing it (and/or the possibility that the relevant actor's construal of it will be quite different from our own) breeds unrealistically high levels of confidence, and ill-advised gambles (Dunning, Griffin, Milojkovic, & Ross, 1990; Griffin, Dunning, & Ross, 1990). Failure to make such allowance similarly breeds undue optimism about the fate of planned social interventions. That is, interventions that are experienced and interpreted very differently by the intended beneficiaries than by the intervention planners and deliverers are likely to produce results that disappoint all concerned.

Consider, for example, the fate of a policy enabling welfare recipients to earn money for socially useful work. The initiative is apt to have been advocated by a social scientist who saw it as a program to boost participants' job skills and personal pride. The relevant initiative, or at least the variant proposed by politicians, is apt to be presented to the public as a "workfare" program to discourage able-bodied adults from "living off" the taxpayers, and to cost-conscious civic bureaucrats as a way of getting snow shoveled from sidewalks or streets freed of litter at low cost. Meanwhile, the initiative is apt to be construed by the welfare recipients, especially in light of the ensuing public discourse, not as a potential benefit to them but as punishment or harassment—as an additional burden to be imposed on the poor by unsympathetic rich folks who are acting out of hostility or prejudice. Given such differences in construal, it is unlikely that the details of the program as it is actually implemented (i.e., the nature of the work, training, and manner of compensation) will remain attuned to the objectives of the social scientist or practitioner who proposed it in the first place, and even less likely that the participants, construing the program as they do, will reap either the anticipated boost in skills or the hoped-for improvement in self-image and social regard.

The same limitation in perspective taking can also promote interpersonal misunderstandings and misattributions. Consider the consequences that occur if John and Mary differ markedly in the assumptions they make about content and surrounding context when they see someone rebuke a ragged individual seeking a handout, or hear a politician endorse "family values," or read about a reported incident of spousal abuse. The two social perceivers will be inclined not only to make different attributions about the relevant actors, but also to reach unwarranted conclusions about each other. That is, on seeing and hearing Mary react, John is apt to make attributions about her that presume she has responded to the same event as he did (attributions that perhaps would have been quite reasonable if she had in fact responded to the same event). Mary, of course, is apt to do the same on hearing John's views. What the two perceivers will fail to recognize, we argue (unless and until they carefully and explicitly probe the divergence in their respective assumptions and construals), is that they have in fact responded to *different* events, or at least to dif ferent social *constructions* of those events. Moreover, there is a distinct risk that Mary and John will exacerbate the problem when they begin to exchange accusations of bias or unreasonableness, and that they will further compound their difficulties if and when they proceed to make attributions about each other's accusations.

Such failures of empathy in perspective taking—or rather failures to treat surprising and seemingly unwarranted responses as a cue that the relevant social actors or observers are in effect responding to different situations—we argue, are ubiquitous in social and political life. Such failures, we contend, play an important role in promoting the correspondence bias (Gilbert & Jones, 1986) or fundamental attribution error (Ross, 1977)—that is, the tendency for observers to attribute actions and outcomes in the social sphere to distinguishing personal dispositions of the actor instead of the situational forces and constraints faced or experienced by that actor. The same failures also play a significant role in the related tendency for observers to offer less situational attributions for particular actions and outcomes than the actors themselves (Jones & Nisbett, 1971).

Our more general contention is that although some aspects of the child's egocentrism disappear through maturation and experience, the process is never completed (see Ross, 1981). The adult, as Piaget well recognized (Inhelder & Piaget, 1958; Piaget, 1962), continues to show important limitations in perspective taking and other aspects of naive or intuitive psychology, especially in confronting new situations and new domains of response. These limitations, we argue, reflect a kind of worldview or lay epistemology that can appropriately be characterized as "naive realism." In the remainder of this chapter we stipulate the main features or tenets of this naive realism, then proceed to discuss some relevant evidence and explore implications for the analysis of social conflict and misunderstanding.

TENETS OF NAIVE REALISM

The layperson's social understanding, we suggest, rests on three related convictions about the relation between his or her subjective experience and the nature of the phenomena that give rise to that subjective experience. For didactic purposes, we find it best to express these convictions or tenets in first-person terms:

1. *That I see entities and events as they are in objective reality, and that my social attitudes, beliefs, preferences, priorities, and the like follow from a relatively dispassionate, unbiased, and essentially "unmediated" apprehension of the information or evidence at hand.*

2. *That other rational social perceivers generally will share my reactions, behaviors, and opinions—provided that they have had access to the same information that gave rise to my views, and provided that they too have processed that information in a reasonably thoughtful and open-minded fashion.*

3. *That the failure of a given individual or group to share my views arises from one of three possible sources—(a) the individual or group in question may have been exposed to a different sample of information than I was (in which case, provided that the other party is reasonable and open minded, the sharing or pooling of information should lead us to reach agreement); (b) the individual or group in question may be lazy, irrational, or otherwise unable or unwilling to proceed in a normative fashion from objective evidence to reasonable conclusions; or (c) the individual or group in question may be biased (either in interpreting the evidence, or in proceeding from evidence to conclusions) by ideology, self-interest, or some other distorting personal influence.*

The first tenet thus asserts, essentially, that I see things as they are, that is, that my beliefs, preferences, and resulting responses follow from an essentially unmediated perception of relevant stimuli and incorporation of relevant evidence. The second tenet further asserts that other rational, reasonable people (provided that they have been exposed to the same stimuli and information as I have, and provided that they process that information in a reasonably thoughtful, objective fashion) will share both my experiences and responses. Empirical demonstrations relevant to these two tenets of naive realism have been provided through a pair of findings from our laboratory. The first finding involves a now much-researched phenomenon termed the *false consensus effect*. The second finding involves a more recently demonstrated and less thoroughly researched phenomenon, one that arises when one research participant generates or hears an impoverished auditory stimulus knowing its identity, while another research participant hears the same stimulus without knowing its identity.

EVIDENCE FOR THE FIRST TWO TENETS OF NAIVE REALISM

The False Consensus Effect

This effect is reflected in the tendency for people who make a given choice to see that choice as more common and more "normative" (i.e., less revealing of personal attributes or idiosyncrasies) than do people who make the opposite choice. In pursuing this phenomenon, Ross, Greene, and House (1977) queried respondents about their reactions to a variety of hypothetical scenarios, administered questionnaires about personal habits, preferences, attitudes, and beliefs, and exposed laboratory subjects to a number of real experimental dilemmas; many investigators subsequently have expanded the relevant body of evidence (see Marks & Miller, 1987; Mullen & Hu, 1988). In perhaps the best known of the Ross et al. (1977) demonstrations, subjects in a study purportedly concerned with "various non-typical communication media" were requested by the experimenter to walk around campus wearing a large sandwichboard sign bearing a message (e.g., "Eat at Joe's") and to note the reaction of other students they encountered. The subjects, however, were given the opportunity to decline the invitation to participate in the study (and return for some later study) if they wished. Immediately after agreeing or refusing to participate and wear the sandwichboard, subjects were asked first to estimate the frequency of agreement versus refusal on the part of other participants and then to make some inferences about the personal attributes of two peers who, they were told, had accepted or declined the experimenter's invitation, respectively.

As predicted, consensus estimates and trait inferences were very different for the two types of subjects. Those who agreed to wear the sandwichboard estimated agreement to be more common than refusal, and less revealing of the individual's personal attributes. Those who refused to wear the sandwichboard offered opposite estimates about the relative commonness of the two responses, and made opposite inferences about their informativeness vis à vis personality.

Although this study was not designed to discriminate between different possible sources of the false consensus bias, it is easy to see how differences in construal could play a role. Subjects who imagined the unfolding scenario for sandwichboard wearers in relatively positive or benign terms (walking relatively unnoticed, or chatting with acquaintances about the psychology experiment and being complimented for being a "good sport"), we suggest, would have been relatively inclined to agree to the experimenter's request, to think that most other "normal" subjects would similarly agree, and to assume that refusal would reflect "uncooperativeness," "uptightness," or some other departure from normal or average personality. By contrast, subjects who imagined the unfolding scenario in less positive or benign terms (i.e., walking through throngs of giggling, finger-pointing students, seeing acquaintances shake their heads and avert their gazes as they hurry off without social acknowledgment) would have been inclined to react quite differently, and to make very different predictions and inferences about the reactions of others. These subjects, we argue, would have been likely to refuse the experimenter's request, to expect others responding to the "same" situation to similarly refuse, and to regard agreement as far more reflective of atypical or extreme personal attributes (e.g., "submissiveness" or inclination to "show off" and make a fool of oneself) than refusal.

Although the original Ross, Greene, and House studies provided no direct evidence for this construal interpretation, such evidence was subsequently provided in an elegant series of studies by Gilovich (1991). Reasoning that if the false consensus effect arose from subjects' insufficient allowance for intersubjective variability in construal, then the effect should be greatest for those response domains that offered the most latitude for interpretation or construal, Gilovich first had an independent panel of judges rate Ross et al.'s various response items in terms of their ambiguity or susceptibility to differences in construal. He then proceeded to demonstrate the predicted positive correlation between the size of the false consensus effect for each item and the latitude for variable construal provided by that item. Gilovich also went on to offer simpler and more direct demonstrations. In one study, for example, two groups of subjects were asked if they preferred the color *aqua* to the color *tan*. Members of one group, however, were given only the color names (which obviously left the subjects to imagine or construe very different hues for each color label) whereas members of the other were given specific color swatches (stimuli that obviously left little if any room for construal differences). As predicted, the subjects responding to color names showed a significant false consensus effect, whereas the subjects responding to color swatches did not. In another study, Gilovich asked his subjects whether they preferred "1960s" or "1980s" music and had them estimate what percentage of their peers would share their preferences. The subjects' estimates once again revealed the predicted false consensus effect. Furthermore, Gilovich showed, the group preferring 1960s music and the group preferring 1980s music had indeed generated different examplars of the two periods—exemplars whose differing merits were recognized readily by subsequent raters. In other words, as predicted, subjects expressing a preference for 1960s music over 1980s music, or vice versa, had construed the respective objects of judgment quite differently, then failed to recognize or make adequate allowance for this construal difference in estimating (and, presumably, in subsequently interpreting) the expressed preferences of their peers.

Such simple demonstration experiments hint at an unfortunate scenario in the domain of political discourse. Issues and events that become the object of social, political, or ethical evaluation are bound to be construed differently by different individuals. Failure by those individuals to recognize the existence of such construal differences, or rather failure to recognize that apparent differences in ethical judgment may arise from and reflect such differences in construal (rather than, perhaps, differences in underlying values or in willingness to be bound by such values) can in turn promote misunderstanding and misattribution. That is, the disputants are apt to make unwarranted inferences about each other's values, beliefs, compassion, wisdom, or sincerity.

Before we return to this troubling scenario, which is a manifestation of the third tenet of naive realism, we wish to offer our readers another very different illustration of the first two tenets. This demonstration, provided in a dissertation study conducted in our laboratory by Elizabeth Newton (1990),

showed in compelling fashion how difficult it can be to separate one's own subjective experience of a stimulus from the objective features of the stimulus that
are available to other perceivers.

The "Musical Tapping" Study

Newton's study, which was designed with the naive realism phenomenon very
much in mind, dealt with a musical stimulus. Subjects in the study were assigned to one of two roles: "tappers" or "listeners." Each tapper was given a
list of 25 well-known songs (a list not made available to the listener) ranging
from "America the Beautiful" to "Rock Around the Clock," and asked to choose
one whose rhythm they then tapped out to a listener sitting across the table.
The tapper was then asked to assess the likelihood that his or her particular
listener would successfully identify the title of the song, and also to estimate
the proportion of students who would be able to do so if given the same listening opportunity. Listeners simply tried first to identify the tune, and after-
ward to estimate the proportion of their peers who would succeed or fail in the
same task.

Before considering Newton's results, it is important once again to contrast
the subjective experiences of the two types of participants in her study (see
Griffin & Ross, 1991). To better appreciate this contrast, imagine yourself first
as the tapper. As you rhythmically tap the opening bars of the tune you have
chosen (let's say "Yankee Doodle" or "Auld Lang Syne"), you inevitably "hear"
the tune and even the words to the song. In fact, many of Newton's tappers reported hearing a full orchestration, complete with rich harmonies between
strings, winds, brass, and human voice. Now imagine yourself as the listener,
unaware of which tune the tapper has undertaken to communicate. For you
there are no notes, words, chords, or instruments; only an aperiodic series of
taps. Indeed, you can't even tell whether the brief, irregular moments of silence between taps should be construed as sustained notes, as musical "rests"
between notes, or as mere task interruptions as the tapper contemplates the
"music" to come next.

This difference in perspectives and subjective experiences is easy enough
to stipulate. The question, however, is whether the tappers were able to separate their private embellishments from the impoverished stimuli they were actually presenting to their listeners—or rather, whether they were able to make
adequate allowance for the relevant differences in perspective and experience
when they were called on to estimate their listeners' success at the identification task. Newton's results provided clear evidence for the inadequate allowance thesis spelled out in the first two tenets of naive realism. The tappers'
predictions of listener success ranged from 10% to 95%, with an average of
50%. Listeners, by contrast, correctly identified only 3 of the 120 tunes presented by the tapper—a success rate of only 2.5%.

Newton went on in a follow-up study to demonstrate that overestimation of listener success was not a reflection of simple optimism or bravado on the part of the tappers. Indeed, she showed that it did not even depend on their having personally performed the tapping task. In this follow-up study, a group of observers were supplied with the name of each tune being tapped (thus allowing these preinformed listeners, like the tappers, to supply their own private orchestration as they heard the impoverished stimulus) and to estimate the subsequent success of noninformed listeners at identifying the tunes. Like the tappers, these preinformed listeners estimated, on average, a 50% accuracy rate on the part of noninformed listeners. That is, like the tappers, they either failed to recognize how the subjective experience of the noninformed listeners would differ from their own experiences or failed to make appropriate allowance for this difference in their predictions. As a consequence, preinformed listeners and tappers alike were poised to make erroneous inferences and attributions about the musical talents and/or effort exhibited by those who did not share their "privileged" subjective experience of the relevant stimuli. Newton's results may prompt students of Piaget to recall his famous example (Inhelder & Piaget, 1958) of the teacher's characteristic inability to set aside his or her own knowledge and mastery of the material being taught and appreciate the perspective of the student being exposed to the information and ideas for the first time.

Our general thesis, once again, is that such failures in perspective taking, or perhaps failures to make adequate allowance for construal differences, are ubiquitous throughout the social sphere. Such failures, we suggest, are apt to be particularly dramatic in cases in which the stimuli and reactions to be evaluated are words and deeds addressed to complex social propositions—words and deeds that are rich and varied in their connotations or associations. Indeed, Ichheiser, another prominent social psychologist who long ago anticipated the tenor of this argument, explicitly distinguished between physical and social stimuli in stating a strong version of the case to be made throughout this chapter:

> Now, the really strange thing is that what every normal person understands by himself as far as things in physical space are concerned, most people do not understand, and even do not want to understand, as far as phenomena in social space are concerned. And any attempt to explain the relativity of social perspectives, and its full implications, usually meets with strong psychological resistance. (Ichheiser, 1951, p. 311)

CONSTRUAL AND SOCIAL ENMITY: THE THIRD TENET OF NAIVE REALISM

The two tenets of naive realism discussed thus far relate to the tendency to assume, often without even considering any alternative, that other social actors and perceivers share one's perspective and one's subjective experience of the objects or events to which one responds. This tendency, in turn, disposes people to make erroneous behavior predictions and unwarranted attributions—predictions and attributions that reflect inadequate inferential allowance for the possibility that other social actors and perceivers might be construing and/or experiencing the relevant events differently than themselves, for the possibility that other actors and observers might, in effect, be responding to very different objects of judgment than the ones to which they themselves were responding. The third tenet of naive realism, which can essentially be derived from the two previous ones, concerns the naive realist's interpretation of differences in response and of disagreements about issues. Given the naive realist's conviction that he or she sees things "naturally"—sees them as they "really are"—then other actors' differing views and responses must reflect something other than a natural, unmediated registering of objective reality.

The naive realist's initial interpretation of differences in opinion is apt to be relatively charitable—that the other party has not yet been exposed to the "way things really are;" that the other party has not yet been privy to the "real" facts and considerations. Indeed, the naive realist may even be so charitable as to concede that the other party may be privy to additional facts and considerations that could moderate the naive realist's own views. In either case, this charitable interpretation of disagreement leads the naive realist to be confident that rational open-minded discourse, in which information and cogent arguments are freely exchanged, will lead to agreement (or at least to a marked narrowing of disagreement). This confidence however is apt to be shortlived, especially in the social and political arena. Repeated attempts at dialogue with those on the "other side" of a contentious issue make us aware that they rarely yield to our attempts at enlightenment; nor do they yield to the efforts of articulate, fair-minded spokespersons who share our views, or even to the evidence presented by whichever media sources we regard as balanced and responsible. (Nor, generally, do those on the other side present new facts and arguments sufficient to persuade us to change sides.)

Another far less charitable interpretation of disagreement, of the failure of others to share our views, involves capacity and effort. Those who fail to arrive at our "truth"—that is, at the views that follow naturally from evidence and logic—may simply be too lazy and/or too limited in intelligence and common sense to reach the right conclusions. This interpretation is comforting, and it is one we sometimes can cling to when the dialogue is limited and the stakes seem low.

A third interpretation of disagreement, however, is more common, especially when our adversaries are persistent, unyielding, energetic, and outspoken, and when the issue is one with hedonic consequences for them or for us. In such cases we are apt to reach the conclusion that people on the other side of the issue are *biased*—by ideology, or by self-interest, or by idiosyncratic values, traits, or features of temperament—and that such bias distorts either their construal of relevant information or their (otherwise unimpaired) capacity to proceed normatively from evidence to conclusions.

This third interpretation is apt to be buttressed by the correlations that one generally observes among others' social and political beliefs, construals, and individual or collective self-interest. Other people in general, and adversaries in particular, the naive realist readily discerns, rarely hold views or advocate propositions whose acceptance would threaten their economic, social, or psychological well-being. In fact, other people generally and adversaries specifically seem to hold views whose general acceptance would advance their individual or collective interests. The naive realist, of course, is apt to be quite correct about the direction (if not, as we shall see, the magnitude) of this correlation between motives and construals or beliefs. What generally seems lacking on the part of the naive realist, however, is the recognition that his or her own interests, ideological beliefs, and construals of facts and evidence are similarly correlated, and that the relevant correlation is equally subject to unflattering interpretation.

It is to this third tenet of naive realism—and more specifically to one's willingness to infer bias on the part of those who fail to share one's own views and perspectives—that we now turn. Again, before discussing specific research evidence and implications, let us make explicit our general contention and its relevance to the concerns of this volume and of the Piagetian perspective that inspired it. We are claiming that adults do come to recognize, in fact even come to assume on the basis of relatively scanty evidence, that certain other individuals or groups fail to share their general perspective and/or their interpretation of particular pieces of information. Indeed, those who participate in or observe outspoken social and political debates could hardly fail to recognize such differences in perspective and construal. However, we are further claiming that even adults persist in feeling that their own perceptions and interpretations are essentially free of distortion, and that other people in general and their adversaries in particular see the world through the distorting lenses of ideology and self-interest.

Again, our presentation of evidence is selective, relying heavily on work done in our laboratory at Stanford. We begin by discussing research documenting the tendency for partisans to see "hostile bias" in the media. We then turn our attention to research on a further tendency that may at first seem a contradiction, but on further examination proves an illustration of our contention about naive realism—that is, the tendency for opposing partisans to overestimate the differences in their respective construals and beliefs.

Biased Perceptions and Perceptions of Bias

Opposing partisans exposed to the same "objective" information are apt to interpret those facts differently. For, as we have noted at several points in this chapter, facts do not necessarily speak for themselves. As Bruner (1957) stated in a celebrated paper that helped to inspire the cognitive revolution throughout all of psychology, people are wont to go "beyond the information given." In the process of assimilating information, they fill in details of context and content, they infer linkages between events, and they adopt dynamic scripts or schemes to give events coherence and meaning (see Fiske & Taylor, 1991; Nisbett & Ross, 1980). In doing so, opposing partisans facing the same objective facts, evidence, and history of events may both find additional support for their pre-existing views and thus become more instead of less polarized in their sentiments and beliefs.

Evidence suggesting such polarization was provided long ago in a classic study by Hastorf and Cantril (1954) that presented Dartmouth and Princeton football fans with a film of a particularly hard-fought game between their teams. Despite the fact that they were being presented with the very same stimulus, the two sets of partisan viewers seemingly "saw" two very different games. The Princeton fans saw a continuing saga of Dartmouth atrocities and occasional Princeton retaliations, whereas the Dartmouth fans saw a hard-hitting contest in which both sides contributed equally to the violence. Moreover, each side thought that the "truth" (i.e., what *they* saw) ought to be apparent to any objective observers of the same events.

Twenty-five years after the classic Hastorf and Cantril (1954) study, Lord, Ross, and Lepper (1979) extended this examination of biased assimilation and its consequences to the evaluation of social science data. Lord et al.'s prediction was that opposing partisans would respond to mixed scientific evidence by accepting evidence supporting their position at face value while attacking or explaining away evidence that was challenging or seemingly disconfirmatory to their position. As a result, partisans would rate those studies whose results supported their own positions to be more convincing and well done than those studies yielding opposite results—even when the objective merits of the relevant research designs and empirical evidence had been held constant. Furthermore, it was predicted, partisans who have had the opportunity to contrast the "sound research" supporting their side with the "slipshod pseudo-science" supporting the other side would end up even *more* convinced that their own views were correct. Thus, through the mechanisms of biased assimilation, the two sides would come away from the same set of mixed evidence even more polarized, and farther apart in their views, than they had been before.

To test these predictions, the investigator recruited capital punishment opponents and proponents and had them read a pair of studies that employed differing methodologies (i.e., a design contrasting homicide rates in adjacent "death penalty" and "no death penalty" states and a design contrasting rates before and after changes in the law permitting executions) and yielded mixed, conflicting evidence about the deterrent efficacy of capital punishment. Although the investigators employed a carefully balanced design, matching the different purported results with the different methodologies, both sides proceeded to accept uncritically the results of the study supporting their position and to identify obvious flaws in the study opposing their position—and thus, as predicted, to become further polarized in their views as they assimilated the relevant findings.

It should be apparent that the same mechanisms that underlie such biased assimilation of evidence, when combined with the features of naive realism described in this chapter, can produce an obvious consequence in terms of interpersonal and intergroup perceptions. To appreciate this consequence, imagine how Lord et al.'s two sets of partisans would have responded to each other's assessments of the evidence and to each other's expressions of increased confidence. Indeed, imagine even how they would respond to a purported neutral third party who evaluated the same two studies and characterized them as "equally flawed," and further insisted that the evidence should encourage both partisan groups, equally, to adopt more moderate, less adamant positions. In such cases, we believe accusations of ideological bias soon would be forthcoming from all quarters. That is, both groups would feel that partisans on the other side, who could look at a body of evidence that objectively favors "our side" but nevertheless insist that it offers support to their side, were either lying or demonstrating the true depths of their unreasonableness. By the same token, both groups of partisans would be apt to feel that a supposedly neutral observer who claims to see equal probative value (or lack of value) in cases of such manifestly unequal merit has thereby shown his or her lack of objectivity.

It was this latter scenario—whereby partisans were led by their own biased perceptions and/or assimilation to perceive bias on the part of third parties—that was put to the test in a study by Vallone, Ross, and Lepper (1985). Capitalizing on long-standing and passionately held differences in opinion that people hold about the Arab–Israeli conflict, Vallone et al. presented pro-Israeli and pro-Arab student partisans (as well as some neutral students) with excerpts from then-current television news coverage of the massacre of civilians in two Palestinian refugee camps located in South Lebanon by so-called "Christian militiamen." Whereas the neutrals (or at least the best informed and most knowledgeable of the neutrals) rated the broadcast summaries as being relatively unbiased on the issue of Israeli responsibility and complicity, the evaluations offered by the two groups of partisans were very different. On measure after measure there was virtually no overlap in the evaluations offered by the two partisan groups (see Fig. 6.2). Pro-Arab and pro-Israeli viewers alike were convinced that the other side had been favored by the media, that their own side had been treated unfairly, and that the relevant biases in reporting had reflected the self-interests and ideologies of those responsible for the program. There was also evidence, reminiscent of Hastorf and Cantril's (1954) findings discussed earlier, that the two partisan groups in a sense "saw" different pro-

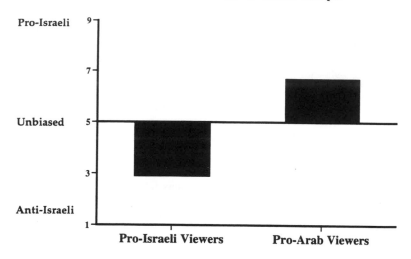

1. Perceived Bias in Media Sample

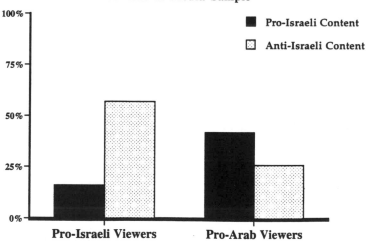

2. Estimated Percentage of Pro-Israeli vs. Anti-Israeli Content in Media Sample

FIG. 6.2.   Assessment of "Beirut Massacre" media coverage by pro-Israeli and pro-Arab viewers.

grams. That is, whereas viewers supportive of Israel claimed that a higher percentage of the specific facts and arguments presented had been anti-Israeli than pro-Israeli, viewers hostile to Israel assessed that balance in opposite terms. Both sides, furthermore, believed that neutral viewers of the program would be swayed in a direction hostile to their side and favorable to the other side.

Overestimating Partisan Differences in Construal

Conflict, misunderstandings, and misattribution, as we have noted, can result when individuals or groups fail to recognize that they have construed issues or events differently and have thus essentially responded to different objects of judgment. However, recent research conducted in our laboratory suggests that naive realism, and its attributional consequences, can lead those who participate in or witness ongoing ideological disputes to *over*estimate rather than underestimate relevant differences in construal. To understand the source of this overestimation we must look again at the third tenet of naive realism—at the attributional possibilities available to the naive realist who finds that others do not share his or her position on a contentious social issue. Once again, for didactic clarity, we use the first-person mode.

Suppose it has become clear to us that others do not share our opinions and perspectives, and that the discrepancy in viewpoints is not the product either of easily corrected differences in access to information or of simple inattention or intellectual impairment on the part of those with whom one disagrees. One attributional possibility remains. That possibility involves the distorting influence exerted by ideological bias and/or self-interest—bias and/or self-interest, of course, on the part of those with whom we disagree, rather than ourselves.

In particular, we can maintain that whereas our own "bottom-up" construals of issues and events reflect the richness, complexity, ambiguity, and even contradictions of objective reality, other partisans' "top-down" construals are a different matter. Other people's construals, governed as they are by ideology and self-interest, are bound (we believe) to manifest a kind of simple, predictable consistency. That is, when it comes to other people, evidence and arguments relevant to beliefs will generally be construed in whatever manner best serves their ideology and self-interest. Thus, other people (especially those on the "other side," but to some degree those on "our side" as well) will be more extreme in the ideological consistency of their construals than we are. This set of assumptions, and the resulting overestimation of self–other and us–them differences, is represented schematically in Fig. 6.3.

Evidence for this phenomenon was provided in a pair of studies by Robinson, Keltner, Ward, and Ross (1995) that compared partisan group members' *actual* differences in construal with their *assumptions* about such differences.

One study dealt with prochoice versus prolife views relevant to the ongoing abortion rights debates (e.g., what kind of abortion scenarios and considerations are common vs. uncommon; also, what positive consequences and what negative consequences would be likely to follow from a tightening of abortion restrictions, etc.). The second study dealt with liberal versus conservative construals of specific events in the racially charged Howard Beach incident in which a Black teenager was fatally injured by an automobile while running away from a group of White pursuers (e.g., who had started and who had exacerbated the initial confrontation, what had been the intentions and motives of the various participants in the incidents, etc.).

Both sides, as expected, provided many instances of construal differences; but almost invariably the magnitude of such differences was overestimated rather than underestimated by the partisans. More specifically, the partisans overestimated the degree of ideological consistency that both sides—especially the other side, but to some extent their own side as well—would show in the assumptions and construals they brought to the relevant issues. What is more, individual partisans in both studies felt that their own views were less driven by ideology than those of other partisans. It is worth noting that nonpartisan or neutral respondents in the study showed the same tendency to overestimate the extremity and ideological consistency of the partisan groups' construals as the partisans did themselves. That is, partisans and nonpartisans alike significantly overestimated the construal gap between the two sides, and in a sense,

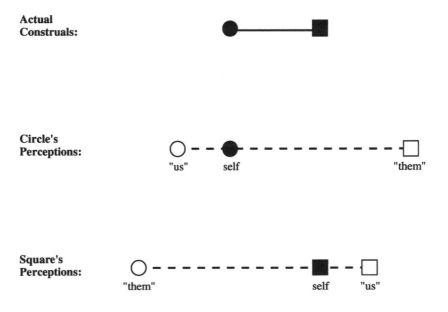

FIG. 6.3. Actual versus perceived differences in partisan group construals.

underestimated the amount of common ground to be found in the assumptions, beliefs, and values shared by the relevant parties.

Informal interviews with students, incidentally, revealed an additional source of these misperceptions and overestimations beyond naive realism, one that is worth mentioning in light of the now numbingly repetitive discussions of political correctness. Students shared with us the fact that they rarely acknowledged to others the degree of ambivalence in their political beliefs—not in talking to their ideological allies (lest their resoluteness come into doubt) and not in talking to their ideological adversaries (lest their concessions be exploited or misunderstood). In fact, most students explained that in the interest of avoiding conflict or being stereotyped, they generally shunned all potentially contentious political discussion. By doing so, it is apparent the students also forfeited the opportunity to learn the true complexity (and the shared ambivalence) in each other's views. The obvious antidote to naive realism and its attributional consequences—that is, the open, sustained, sympathetic sharing of views and perspectives—was rarely employed by the students. Ironically, in attempting to avoid discomfort and giving offense, many students failed to discover that their particular position on the political spectrum (i.e., that of self-labeled "realistic" liberal, or "compassionate" conservative) was one shared by a great number of their peers.

The underestimation of common ground in campus debates was been nicely demonstrated in a follow-up study by Robinson and Keltner (1994) that focused on instructors' views about the proper balance of traditional and nontraditional materials in the basic English literature course. The main finding was that the suggested reading lists of self-labeled "traditionalists" and "revisionists" actually overlapped considerably—despite the traditionalists' beliefs that there would be no overlap at all. The same authors (Keltner & Robinson, 1993) further showed that reducing partisans' misperceptions about each other's construals and beliefs will not only lead those on opposite sides of an issue to view each other more favorably, it will also facilitate their search for integrative agreements. A provocative discussion of the role that erroneous construals can play in social policy disputes has been offered by Doob and Roberts (1984), who found that public perceptions of undue judicial leniency to criminals was based in part on erroneous factual beliefs and construals, and that inclusion of factual details vis à vis particular cases drastically reduced the tendency for respondents to feel that the relevant perpetrators deserved harsher treatment.

BARRIERS TO DISPUTE RESOLUTION

The various features of egocentrism and naive realism described in this chapter not only give rise to social misunderstanding and conflict, they also create barriers to successful negotiation and dispute resolution. Once again, the sample of research we review is limited mainly to work done in our laboratory. (See Ross & Stillinger, 1991; also Mnookin & Ross, 1995, and Ross & Ward, 1995, for more detailed accounts.)

The Pursuit and Perception of Equity

In attempting to resolve disputes and end conflict, indeed in any bargaining or negotiation, the relevant parties seek to achieve "gains in trade." By exploiting differences in their present needs, preferences, and opportunities, the two parties hope to exchange resources, concessions, and costs in a manner that leaves both of them better off than they were before (or at least better off than they would be in the absence of an agreement). In a sense, it is thus not agreement but disagreement that provides the vehicle for successful negotiation, insofar as it is the differences in the parties' subjective evaluations, expectations, and preferences (along with the differences in their objective circumstances) that make the negotiation process a nonzero sum game. At the same time, however, differences in subjective understanding and construal create barriers to dispute resolution. One particular barrier arises from the fact that the parties to a negotiation seek more than a simple advance over the status quo—they demand and feel entitled to receive fairness or equity (see Adams, 1965; Homans, 1961; also Berkowitz & Walster, 1976; Walster, Berscheid, & Walster, 1973). Attempts to satisfy the equity criterion—that is, to forge an agreement that allocates gains and losses in a manner proportionate to the strength and legitimacy of the negotiating parties' respective claims (see Bazerman, Loewenstein, & White, 1992)—will thus be made more difficult by the features of naive realism discussed throughout this chapter.

Disputants are apt to construe the history of their conflict (i.e., who did what to whom in the past, and with what justification, provocation, and intent) in very different terms. They similarly are apt to have divergent expectations about the present (i.e., whose intentions are hostile and whose are merely self-protective) and about the future (i.e., who will grow stronger with the passage of time and whose assurances can be taken at face value and trusted). As a result, disputants are likely to disagree vehemently about the balance of any proposal that seeks to give both parties what they feel they need and deserve. Moreover, in accord with the tenets of their naive realism, the disputants are apt to misattribute each other's cool response to the proposal in a way that heightens enmity and mistrust. That is, each party is likely to feel that the other is being disingenuous in its public pronouncement of concern and disappointment, that the other is merely engaging in "strategic" behavior designed to secure sympathy from third parties and win further concessions. And each party responds with anger and suspicion when it hears its own response characterized in such uncharitable terms. No laboratory experiment, unfortunately, is required to demonstrate the pattern of costly stalemates, misattributions, and ever-growing enmity predicted by our analysis. The news media, with their continual accounts of ethnic strife and intergroup conflict, provide all the evidence one could wish.

A pair of recent laboratory studies (Diekmann, Samuels, Ross, & Bazerman, 1994) conducted at Northwestern and Stanford, however, offer a more hopeful, or at least more subtle account of the interplay between equity concerns and self-interested construal biases. Both studies confronted subjects with hypothetical resource allocation problems. Furthermore, in both studies the potential recipients of those allocations (i.e., either candidates from two different schools competing for shares of a scholarship fund or managers of two different divisions of a large company seeking shares of a bonus pool) presented equally strong, albeit rather different, records of accomplishment. Both studies contrasted the response of *allocators* (i.e., those recommending specific splits of the resources in question) and *evaluators* (those assessing the fairness of specific splits enacted by others).

The findings from these studies revealed the specific manner in which the participants' individual or group interests, as opposed to fairness and/or equality norms, manifested themselves. That is, allocators tended to opt for equality or a 50/50 split, even in circumstances in which they could have cited differences in accomplishments or other bases for claims if they had wanted to justify an unequal split. Similarly, evaluators who received a 50/50 split tended to rate that division as perfectly fair, even when they too could have pointed to the differences in accomplishments or bases for claims to justify a contention that they, or the representative from their school, deserved the larger share. Self-interested bias was apparent only among subjects who received, or saw a member of their group receive, a much greater than 50% share. Only then did subjects' assessments of fairness and perceptions of entitlement show the distorting influence of self-interest. Only then did they claim that their own accomplishments, or those of a member of their own group, were more significant and more worthy of financial recognition than those of rival claimants. Biases reflecting self-interest, in short, did not overcome all tendencies toward fairness, equality, and equity. But such biases did make advantaged recipients willing and able to justify, after the fact, an inequality of resources that few personally would have recommended, demanded, or imposed.

There is a footnote to be added to this account of the Diekmann et al. study. When asked to predict how others would respond in the same study, subjects made the same error shown by participants in the Robinson et al. (1995) study (described earlier in this chapter) dealing with perceptions of ideological consistency and extremity. That is, subjects were overly cynical and uncharitable in their predictions. They greatly overestimated the degree of partisan bias that other allocators and evaluators would show (and, as a result, they probably would have overestimated the difficulty of negotiating a mutually acceptable allocation of the relevant resource).

Biased Construal and Reactive Devaluation

Disputants who seek equity rather than a mere advance over the status quo—especially those who seek equity in light of their differing construals of past events and present needs and entitlements—thereby erect a formidable barrier for those negotiating on their behalf, and any third party mediators, to overcome. Cognitive and motivational biases alike lead both sides in the dispute to feel that it is they who have acted more honorably in the past, they who have been more sinned against than sinning, and they who are seeking no more than that to which they are entitled. Both sides, moreover, are apt to feel that it is *their* interests that most require protection in any negotiated agreement—for example, by avoiding ambiguities in language that could provide "loopholes" by the other side (at the same time, avoiding rigidities in formulation that could compromise their own side's "legitimate" need to protect itself against presently unforeseeable developments). When the other side makes similar claims, or when third parties offer evenhanded commentary about the legitimacy of the disputants' respective claims, of course, accusations about unreasonable hostility or devious strategic intent are apt to follow.

The same biases apply to the interpretation or construal of proposed terms of agreement and concessions asked of the two sides. Thus the "impartial review board" proposed by the mayor's task force to deal with allegations of racist-inspired police brutality is apt to be construed very differently by members of the outraged minority community ("a bunch of political hacks who will take the word of the police over folks like us") than by the skeptical and beleaguered police force ("a bunch of civilians who don't understand our problems and frustrations and who will try to placate voters"). Acceptance of such a review board, accordingly, would be seen by each side as a major concession to the other side. Moreover, when each side hears the other side's characterization of the content and equitability of the proposal, the result is likely to be heightened enmity and distrust.

Beyond the barriers posed by biased assessment of content and context, there is a further problem resulting from the dynamics of the negotiation process. The evaluation of specific package deals and compromises may *change* as a consequence of the knowledge that they actually have been put on the table, especially if they have been offered or proposed by one's adversary. Evidence for such "reactive devaluation" has been sought in a variety of laboratory and field settings in which subjects evaluated a variety of actual or hypothetical dispute resolution contexts and proposals (e.g., arms control proposals by then Soviet leader Gorbachev, university proposals concerning divestment vis à vis South Africa, and a professor's offer of various forms of recognition and compensation to an aggrieved research assistant).

Three findings suggestive of reactive devaluation have emerged from this research (see Ross, 1995; also, Lepper, Ross, Tsai, & Ward, 1994; and Stillinger,

Epelbaum, Keltner, & Ross, 1990). First, it appears that the terms of a compromise proposal for bilateral concessions are rated less positively when they have been put forward by the other side than when the same terms ostensibly have been put forward by an apparently neutral third party (or, of course, when those terms have been proposed by a representative of one's own side). Second, it appears that those concessions that actually have been offered are rated less positively than alternative concessions that have not been offered or have been "withheld." Finally, it appears that a given compromise is rated less positively after it has actually been put on the table or unilaterally enacted by a party with the power to do so—less positively, that is, than it had been rated beforehand, when it was merely a hypothetical possibility.

A particularly compelling demonstration of the before being proposed versus after being proposed change in evaluation was provided in Stillinger et al.'s (1990) study of student responses to university plans concerning financial divestment from South Africa. Stillinger et al. were able to measure students' evaluation of the plan ultimately adopted by the university—a plan calling for selective or partial divestment, which fell short of the students' demand for full divestment—on two occasions; once before the adoption of the plan was announced (when it was merely one hypothetical possibility among many) and then shortly after the announcement. For comparison purposes, they also measured students' responses to an alternative plan—a seemingly modest proposal to increase university investment in companies that had left South Africa, but to otherwise retain its current investments. The results were dramatic. Students' evaluation of the university's actual concession became more negative after the relevant announcement, and evaluations of the initially unattractive alternative became increasingly positive (see Figure 6.4).

A range of mechanisms and explanations have been proposed to account for this bias in construal and evaluation, including the "rational" tendency to view an adversary's willingness to offer a given resource or concession as informative regarding its scarcity, value, and significance. However, at this point it is also clear that less rational, more motivational processes are involved. Specifically, reactive devaluation seems to occur even when the source of the concession is not a hostile adversary, and the relevant decrease in perceived value or attractiveness reflects a more general tendency for people to devalue that which is at hand, or readily available, relative to that which seems unavailable or is withheld (see Brehm, 1966; Brehm & Brehm, 1981; Wicklund, 1974). Regardless of why reactive devaluation occurs, its potential contribution to the maintenance of negotiation deadlocks and ensuing cycle of heightening enmity and mistrust should be clear. That is, preliminary proposals or even small unilateral concessions are apt to be dismissed by the recipient as "trivial," "token," and "insincere." Each side, moreover, is apt to interpret the other side's negotiation behavior and rhetoric as at best "strategic" and at worst dishonest, as dictated by animus and "out of touch with reality."

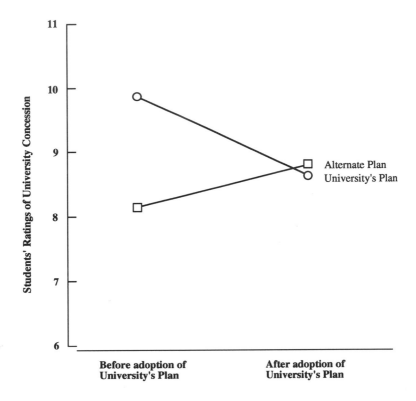

FIG. 6.4.   Students' ratings of university's plan and alternative plan before and after university's announcement.

Indeed, one important role played by the mediator in any conflict is to short circuit this process—to obscure the parentage of specific proposals and concessions, and to encourage more positive (and accurate) attributions on the part of the disputants as they struggle to reach terms of agreement that are personally and politically bearable. To this end, skilled mediators may oblige the disputants to clarify their priorities and interests, in particular to have each side indicate concessions it may value more highly than its adversaries and vice versa. The mediator then is free to propose possible exchanges of concessions that are not only based on but also readily attributable by the parties to their own particular expressions of priority.

CONFLICT, CONSTRUAL, AND VALUES

Parties involved in conflict often attribute the existing stalemate to differences in basic values and/or incompatibility of basic interests. We, the authors of this chapter, have no doubt that some conflicts *do* reflect irreconcilable differences in the parties' values, interests, needs, or objectives. We recognize, further, that some conflicts have little chance of being resolved until one party can impose its will on the other or until objective circumstances change in a way that creates greater commonality of interests. Indeed, we are sympathetic to the view, voiced by many critics of the contemporary dispute resolution movement, that conflict resolution is not always a desirable goal—that sometimes wrongs must be righted, structural changes accomplished, or power redistributed under circumstances in which any genuine resolution demands that the objectives and interests of one party to the dispute be compromised to a degree that it will deem unacceptable and resist as long as it has any means to do so. We also feel, however, as the analysis offered throughout this chapter attests, that many and perhaps even most conflicts are far more tractable than they seem; that disputants are often constrained not by objective circumstances but by cognitive, perceptual, or motivational biases; and that incompatibilities in basic needs, interests, and values are often more apparent than real.

It is to this latter set of observations that we turn our attention in our concluding discussion. We first consider apparent conflicts in basic values, once again focusing on the role of social construal and the limitations of naive realism. We then close on a more optimistic note by pointing out that egocentrism or the assumption of self–other similarity, at least when it is consciously adopted as a charitable working hypothesis about one's adversaries, can forestall erroneous interpersonal influences and promote rather than inhibit the process of reconciliation and conflict resolution.

Apparent versus Real Value Differences

Our most general contention is that perceivers are apt to misattribute behavior, especially behavior that they abhor, to the values (or lack of values) held by the relevant actors. More specifically, we contend that people concerned with particular social issues are bound to find various other individuals or members of other groups or cultures (or even members of their own group or culture at an earlier moment in history) speaking and acting in ways that seemingly reflect indifference to values that the perceivers hold dear, and indeed values they deem to be essential features of any civilized or humane standards of moral conduct. In proceeding from such evidence to any conclusions about the values of the relevant actors, we argue, the perceivers are once again displaying convictions and biases that we have associated in this chapter with naive realism. That is, they are assuming their own construal of the issues or evidence in question to be a veridical, unmediated registering of reality, and they are perceiving the connections between their own values and the specific policies or positions they advocate in light of that "objective reality." They are further reasoning (or tacitly assuming without deeper thought) that other very different policies or positions accordingly reflect an absence of, or weaker adherence to those values, accompanied by a greater commitment to some other, nonuniversal values or perhaps simply by a closer adherence to the dictates of self-interest.

Thus advocates and opponents of universal health care (or of restrictive abortion laws, or of capital punishment, or of particular affirmative action policies) are apt to assume, often wrongly, that their adversaries simply do not place the same weight that they do on compassion, equality, personal responsibility, or some other widely shared value. What such adversaries fail to recognize is the extent to which their ideological opponents proceed from different construals and factual assumptions, and more importantly, from very different perceptions concerning the linkages between relevant perceptions, political positions, and values. Thus, capital punishment opponents may indeed place a higher value on compassion or equality and a lower value on personal responsibility than proponents, but these opponents may also see the death penalty issue (perhaps because of what they assume to be true about crime and criminals) as much more "about" compassion and equality, and much less about responsibility than do proponents. Hence mutual misattributions are made, as the two sides essentially evaluate objects of judgment that are different in substance and different in their association to various values, and each side sees the other side as unreasonable and lacking in ethical maturity—both in its political position and its way of construing the relevant factual issues and linking those issues to universal values.

As we noted somewhat earlier in this chapter, the conviction that the other side has acted out of pure self-interest or ideological bias with little concern for or appreciation of universal values often gains support from real-world observation. If we examine the political landscape at all closely, we cannot help but notice that other people's views, construals, assumptions, and political positions generally do prove to be suspiciously congruent with their overall ideology and their personal or group interests. Furthermore, those on the other side (and even those on our side) seem disinclined to express the kinds of reservations and sources of ambivalence that we know to be characteristic of our views. What we often fail to note, of course, is the same potentially telling congruence among our own beliefs, assumptions, and interests. And we forget that other individuals—both on our own side and on the other side of the debate—may, like us, hold more ambivalent and complex views than they are comfortable about expressing to anyone but trusted intimates. When the naive realist hears spokespersons for the other side appeal to universal values such as equality, equity, self-determination, reverence for life, or compassion for those weaker than oneself, the appeals are seen as cynical or at best misguided. The real situation—at least when that situation is appraised dispassionately—could lead the ethical actor and possessor of universal values to only one position (or so the naive realist believes); that is, the position that he or she happens to hold. In a sense the failure is one of attributional "charity." Partisans on the other side, to be sure, do see the world through the prism of their beliefs, expectations, needs, and interests—but the impact is apt to be less powerful, pervasive, and distorting than we assume (in fact, no more powerful, or average than that exerted by the same influences on our own views). Moreover, the congruencies between construals and beliefs that we note in others are a product neither of a particular group or ideology but rather of the way human beings in general, including ourselves, go "beyond the information given" (see Bruner, 1957; Nisbett & Ross, 1980; Ross & Lepper, 1980).

Egocentrism, Naive Realism, and Golden Rules

Through maturation and experience, social perceivers come, as we have noted, to recognize that different actors not only have different preferences or tastes but also different perspectives and perceptions—that their own construals or constructions of social actions and entities may not be shared by their peers. Such insights about the diversity of subjective responses can, of course, be very helpful in promoting more accurate social predictions and inferences. Indeed, we argued earlier in this chapter that the wise social perceiver should, at least tentatively, assume surprising or seemingly inappropriate responses on the part of others to be symptoms of exactly such construal differences, rather than prematurely and uncharitably inferring negative personal traits (or, we would now add, inferring deficiency or marked differences in personal values). However, the "naive" conviction that others share our way of responding to the world—especially when such a conviction is adopted mindfully and selectively rather than assumed mindlessly and indiscriminately—similarly can be helpful; for it too can spare us premature and erroneous assumptions about the values adhered to by others.

The so-called Golden Rule, which is an essential feature not only of Christianity but of virtually all of the world's major religions, holds that we should do unto others as we would have them do unto us (or, in the less presumptuous version of the rule favored by other sages, *refrain* from doing unto others what we would have them *not* do unto us). The English philosopher Thomas Hobbes (cited in Leakey & Lewin, 1992) extended this prescription from presumptions of behavior preference to assumptions about others' subjective responses, offering the following advice: "Given the similitude of the thoughts and passions of one man to the thoughts and passions of another, whosoever looketh into himself and considereth what he doth when he does think, opine, reason, hope, fear, etc., and upon what grounds, he shall thereby read and know what are the thoughts and passions of all other men upon the like occasions" (p. 296).

Although there is room to debate the wisdom of relying too heavily on such advice, which both codifies naive realism and provides a recipe for the false consensus effect, we think such a tentative assumption or presumption can help guard us against errors that may be even more serious in their consequences. We would, however, be inclined to sharpen somewhat the good philosopher's advice. That is, assume tentatively that others share your most important values and preferences—that others, like you, value friendship and family highly, that others, like you, believe that justice must be served (albeit tempered with mercy). Assume further that self-determination, personal responsibility, fair play, compassion for those less fortunate, and other values you regard as essential to moral conduct are shared (although perhaps not ordered identically) by your peers and adversaries alike. And, when others respond in a way that seems unreasonable, unconscionable, or simply bizarre, do not give up such assumptions unless and until you have ruled out the possibility that your peers or adversaries have proceeded from very different construals or interpretations of the relevant objects of evaluation. In short, our advice is to proceed from the naive but charitable assumption that when people respond to important objects of social evaluation in ways that are surprising and/or offensive, it is generally their perceptions, assumptions, associations, and construals, rather than their basic values, that differ from our own and that must be addressed in the process of seeking reconciliation.

ACKNOWLEDGMENTS

We owe a debt of gratitude to Ed Reed and Elliot Turiel for insightful comments and suggestions that guided our revisions. We also would like to acknowledge the Jean Piaget Society, whose invitation to discuss the nature and implications of our work at its annual meeting was the initial impetus for this chapter.

REFERENCES

Adams, J. S. (1965). Inequity in social exchange. In L. Berkowitz (Ed.), *Advances in experimental social psychology* (Vol. 2, pp. 267–299). New York: Academic Press.

Asch, S. E. (1952). *Social psychology*. New York: Prentice-Hall.

Bandura, A. (1990). Selective activation and disengagement of moral control. *Journal of Social Issues, 46*, 27–46.

Bazerman, M. H., Loewenstein, G. F., & White, S. B. (1992). Psychological determinants of utility in competitive contexts: The impact of elicitation procedures. *Administrative Science Quarterly, 37*, 220–240.

Berkowitz, L., & Walster, E. (Eds.). (1976). *Advances in experimental social psychology* (Vol. 9). New York: Academic Press.

Brehm, J. W. (1966). *A theory of psychological reactance*. New York: Academic Press.

Brehm, S., & Brehm, J. W. (1981). *Psychological reactance: A theory of freedom and control*. New York: Academic Press.

Bruner, J. S. (1957). Going beyond the information given. In H. Gruber, K. R. Hammond, &

R. Jesser (Eds.), *Contemporary approaches to cognition* (pp. 41–69). Cambridge, MA: Harvard University Press.

Dawes, R. M. (1991). Social dilemmas, economic self-interest, and evolutionary theory. In D. R. Brown & J. E. Keith Smith (Eds.), *Frontiers of mathematical psychology: Essays in honor of Clyde Coombs* (pp. 53–79). New York: Springer-Verlag.

Diekmann, K. A., Samuels, S. M., Ross, L., & Bazerman, M. H. (1994). *Self-interest and fairness in problems of resource allocation.* Unpublished manuscript, Northwestern University, Evanston, IL.

Doob, A. N., & Roberts, J. V. (1984). Social psychology, social attitudes, and attitudes toward sentencing. *Canadian Journal of Behavioural Psychology, 16,* 269–280.

Dunning, D., Griffin, D. W., Milojkovic, J., & Ross, L. (1990). The overconfidence effect in social prediction. *Journal of Personality and Social Psychology, 58,* 568–581.

Fiske, S. T., & Taylor, S. E. (1991). *Social cognition* (2nd ed.). New York: McGraw-Hill.

Flavell, J. H. (1963). *The developmental psychology of Jean Piaget.* Princeton, NJ: Van Nostrand.

Flavell, J. H. (1985). *Cognitive development* (2nd ed.). Englewood Cliffs, NJ: Prentice-Hall.

Gilbert, D. T., & Jones, E. E. (1986). Perceiver-induced constraint: Interpretations of self-generated reality. *Journal of Personality and Social Psychology, 50,* 269–280.

Gilovich, T. (1981). Seeing the past in the present: The effect of associations to familiar events on judgments and decisions. *Journal of Personality and Social Psychology, 40,* 797–808.

Gilovich, T. (1991). *How we know what isn't so: The fallibility of human reasoning in everyday life.* New York: The Free Press.

Griffin, D., Dunning, D., & Ross, L. (1990). The role of construal processes in overconfident predictions about self and others. *Journal of Personality and Social Psychology, 59,* 1128–1139.

Griffin, D., & Ross, L. (1991). Subjective construal, social inference, and human misunderstanding. In M. P. Zanna (Ed.), *Advances in experimental social psychology* (Vol. 24, pp. 319–359). San Diego, CA: Academic Press.

Hastorf, A., & Cantril, H. (1954). They saw a game: A case study. *Journal of Abnormal and Social Psychology, 49,* 129–134.

Higgins, E. T., Rholes, W. S., & Jones, C. R. (1977). Category accessibility and impression formation. *Journal of Experimental Social Psychology, 13,* 141–154.

Homans, B. C. (1961). *Social behavior: Its elementary forms.* New York: Harcourt Brace Jovanovich.

Ichheiser, G. (1949). Misunderstandings in human relations: A study in false social perception. *American Journal of Sociology, 55* (Suppl.).

Ichheiser, G. (1951). Misunderstandings in international relations. *American Sociological Review, 16,* 311–315.

Inhelder, B., & Piaget, J. (1958). *The growth of logical thinking from childhood to adolescence.* New York: Basic Books.

Jones, E. E., & Nisbett, R. E. (1971). The actor and the observer: Divergent perceptions of the causes of behavior. In E. E. Jones, D. Kanouse, H. H. Kelley, R. E. Nisbett, S. Valins, & B. Weiner (Eds.), *Attribution: Perceiving the causes of behavior* (pp. 79–94). Morristown, NJ: General Learning Press.

Kelly, G. (1955). *The psychology of personal constructs.* New York: Norton.

Keltner, D., & Robinson, R. J. (1993). Imagined ideological differences in conflict escalation and resolution. *International Journal of Conflict Management, 4,* 249–262.

Krech, D., & Crutchfield, R. S. (1948). *Theory and problems of social psychology.* New York: McGraw-Hill.

Leakey, R., & Lewin, R. (1992). *Origins reconsidered: In search of what makes us human.* New York: Anchor Books.

Lepper, M., Ross, L., Tsai, J., & Ward, A. (1994). *Mechanisms of reactive devaluation.* Unpublished manuscript, Stanford University, Palo Alto, CA.

Lewin, K. (1935). *A dynamic theory of personality.* New York: McGraw-Hill.

Lord, C. G., Desforges, D. M., Fein, S., Pugh, M. A., & Lepper, M. R. (1994). Typicality effects in attitudes toward social policies: A concept-mapping approach. *Journal of Personality and Social Psychology, 66, 658–673.*

Lord, C. G., Ross, L., & Lepper, M. R. (1979). Biased assimilation and attitude polarization: The effects of prior theories on subsequently considered evidence. *Journal of Personality and Social Psychology, 37,* 2098–2109.

Marks, G., & Miller, N. (1987). Ten years of research on the false consensus effect: An empirical and theoretical review. *Psychological Bulletin, 102,* 72–81.

Mnookin, R., & Ross, L. (1995). Strategic, psychological, and institutional barriers: An introduction. In K. Arrow, R. Mnookin, L. Ross, A. Tversky, & R. Wilson (Eds.), *Barriers to the negotiated resolution of conflict* (pp. 3–27). New York: Norton.

Mullen, B., & Hu, L. (1988). Social projection as a function of cognitive mechanisms: Two meta-analytic integrations. *British Journal of Social Psychology, 27,* 333–356.

Newton, E. (1990). *Overconfidence in the communication of intent: Heard and unheard melodies.* Unpublished doctoral dissertation, Stanford University, Stanford, CA.

Nisbett, R. E., & Ross, L. D. (1980). *Human inference: Strategies and shortcomings of social judgment.* Englewood Cliffs, NJ: Prentice-Hall.

Orwell, G. (1949). *1984: A novel.* New York: Harcourt, Brace.

Piaget, J. (1926). *The language and thought of the child.* New York: Harcourt, Brace.

Piaget, J. (1928). *Judgment and reasoning in the child.* New York: Harcourt, Brace.

Piaget, J. (1962). *Play, dreams and imitation in childhood.* New York: Norton.

Rapoport, A. (1960). *Fights, games, and debates.* Ann Arbor: University of Michigan Press.

Read, S. J. (1984). Analogical reasoning in social judgment. The importance of causal theories. *Journal of Personality and Social Psychology, 46,* 14–25.

Read, S. J. (1987). Similarity and causal use of social analysis. *Journal of Experimental Social Psychology, 23,* 189–207.

Robinson, R. J., & Keltner, D. (1994). *Much ado about nothing? Revisionists and traditionalists choose an introductory English syllabus.* Manuscript submitted for review.

Robinson, R. J., Keltner, D., Ward, A., & Ross, L. (1995). Actual versus assumed differences in construal: "Naive realism" in intergroup perception and conflict. *Journal of Personality and Social Psychology, 68,* 404–417.

Ross, L. (1977). The intuitive psychologist and his shortcomings: Distortions in the attribution process. In L. Berkowitz (Ed.), *Advances in experimental social psychology* (Vol. 10, pp. 173–220). New York: Academic Press.

Ross, L. (1981). The "intuitive scientist" formulation and its developmental implications. In J. Flavell & L. Ross (Eds.), *Cognitive social development: Frontiers and possible futures* (pp. 1–42). New York: Cambridge University Press.

Ross, L. (1995). Reactive devaluation in negotiation and conflict resolution. In K. Arrow, R. Mnookin, L. Ross, A. Tversky, & R. Wilson (Eds.), *Barriers to the negotiated resolution of conflict* (pp. 30–48). New York: Norton.

Ross, L., Greene, D., & House, P. (1977). The false consensus effect: An egocentric bias in social perception and attribution processes. *Journal of Experimental Social Psychology, 13,* 279–301.

Ross, L., & Lepper, M. R. (1980). The perseverance of beliefs: Empirical and normative considerations. In R. A. Shweder & D. W. Fiske (Eds.), *New directions for methodology of behavioral science: Fallible judgment in behavioral research* (pp. 17–36). San Francisco: Jossey-Bass.

Ross, L., & Nisbett, R. (1991). *The person and the situation: Perspectives of social psychology.* New York: McGraw-Hill.

Ross, L., & Samuels, S. M. (1993). *The predictive power of personal reputation vs. labels and construal in the Prisoner's Dilemma game.* Unpublished manuscript, Stanford University, Palo Alto, CA.

Ross, L., & Stillinger, C. (1991). Barriers to conflict resolution. *Negotiation Journal, 8,* 389–404.

Ross, L., & Ward, A. (1995). Psychological barriers to dispute resolution. In M. P. Zanna (Ed.), *Advances in experimental social psychology* (Vol. 27, pp. 255–304). San Diego, CA: Academic Press.

Spellman, B. A., & Holyoak, K. (1992). If Saddam is Hitler then who is George Bush: Analogical mapping between systems of social roles. *Journal of Personality and Social Psychology, 62,* 913–933.

Stillinger, C., Epelbaum, M., Keltner, D., & Ross, L. (1990). *The reactive devaluation barrier to conflict resolution.* Unpublished manuscript, Stanford University, Palo Alto, CA.

Thomas, W. I., & Znaniecki, F. (1918). *The Polish peasant in Europe and America: Monograph of an immigrant group.* Boston: Badger.

Tversky, A., & Kahneman, D. (1981). The framing of decisions and the psychology of choice. *Science, 211,* 453–458.

Tversky, A., & Kahneman, D. (1986). Rational choice and the framing of decisions. *Journal of Business, 59,* 250–278.

Vallone, R. P., Ross, L., & Lepper, M. R. (1985). The hostile media phenomenon: Biased perceptions and perceptions of bias in media coverage of the "Beirut Massacre." *Journal of Personality and Social Psychology, 49,* 577–585.

Walster, E., Berscheid, E., & Walster, G. W. (1973). New directions in equity research. *Journal of Personality and Social Psychology, 25,* 151–176.

Wicklund, R. A. (1974). *Freedom and reactance.* Potomac, MD: Lawrence Erlbaum Associates.

7

Values, Knowledge,
and Piaget

Terrance Brown
Chicago, Illinois

Five of the chapters in this book were originally presented as plenary addresses at the 23rd Annual Symposium of the Jean Piaget Society in Philadelphia in 1993. The theme of that symposium, Values and Knowledge, was chosen for two main reasons. One was that values constitute one of the most pressing concerns of parents, educators, developmental psychologists, clerics, criminologists, people who deal with at-risk populations, and societies in general. Second, the function of values in the construction and use of knowledge—in mental adaptation generally—is worthy of examination. Although he abandoned the topic of values rather early in his career, Piaget created one of the most important paradigms for studying values in his book *The Moral Judgment of the Child* (1932/1965). As time went on, he came to view values as a somewhat necessary evil in the march toward logical rationality (whose role in human affairs he greatly overvalued) and relegated them to a confused and secondary role in the construction of reason. Was he right? Why not put all of these issues on the table, re-evaluate their importance, and reassess our thinking on them? In the present chapter, I first review Piaget's thought with respect to values. I then critique Piaget's functional analysis of evaluative activity and examine alternative interpretations, and, finally, I formulate a conception of how values function and develop within the constructivist paradigm.

PIAGET AND VALUES

Piaget was both passionate and ambivalent about values throughout his career. In his earliest works, he often seemed concerned with little else. Not only are

there poems of tender feeling concerning the beauty of the first snow in win-
ter and the wish to lead a lover to summits above the human plane, but there
is also, in *La Mission de l'Idée* (1915), a plaint against the poverty of the real:

> The poet feels a higher beauty
> That his verses cannot capture
> And half destroy.
> In his soul,
> He hears a symphony of enchanted virtuality,
> A procession of dreams,
> Colored and alive.
> But reality can express one of these alone,
> And that by robbing it
> Of its true life (p. 10)

A bit later, in an autobiographical novel written as his adolescence ended,
Piaget (1918) appeared to be more enthusiastic about reality when he resolved
to create a biological theory of good and evil:

> You are going to create an ethics based on science and scandalize men by show-
> ing Good to be biological equilibrium, a mechanical law of material evolution.
> . . . You will bring forth a completely experimental religious psychology and show
> faith to be another form of biological equilibrium, prayer to be a reunification of
> the self, conversion to be an unconscious process aiming, in the same way mys-
> ticism does, at equilibrating sexuality. . . . Above all, you are going to combat all
> metaphysics and show that the simplest decisions of the will include Christian
> faith in all its beauty. (pp. 137–138)

Fifteen or so years later, this project developed scientific teeth with the publication of *The Moral Judgment of the Child* (1932/1965), a pioneering study
from which several chapters of this book derive, and it was still fitfully alive in
the early 1950s when Piaget published a study on patriotic feeling (Piaget,
1951/1976) and gave his lectures on *Intelligence and Affectivity* (Piaget, 1953–
1954/1981). However, as time went on, Piaget's focus underwent a subtle shift.
Where once he had believed that good and evil were universal, objective, and
capable of being known, he came to believe that all values except logicomathe-
matical necessity and empirical truth are subjective, diverse, and difficult to
study. Where he once imagined that evaluation led to higher forms of knowledge, he came gradually to the conclusion that evaluation, although preliminary to all knowledge construction, can neither lead to nor modify knowledge
in any way (Piaget, 1953–1954/1981, 1965/1971, 1966). In the end, Piaget no
longer expressed interest in subjective forms of value and in one of his rare self-
contradictions, even attempted to displace the problem onto another discipline, that is, neurology (Bringuier, 1977/1980). Despite his apparent change
of mind, Piaget's ever more negative and restrictive statements about the role
and the importance of values provide many of the elements needed to formu-

late a naturalistic theory of evaluation. I believe, moreover, that the chapters in this book deal with one or another aspect of Piaget's grudging, nascent theory, a theory that was never fully realized because Piaget did not achieve for evaluative phenomena what he achieved for sensation and motricity: an accurate functional analysis. I argue that conviction by examining Piaget's own words.

THE RECORD

L'Introduction à l'Épistémologie Génétique

Early on, Piaget began to realize that, if for no other reason than want of time, he would not be able to realize his adolescent ambition to explain every aspect of human mental processes biologically and would have to choose. One of the choices he made was to lay aside the problem of values. The 1950 summation of his epistemology gives the fullest account of the reasons for that decision. In that work, Piaget laid out the conditions under which he believed epistemology could be extracted from philosophy and made a science:

> Philosophy has for its aim the whole of the real—of external reality, of the mind, and of the relations between the two. Because it embraces everything, reflective analysis is the only method it has available. Since no aspect of reality can be omitted, the systems that philosophers construct necessarily involve evaluation alongside investigation. For that reason, philosophical systems sooner or later manifest irreducible oppositions traceable to the diversity of values presented to human consciousness. Whence the heterogeneity of the broad philosophical traditions that periodically reappear in the history of metaphysics. . . .
>
> By contrast, a science delimits its aim and begins to gain acceptance as a scientific discipline only when that delimitation succeeds. Moreover, in pursuing answers to particular questions, it constructs methods that allow it to bring new facts together and to coordinate their interpretation within a circumscribed domain. The upshot of all of this is that philosophers often disagree because of the inevitable differences of values that separate conceptions bearing simultaneously on the universe and the internal life, while scientists achieve a relative accord of minds. But science does so only insofar as it solicits agreement for solutions of restricted problems using equally restricted methods. . . .
>
> When a discipline like experimental psychology separates itself from philosophy and establishes itself as an autonomous discipline, [it means that its representatives have] agreed to give up certain types of divisive discussion and to commit themselves, by convention or "gentlemen's agreement," to consider only questions that can be approached exclusively through the use of certain common or communicable methods. In the constitution of a science, there is, therefore, a necessary renunciation. There is a decision to give the most objective exposition possible of the results achieved or the explanations sought within the domain delimited and to leave outside of the discussion the perhaps even stronger pre-

occupations one holds in his heart of hearts. In this way, an accord of minds becomes realizable. . . . Such renunciations often appear as an impoverishment. In fact, however, it is always because of such delimitations that human knowledge is able to progress. (Piaget, 1950, pp. 13–15)

In these paragraphs Piaget takes tentative descriptive hold of one of the features central to any naturalistic theory of values: When problems are so broad or so difficult that they outstrip our ability to solve them exactly or scientifically, we fall back on inexact, philosophical, or unscientific methods. Exact or scientific solutions are achieved, according to Piaget, by delimiting problems in such a way that investigative methods communicable to and reproducible by others can be used. To be scientific, such methods must be employed even if doing so means that one cannot study the things he or she cares about most. In contrast, inexact or philosophical solutions are achieved by reflection and evaluation, values being conceived as a set of decision criteria not wholly appreciated by the subject and unavailable to the scrutiny of others. Judgments based on such criteria produce both internal inconsistency and external conflict with the equally unconscious and inconsistent evaluative judgments of other people. Whatever comfort philosophizing may bring to frightened little men faced with an incalculably complex world, it serves no epistemological purpose. Philosophic methods work against the "accord of minds" and are inimical to science. (Piaget, 1966, would later concede that philosophy could lead to rational formulations of questions.) Although Piaget's delineation of science and philosophy may be acceptable enough as pure description, it is not acceptable as an explanation. In fact, it sheds little if any light on the role that evaluation plays in constructing knowledge and provides few clues as to how evaluation and scientific methods interact. In subsequent works, Piaget sharpened his description.

Insights and Illusions of Philosophy

Fifteen years after the previously mentioned text was written, Piaget restated his basic argument in *Insights and Illusions of Philosophy* (1965/1971) and elaborated on the "reflective analysis" cited as the method of philosophers in the passage just given. (In this text, Piaget refers to the "reflective analysis" as "subjective reflection.")

> In putting an argument across to an opponent . . . one is very conscious of one's own strategies, whereas, when one convinces oneself by reflection, there is the constant risk of being the victim of one's unconscious desires. In the case of philosophical reflection these unconscious desires are connected with one's deepest intellectual and moral values, which are or appear to be the most disinterested, so that the more altruistic the cause the greater the risk of self-persuasion, to the evident detriment of objectivity and of the truth-value of the results obtained. . . .

Although speculative reflection is a fertile and even necessary heuristic introduction to all inquiry, it can only lead to the elaboration of hypotheses. . . . As
long as one does not seek for verification by a group of facts established experi-
mentally or by deduction conforming to an exact algorithm (as in logic), the criterion of truth can only remain subjective, in the manner of an intuitive satisfaction, of "self-evidence," etc. When it is a question of metaphysical problems
involving the coordination of values judged to be of essential importance, problems which thus introduce factors of conviction or faith, speculative reflection
remains the only method possible; but remaining bound up with the whole personality of the thinker, it can only lead to a wisdom or rational faith, and is not
knowledge from the point of view of objective or interindividual criteria of truth.
When it is a question, on the other hand, of the more delimited or delimitable
problems of epistemology, then an appeal to facts or to logico-mathematical deduction becomes possible. (Piaget, 1965/1971, pp. 11–12)

This adds several important ideas to Piaget's previous analysis. To begin
with, rather than just being something people do when they cannot do science,
as the 1950 text implied, in these passages Piaget admitted that evaluative reflection is a necessary preliminary to all knowledge construction. Second, and
important from the point of view of contemporary theories, Piaget here put
forth the view that speculation, guided as it must be by evaluation, is heuristic
in nature. Third, Piaget differentiated evaluation in terms of truth from evaluation according to other criteria. Fourth, Piaget posited that there are subjective and objective—by which he meant intersubjective—evaluative criteria.
Fifth, he asserted that values and feelings are somehow connected. Finally, he
put forth the idea that values and personality are deeply intertwined. These
additions and clarifications are good as far as they go, but they do not move
Piaget's conception of values beyond the descriptive level. Piaget was still trying to distinguish philosophy from science rather than to analyze values and
evaluation per se. For an analysis of that kind, one must turn to the Sorbonne
lectures on the relation between intelligence and affectivity (Piaget, 1953–
1954/1981).

Intelligence and Affectivity

The texts cited so far have not examined the terms values and evaluation carefully. Assuming, apparently, that these concepts are understood and unproblematic, they proceed directly to examine the role values and evaluation play
in the speculative reflection associated with philosophy. But elsewhere, Piaget
(1953–1954/1981) did attempt to say what values and evaluation are and to
identify the functions they serve. Shortly after L'Introduction à l'Épistémologie Génétique was published, Piaget was enjoined by students to stop isolating
intelligence from the rest of mental life and to address the problem of affectivity. In the lectures that resulted, he provided an in-depth analysis of how values, affectivity, and interest relate to one another; of the parallels between cog-

nitive and affective development; and of the nature of value structures and their construction.

With regard to the first of these topics, Piaget's (1953–1954/1971) basic thesis was that there are no such things as purely cognitive or purely affective behaviors. All behavior has both cognitive and affective aspects, and "on either plane, development is achieved through progressive equilibration" (p. 73).

> Behavior cannot be classified under affective and cognitive rubrics. If a distinction must be made, and it appears one should, it would be more accurate to make it between *behaviors related to objects and behaviors related to people*. Both have structural or cognitive and energetic or affective aspects. In behaviors related to objects, the structural aspects are the various empirical and logico-mathematical knowledge structures while the energetic aspects are the interests, efforts, and intra-individual feelings that regulate behavior. In behaviors related to people, the energetic element is made up of interpersonal feelings. Ordinarily, these are emphasized exclusively. They contain a structural element, however, which comes from [constructing a conscious conceptualization] of interpersonal relationships and leads, among other things, to the constitution of value structures. (p. 74)

The affective aspect of behavior, Piaget contended, serves two functions. On the one hand, it has a synchronic component that determines the intensity of behavior by regulating energy. On the other, it has a diachronic component that determines the content of behavior by assigning value. These two functions interact to form interest. Interest, Piaget argued, is the affective aspect of assimilation, whereas understanding is the cognitive aspect. Because affectivity is essentially quantitative and dynamic in nature whereas cognition is structural and qualitative, there is no possibility that affectivity could affect the final form that knowledge structures take: "Affectivity can cause accelerations and retardations in the development of intelligence . . . it can disturb intellectual functioning and modify its contents, but . . . it can neither engender nor modify structures" (Piaget, 1981/1987, p. 73).

Piaget's second major thesis in this work is the idea that affectivity develops and that, in fact, it goes through a series of stages analogous to and correlated with the stages through which cognition passes. In a table laying out parallel stages of intellectual and affective development, Piaget divided development into two great periods. He called the interval from birth to about 2 years the period of sensorimotor intelligence and intraindividual feelings and divided it into three substages. During the first substage of this period, the baby exhibits inborn affects, just as he or she exhibits inborn instincts and reflexes. The function of these inborn feelings is to determine when (evaluation) and with what vigor (energy regulation) schemes will be employed. With each succeeding substage, new affects are found. The second great developmental period indicated in Piaget's table (verbal intelligence and interpersonal feelings) extends from 2 to about 15 years. Piaget characterized it as "the period of verbal or socialized intelligence" (p. 44). As he did with sensorimotor intelligence, he divided this period into three substages and listed the characteristic cognitive and affective features of each. The basic argument concerning verbal or socialized intelligence is that, with the advent of evocative memory made possible by a newly developed capacity for using symbols and signs, feelings, like perceptions, can be evocatively remembered, communicated, and objectified. Children can now remember feelings caused by their own actions or by the actions of other people. They will, therefore, take those memories into account when formulating actions in the future. If touching the stove caused pain, they will not touch it anymore. If mother became angry when they jumped up and down on the couch, they will be careful not to repeat that action—at least when Mom is watching. Also, because of their newfound ability to conceptualize and communicate, children become capable of sharing feelings and generalizing their own affects into behavioral norms. They will, for instance, become convinced that for all children "it is 'ouchy' to touch the stove" or that for all children "it is bad to jump up and down on the couch." Piaget elaborated these newfound capacities into a general theory of interpersonal exchanges. Interpersonal feelings, Piaget insisted, cannot be reduced to the two tenets of utilitarian theories of value, that is, that behavior is based on interest (in the sense of personal profit) and that selfishness holds primacy over altruism. Interpersonal feelings, argued Piaget, arise through much more complex processes having to do with how we evaluate other people's actions. For interactions to be adaptive, they must be mutual. They must conform to values of equality, fairness, justice, and the like. They cannot just be ruled by utilitarian values of "get ahead at any price" or "be altruistic only if you can see some profit in it." (Piaget's conception of interpersonal exchanges first appeared in 1941 in an article entitled "Essai sur la théorie des valeurs qualitatives en sociologie statique [«Synchronique»]." It forms the basis of his sociological theory, identified by Mays, 1982, as closely related to the sociological theory of Homans cited in Ross and Ward's article, chap. 6, this volume. An English translation can be found in Piaget, 1967/1995.) It was not lost on Piaget that the idea of normalized scales of values contradicted his general thesis that affectivity cannot influence structure. He resolved the contradiction in the following manner.

> As early as the fifth or even the fourth [substage of sensorimotor intelligence] . . . "affective structures" were encountered. These included seriated scales of interests and values involving symmetrical and asymmetrical relations; moral feelings something like operatory rules of affectivity; and the will, which we described as a regulation of regulations analogous to reversible operations. The existence of these structures contradicted, or at least seemed to contradict, the third part of our hypothesis [i.e., that affectivity can neither engender nor modify structures]. We resolved the paradox by recognizing that . . . affective structures are isomorphic with cognitive structures, [that] they are not a special and separate sort of structure that is different in kind from intellectual structures. . . .

Affective structures have to do with an intellectualization of the affective aspect of our exchanges with other people. While at lower levels values result simply from projecting feelings onto objects, at the level of interpersonal exchanges the expression of values in the form of value judgments is an intellectualized expression. A second instance of this intellectualization of feeling is evident in our demonstration that schemes arising from interpersonal relationships are subsequently internalized and applied by the individual to himself. (Piaget, 1981/1987, pp. 73–74)

In sum, then, in his fullest statement on the subject, Piaget viewed affectivity as an aspect of all behavior and linked values and evaluation to the affective system. Affectivity had a synchronic dimension concerned with the regulation of energy and a diachronic dimension concerned with the assignation of value. These two aspects interacted to form interest, the regulator of all assimilation. Moreover, Piaget argued that, in concert with action and thought, feelings develop by equilibration. Thus, one finds stages of affective development that are parallel with the stages of cognitive development. When intelligence becomes mediated by symbols and signs, it becomes possible for children to conduct reciprocal interpersonal exchanges and to construct value scales that will serve as norms of behavior. Such value scales constitute affective *structures*. They are produced through the intellectualization of feelings and are cognitive in nature.

THE SELF AND SOCIETY

There remains a final topic more general than the theory of values but central to Piaget's thinking on values and much in evidence in the chapters of this book. This is the concept of the self. Its relevance to a theory of values is quite simple. If Piaget is going to speak of subjective as opposed to objective values, then what is the nature of the subject and what does he mean by objective values?

The Subject

In his chapter in this book, Reed outlines how, in Western society, our concept of the self has developed from Rousseau's notion that children are born with autonomous souls that are pure in nature. It is only through socialization into adult society that they become selfish and evil. Reed goes on to analyze the twists and turns this idea has undergone in the writings of Hegel, Marx and Engels, Dewey, and so forth. Piaget's thinking about all of this was very different.

In *The Social Psychology of Childhood,* Piaget (1967/1995) distinguished the self from the personality and put forth the thesis that the self does not exist primordially. At first, infants are selfless, not in the sense of being altruistic but in the sense of being undifferentiated from their environment. Contrary to Rousseau, the major developmental task in self-formation is not, therefore, to degenerate from altruism to selfishness through the offices of adult socialization. Rather, the great task is to distinguish the self from the nonself. Further, the nonself has to be sorted into objects that are other selves and those that are not. There is, therefore, a tripolar differentiation of self, object, and other. In Piaget's view, this implies that self-construction and socialization go hand in hand. Moreover, Piaget argued that children do not achieve complete selfhood and socialization the first time around but construct it in stages. Relating selfhood to the locus of control, he envisioned it as developing from primitive anomy through heteronomy to autonomy.

Although this corrects the erroneous developmental sequence posited by Rousseau, it does not represent Piaget's full thinking on the matter. The self, for Piaget, was the psychological subject and, as such, the repository of subjective values. Knowledge, he believed, was constructed by a different kind of subject, one abstracted from many psychological subjects. This epistemic subject was the seat of objective values. About the epistemic subject, Piaget had this to say:

> There are thinkers who dislike "the subject," and if this subject is characterized in terms of its "lived experience" we admit to being among them. . . . The "lived" can only have a very minor role in the construction of cognitive structures, for these do not belong to the subject's consciousness but to his operational behavior, which is something quite different. Not until he becomes old enough to reflect on his own habits and patterns of thought and action does the subject become aware of structures as such. . . .
>
> If, then, to account for the constructions we have described we must appeal to the subject's acts, the subject here meant can only be the epistemic subject, that is, the mechanisms common to all subjects at a certain level, those of the "average" subject. . . . Everyone grants that structures have laws of composition, which amounts to saying that they are regulated. But by what or by whom? If the theoretician who has framed the structure is the one who governs it, it exists only on the level of a formal exercise. To be real, a structure must, in the literal sense, be governed from within. . . . So we come back to the necessity of some sort of functional activity; and, if the facts oblige us to attribute cognitive structures to a subject, it is for our purposes sufficient to define this subject as the center of functional activity. . . .
>
> But why postulate such a center? If structures exist and each is regulated from within, what role is left for the subject? . . . Why not eliminate it altogether, as certain contemporary structuralists dream of doing? . . .
>
> If cognitive structures were static, the subject would indeed be a superfluous entity. But if it should turn out that structures tend to become connected in some way . . . then the subject regains the role of mediator. It will either be the "structure of structures," the transcendental ego of a priorist theories, or, perhaps, more modestly, the "self" of psychological theories of synthesis. . . . Or, lacking this overarching power of synthesis, and having no structures at its disposal un-

til it constructs them, the subject will, more modestly, but also more realistically, have to be defined in the terms we earlier proposed, as the center of activity. (Piaget, 1968/1970, pp. 68–70)

In *Possibility and Necessity,* Piaget (1981/1987, 1983/1987) examined how this abstract epistemic creature constructs *objective values* through its own action. He considered such construction to be one of the central issues in epistemology. However, he would never return to the issue of subjective values. In an interview with Bringuier late in his career, he even professed to have lost all interest in that subject.

Bringuier: Now, your approach to the problem of human evolution and stages is strictly from the point of view of intelligence, isn't it?
Piaget: Yes.
Bringuier: You don't deal with the affective level at all?
Piaget: Only because I'm not interested in it. I'm not a psychologist. I'm an epistemologist. (He smiles, as if he had played a trick on me.)
. . .
Bringuier: But how can one be interested in someone—in a child, to be specific—with regard to his intelligence, the development of his intelligence alone, and not be interested in his affective side? Can they be separated?
Piaget: Obviously, for intelligence to function, it must be motivated by an affective power. A person won't ever solve a problem if the problem doesn't interest him. The impetus for everything lies in interest, affective motivation.
Bringuier: You like one thing, you dislike something else.
Piaget: That provides the motivation, of course. But take, for instance two boys and their arithmetic lessons. One boy likes them and forges ahead; the other thinks he doesn't understand math; he feels inferior and has all the typical complexes of people who are weak in math. The first boy will learn more quickly, the second more slowly. But, for both, two and two are four. Affectivity doesn't modify the acquired structure at all. If the problem at hand is the construction of structures, affectivity is essential as a motivation, of course, but it doesn't explain the structures.
Bringuier: It's strange that affectivity doesn't appear at the level of structures, regardless! An individual is a whole.
Piaget: Yes, but in the study of feelings, when you find structures, they are structures of knowledge. For example, in feelings of mutual affection there's an element of comprehension and an element of perception. That's all cognitive. In behavior you have—and I think all scholars are agreed on this point—a structure of behavior and a motivating force of behavior. There is motivation on the one hand, and mechanism on the other.

Bringuier: But if everyone conforms to structures, as you say, you lose sight of individuality, of the unique qualities of each person.
Piaget: You're forgetting what I told you about accommodation. There is great diversity in structures. And the same structures, implied by different individuals . . .
Bringuier: Everyone has his own style of accommodation . . .
Piaget: Of course. Accommodation gives rise to unlimited differentiations. The same structures are very general. The fact that number is the same for everyone, and the series of whole numbers is the same for everyone, doesn't prevent mathematicians, taken one by one, from being unique individuals. There is such diversification of structures . . .
Bringuier: Still, to hear you talk about affectivity, for instance, one would think it was one of psychology's poor relations, in the sense that it becomes simply a motivating force.
Piaget: Why not at all! I think that it's a problem that's beyond us today. In fifty years we'll be able to talk about it intelligently, because it's considerably more difficult, and we don't have the neurological data. (Bringuier, 1977/1980, pp. 49–52)

This is disappointing to those interested in the self and subjective values. Piaget did, however, have something interesting to say about another aspect of those topics. Children are born into societies with elaborate value systems that they eventually acquire. All of the chapters in this book except Ross and Ward's—Nucci's, Okin's, Reed's, and Užgiris', in particular—are concerned in one way or another with how such acquisition is effected. None of the authors here, but many authors writing currently, have conceived the issue of acquisition in terms of an opposition between individual and social construction. About that issue, Piaget had much to say.

Individual Versus Social Construction

Piaget saw the idea that society constructs values and then transmits them directly to children as just one more manifestation of empiricism, of the belief that knowledge comes from the outside, that it increases by accretion rather than evolution, that it has no structure. To him, the idea was incomprehensible. For Piaget, all knowledge, including axiological knowledge, was structured and could only be acquired through a process of assimilation. This ensures an interpretive and synthetic role for the individual mind.

This conviction has led many scholars to claim that Piaget believed knowledge to be individually constructed (Shweder, 1984; Tudge & Rogoff, 1989). The argument often proceeds along the lines that, because it was derived by generalizing biological adaptive functions, Piaget's theory is necessarily opposed to the idea of social construction. That conclusion is, in fact, a non-sequitur. The fact that intelligence arises from internalizing the functions of organic evolution does not make intelligence individual any more than the fact that genes reside in individuals makes organic evolution individual. In organic evolution, interaction between individually embodied genes by means of sexual recombination is a major source of variation. Selection, also, has significance only when it works on populations. In parallel, the full functioning of intelligence, as Piaget explicitly insisted, depends on the communicative interaction of individuals in populations or societies. On that view, intercourse between minds is a functional analog of intercourse between bodies in constructing adapted forms. In that view also, social selection or evaluation has a profound effect on which ideas survive.

However, Piaget's position on this question did not rest on the analogy with population genetics only. It also rested directly on sociological theory. Piaget, in fact, served for a time as department chair of sociology at the University of Geneva (Piaget, 1976a), produced extensive sociological writings (Piaget, 1967/1995), and carried out empirical studies on social influence (Piaget, 1932/1965). His theory lists "social experience" as one of the four factors responsible for the ontogenetic development of knowledge (Piaget & Inhelder, 1966/1969) and makes society the veritable "epistemic subject" in the historical evolution of knowledge (Piaget & Garcia, 1983/1989).

Numerous misinterpretations to the contrary, Piaget held that individual and social contributions to the construction of knowledge can, up to a certain point, be distinguished analytically but cannot, except at superficial levels, be distinguished operationally. The pitfall to be avoided, according to Piaget, is to suppose that precise differentiation of individual and social determinants is possible and to hold that one or the other is primary (Brown, 1988). That, unfortunately, is what many of his social constructionist critics attempt to do.

ASSESSING PIAGET'S THOUGHT ON VALUES

Reviewing the written record, it becomes apparent that Piaget argued the question of values in two incompatible ways. On the one hand, he argued that subjective values are a method of philosophy used to tackle complex problems unamenable to exact solution, in which case they produce, at best, possible rather than true positions. On the other hand, he argued that subjective values determine the content of motivation but do not themselves play any role in constructing even approximate solutions. Because the first of these arguments itself contains an ambiguity, the trouble does not end there. As a philosophical method, subjective values are both a means of knowledge and, in certain cases, a content of it. As a means of knowledge the fact that individual knowers have different subjective values leads to disagreement and, therefore, to beliefs that do not qualify as knowledge. As a content of knowledge, when other subjects are taken as the "object" of kowledge, their subjective values must be evaluated objectively.

Piaget tried to get around all of these difficulties by saying that, whereas psychologists might have to deal with subjective values or even "lived experience," epistemologists do not. By properly delimiting problems, they need consider two things only: (a) the "epistemic subject" from whom all values except objective values have been abstracted, and (b) how scientific thought "proceeds from a state of less knowledge to a state of knowledge judged superior" (Piaget, 1950, p. 18). Along with Bringuier, I wonder whether it is as easy as all that. Whereas it would be illegitimate to question Piaget's personal disinterest in people's lived experience, it is not illegitimate to ask whether his conception of the epistemic subject is adequate for a theory of knowledge. By his own admission, subjective values play a role in discovery. Are they, therefore, as dispensable as Piaget believed?

In fact, Bringuier's questions put Piaget's back against the wall. Piaget's remark, "We don't have the neurological data," suggests that it was because he did have the neurological data that he was able to talk intelligently about intelligence, cognition, and knowledge structures. Obviously, that was not the case. However, unable to come up with a coherent functional account of affectivity (and, therefore, values), he resorted to a re-equilibration strategy that in better moments he despised: displacement of a problem onto another discipline. The pity of it all is that Piaget was so close to solving the riddle of why people have feelings. Had he been truer to himself, he would have realized that the answer to that question lies, as he had shown in the case of intelligence and knowledge, not in neurology, but in biology taken in the sense of natural history, in the sense of Darwin. Had he stuck with his original inspiration, he would have created a natural place for values within the theoretical edifice he had erected. That edifice, after all, had its foundations in the functional analogies between organic and psychosocial evolution. But Piaget was, in the case of values, motivation, and affectivity, frightened off by the legacy of his history: by his parents' personalities, by the chaos of World War I, by his adolescent abhorence of uncertainty, by his disappointment with philosophy, and, significantly, by his distrust of Charles Darwin (Brown, 1980). In the end, his affective evaluations led, as he himself might have predicted, to a theory of knowledge that is impoverished and distorted. In what follows, I argue that that would not have had to be the case.

A PIAGETIAN CONCEPTION OF VALUES AND EVALUATION

Selecting and reorganizing Piaget's various assertions concerning values, one arrives at the following list:

1. Evaluation in terms of subjective criteria is a method of philosophy, that is, the reflective analysis preliminary to all knowledge construction.
2. There are both subjective and objective values; logical necessity and truth are objective values.

3. Subjective evaluation is heuristic in nature.

4. Subjective values are both intra- and interpersonally diverse and lead to conflicts.

5. Evaluation is a function of the affective system. Awareness of evaluative activities comes in the form of feelings. Values can be studied in terms of tastes, preferences, interests, choices, decisions, judgments, motivations, and feelings.

6. Values are bound up with personality.

7. There are different kinds of values, for example, intellectual values, values regulating social exchanges, and so on.

8. Infants are provided with a system of values by biological evolution. These are the rudimentary forms out of which all other values are constructed.

9. Values are somehow related to motivation.

10. Values are central to interpersonal exchanges.

11. Value structures result from the intellectualization of values and constitute a form of knowledge.

Good as far as it goes, Piaget's list remains descriptive rather than explanatory for the simple reason that, even reordered in this way, it lacks any feeling of necessity. This is quite surprising from a man who insisted throughout a very long career that the empiricist renunciation of causality was wrong. The essence of explanation, according to Piaget, was that it lent necessity to compositions of events that at the descriptive level remained contingent (Piaget, 1963/1968, 1971/1974). More surprising still is the fact that he himself had pioneered an approach that could have given his description of values and affectivity the very feeling of necessity it lacks. However, as already mentioned, Piaget seemed unwilling to do for values and evaluation what he did for knowledge. He was unwilling to draw functional analogies between mental and biological functioning insofar as values were concerned. For that reason, they were not fully and consistently integrated into his conception of intelligence but remained sequestra on the fringes of cognition. My task, then, in creating an explanatory theory of values is to frame Piaget's description of evaluative phenomena within his own interpretive framework. That means starting with inorganic evolution.

Directionality, Value, and Selection[1]

Under most definitions, values are unknown in the inorganic world, but directionality is not. In fact the inorganic world moves in the direction of thermo-

---

[1] Parts of this and the next two sections summarize work previously published (Brown, 1990, 1994; Brown & Weiss, 1987).

dynamic equilibrium, of entropy, of an even distribution of matter and energy. If one were to consider nature a regulating system, one might then say that it values entropy and selects out those randomly occurring situations in which entropy is greatest. This, however, imparts an intentionality to natural processes with which most educated persons are uncomfortable. By pure chance and at some date long removed, inorganic evolution produced the first teleonomic systems, the first systems capable of regulating, within certain limits, their own evolution. Rather than being disorganized by random changes occasioned by interaction with the environment, such systems compensate or reverse modifications that might undo them. Once created, the system itself controls which transformations will be permitted and which will be reversed or compensated. With their creation, a new process of selection began. Something besides entropy had "value."

Eventually, through random change and selection in terms of functional stability, arrangements of causal mechanisms evolved that allowed information to be stored, replicated, and passed on through reproduction. This led, ultimately, to the familiar story of Darwin's "inherited constitution," "variation," and "natural selection." It also led to new evolutionary epistemologies and to Piaget's core hypothesis about intelligence. Intelligence, Piaget contended, results from reproducing the functions of organic evolution by internal, psychological means. In the event nature did not devise a system that could create new adaptive organs in any literal sense. Rather, it devised a system that could vary and select forms of behavior, and these, in turn, could invent new material "organs" in the form of tools.

Piaget wrestled with the problem of how adaptive functions are realized psychologically right up to the end of his life. In *Le Possible, l'Impossible et le Nécessaire* (Piaget, 1976b) and again in *Possibility and Necessity* (Piaget, 1981/ 1987, 1983/1987), he argued that the central problem of constructivist epistemology is to understand how actions or ideas that have not existed previously can be created. He then explained why his theory of mental operations is insufficient to resolve that problem and why, therefore, it is necessary to add "new dimensions and complementary forms of organization" to that theory (p. 286). Piaget's analysis led to distinguishing two great systems at the heart of cognitive activity. One functions to produce understanding; the other functions to produce success (cf. *Réussir et Comprendre*, Piaget, 1974b). In order to account for how these functions are accomplished, Piaget distinguished three kinds of schemes: presentative, procedural, and operational. *Presentative schemes* correspond in many ways to Piaget's idea of atemporal operational structures. They "bear on the permanent and simultaneous characteristics of comparable objects;" their goal is understanding (p. 286). In contrast, *procedural schemes* correspond in many ways to Piaget's notion of schemes of action. They bear on particular and heterogenous situations; their goal is success. Finally, *operatory schemes,* formed by putting presentative content to procedural purpose, bear on understanding procedures, on reproducing them by deductive means.

> In opposition to the "real," constituted by presentative and operatory schemes (the latter only insofar as they are structural) . . . the formation of new "possibilities" is subordinated to two conditions. The first condition is the constitution of free combinations among the facts or context of an unresolved problem and the procedures employed or attempted in order to resolve it. Such combinations can be either more or less directed or more or less random. They enjoy, therefore, freedom to grope or make errors, without worrying about formal combinatorics which remain a special case of higher level. The second condition is that there is selection among these combinations in order to correct errors. Such selection is effected in two ways. On the one hand, external selection is effected in function of the results obtained by whatever procedures are attempted. On the other hand, internal selection is effected in function of the presentative and operatory schemes already organized (system I) or of the procedural schemes already tested and transferable (system II). . . . In short, the opening up of new possibilities essentially arises from the procedures of the second system. (Piaget, 1976b, pp. 287–288)

This leaves no doubt that in Piaget's theory as he left it both psychological variation and psychological selection are associated with the procedural system. Variation is a matter of creating possibilities; selection is a matter of assessing their functional effect (i.e., schemes that achieve or produce progress toward a goal are conserved) or of assessing consistency with existing structures (i.e., schemes that succeed in isolation but conflict with existing schemes may be modified or repressed—cf Piaget, *La Prise de Conscience,* 1974a). The revised theory has the great merit of reintroducing the psychological subject into Piaget's theory in terms of the center of procedural control. At the same time, it has the disadvantage of holding onto the idealistic illusion that, on all levels, selection in mental evolution is effected by assessing possibilities directly in terms of a single and determinable value, that is, whether or not adaptive equilibrium is improved. On that point, I believe, Piaget got into trouble.

The Hierarchy of Teleonomic Frameworks

Stated in the simplest terms, Piaget's last version of his theory does not grasp how, when problems are enormously complicated as most adaptive problems are, people make adaptive choices. One way they choose, according to Piaget, is by matching the results with the goals of thought or action. But that could ensure adaptation only insofar as the goal itself is adaptive. Piaget never examined how the adaptivity of goals is determined. Another way people make choices is by assessing the consistency of new possibilities with what is already believed or known. Ross and Ward (chap. 6, this volume) demonstrate empirically the kind of errors that selective criterion can lead to at the level of individual decisions. History provides profound lessons on the kind of errors it can lead to at the cultural level, for example, the Church's treatment of Galileo, the Nazi's treatment of relativity theory. In short, Piaget's theory of mental adaptation founders because it subordinates mental selection to goals but provides no conception of how goals are determined or how their adaptivity is assured. This results in the paradoxical claims that intention is the criterion of intelligence but mental selection is after the fact and not intentional. Apparently, on the issue of selection, Piaget could not free himself from dependence on the biological morphism. Intention requires that adaptation be anticipated, something unknown in biological evolution.

Piaget was able to sustain his belief that selection in terms of success or coherence might be possible because, in line with his principles of "impoverishment" and "renunciation," he bracketed motivational issues and limited his investigations to the solution of rather simple problems, for example, how to judge equivalence of volume when liquid is poured from one container to another. For such problems, once the goal is accepted by the subject, objective evaluation of means in terms of progress toward that goal or coherence with what is already known seems possible (although careful scrutiny of children's problem-solving procedures casts doubt even on that intuition (see Blanchet, 1986). However, most of the problems human beings face are not so simple. Consider, for example, the decision hierarchy facing a college student sitting on the edge of the bed each morning: Is life worth living? If so, how should I live it? What sort of person do I want to be? Do I really want to be a teacher? Should I marry Sally? Do I want kids? How many? How would I raise them? What should I have for breakfast? Did Brown really mean what he said about values? Should I change my major? Is that Webern? People call that beautiful? What should I do today? Should I call my mother? Can I pay this bill? When should I leave for class? Where are my bus tokens? Where are my shoes?

On the one hand, this list can be viewed from the motivational point of view: Why did the student ask these and not other questions? On the other it can be viewed from the point of view of the great differences in scale involved and the attendant differences in complexity of the decisions required. For any theory of knowledge to be complete, both perspectives must be considered. Insofar as Piaget dealt with the first perspective at all, he did so at the very end of *Possibility and Necessity*, where he reframed the basic motivational idea inherent in his theory of equilibration (Piaget, 1975/1985) in terms of presentative and procedural systems. Although this final formulation remains subject to the objections already raised, it does indicate that Piaget's attempts to understand possibility and necessity forced him to readmit the psychological subject in both its statistical and "lived experience" forms back into his epistemological theory.

Disturbances function to drive transitions, which then turn out to be compensations despite their appearing to be spontaneous activities unrelated to equilibration. . . . In this way a relationship is established between the structuring, organizing activities of the epistemic subject and the needs and specific capacities of the psychological subject, which depend on the subject's history: structure as such does not, in fact, include "needs," yet it can present gaps. To be precise, one would have to distinguish the individual capacities of a psychological subject from the variable strength or diversity of composition in an epistemic structure. The fact that psychological subjects may have many traits in common can only induce us to replace the dichotomy of the psychological and epistemic by a trichotomy suggested by the work presently conducted by B. Inhelder [Inhelder & Cellérier, 1992]: the individual, the common or general psychological (still temporal and causal), and the epistemic, which is nontemporal and exclusively implicational. (Piaget, 1983/1987, p. 153)

From the perspective of the widely varying complexity of adaptive problems, one sees that the questions at the beginning of the student's list have, at least as long as human history has been recorded, eluded rigorous solution, whereas the questions at the lower levels are rather easily solved. One sees further that Piaget's idea that problems can be solved in terms of success or coherence applies only at the lower levels of this hierarchy. At the upper levels of the hierarchy, decisions cannot be made on the basis of Piaget's selective criteria and the selection of means proceeds, as does selection of the goals themselves, according to subjective evaluative criteria. It is at this point that a theory of affectivity enters.

AFFECTIVITY AS A SYSTEM
OF EVALUATIVE HEURISTICS

In a prophetic but neglected book, *The Biological Origins of Human Values,* Pugh (1977) demonstrated why rigorously logical decisions are impossible in most of the situations adapting organisms face and why, therefore, accounts of human intelligence cannot be based on logical rationality only. Instead, Pugh argued, intelligence is a value-directed system, a key feature of which is the use of heuristics for estimating adaptive value and selecting among possibilities of action or thought. In mathematics, heuristics have been employed in conceptualized form for centuries; in intuitive form, they have been around forever. They have also played a central role in artificial intelligence since its inception. The idea that intelligence makes use of heuristics is nothing new. What was original about Pugh's hypothesis was that he attributed the heuristics at the core of human intelligence to the affective system. Rather than suggesting, as Piaget had done, that affectivity has to do with the energetics of behavior without influence on its structure, Pugh posited that, in fact, affectivity provides a method for inventing provisional or "good-enough" knowledge structures. Further, Pugh interpreted feelings as the conscious manifestation of evaluative activity and demonstrated that the affective heuristics needed to solve complex problems are multiple, particular to various levels of the goal–subgoal hierarchy, specific to different tasks, and often contradictory. He provided a provisional classification of the types of values needed to engineer intelligence and struggled with the problem of how value conflicts are resolved. Although he appreciated that a developmental theory was necessary both for constructing the knowledge base that value-governed systems employ and for developing what he called "secondary" values, he did not provide one.

Heuristics

Pugh's full argument and ingenious examples cannot be reproduced here, but several of his central concepts can. I start with his idea that human values are heuristic methods for estimating adaptation.

In his famous reintroduction of the subject of heuristics into mathematics education, Polya (1945/1957) pointed out that this discipline concerns the methods and rules used in invention and discovery. Heuristic reasoning, Polya contended, is not reasoning in the strictly logical sense, and it does not aim at rigorous solutions. Rather, heuristic thinking is makeshift or provisional. It attempts to come up with solutions that are only approximate or likely. Often problems are so difficult that one has to settle for such solutions, at least until rigorous answers can be worked out. "We need heuristic reasoning when we construct a strict proof as we need scaffolding when we erect a building" (p. 113).

Pugh applies heuristic principles to epistemology in general. The reason that heuristic methods are necessary for solving adaptive problems, Pugh pointed out, is that the number of possibilities open to intelligent beings is large beyond imagining. For example, in order to be certain about what we should eat, we would need to know the nutritional value and long-term effects of every food available. We would also need incredible amounts of memory, processing capacity, and time in order to store and sort through the data. In every respect we are deficient. Despite decades of nutritional science and eons of nutritional superstition, our knowledge of the long-term effects of diet remains uncertain. Complicating our insufficient knowledge is the fact that few of us have either the capacity or the time to examine carefully what little is known about a given food. For example, it now appears that the benefits and dangers of eating butter are better determined by the simple fact that people like butter than by the myriad studies on cholesterol and atherosclerosis that forbid it. So far at least, nature's simple heuristic for estimating the adaptive value of eating butter outstrips medical science and does so quickly without government support.

The use of affective heuristics, Pugh continued, is found in every domain of knowledge. By substituting a sweet tooth for knowledge about the nutritional value of sugar, by substituting lust for certitude about the reproductive value of sexual union, by substituting attachment for certainty about the adaptive advantages of relating to other people, by substituting interest in the somewhat unfamiliar, boredom with the everyday, and fear of the truly strange for elaborate theories about the ZPD, nature gets around the practical impossibility of finding rigorous solutions to all of these adaptive problems. More often than not, such affective heuristics mimic full-blown selective processes even though they are only indirectly related to them. Most of the time, feelings lead in the direction that biological selection would have led had the genetic system done the selecting.

Feelings and Affective Processes

With becoming candor, Pugh recognized that he did not understand how values are assigned. However, he did recognize that, as is the case with the five senses, evaluative processes are present from birth, that they are part of the sensorimotor system, and that the conscious manifestation of evaluative activities takes the form of what "folk psychology" (Block, 1980) calls feelings. In the later section on affective development, I develop the idea that in certain ways feelings are analogous to percepts and correspond, in general, to what Piaget called the "figurative" aspects of knowledge.

The Complexity of Values

In his own attempts to simulate decision systems for complicated situations, Pugh, like Piaget, did not at first appreciate the complexities of evaluation. Asked to design a program that would decide busing patterns ensuring desegregation, he employed the single value of optimal desegregation, a bit like Piaget employed the single value of optimal equilibrium. The result was that the children of neighboring families or even the children of the same family were assigned dramatically unequal distances to travel and, therefore, very unequal times to go to and from school. A child might have to catch the bus an hour earlier and come home an hour later than a sibling or the child next door. Also, siblings or neighboring children might have to go to schools on opposite sides of town. By human standards, his single-valued decision system was not very smart.

Even ignoring the complex interplay of values that led to the decision to bus children in the first place, it was obvious that intelligent busing decisions required doing more than simply optimizing desegregation. It was important that all children be treated pretty much the same, that no child be required to go too far or to spend too much time on the bus, and that children from the same family and neighborhood attend the same school. In the end, it was necessary to weight possibilities according to a multidimensional value system in order to find solutions that mimicked the decisions real people would make.

From this and other simulation problems, Pugh concluded that surrogate evaluative heuristics are, in the combinations needed to solve complex problems, neither simple, coherent, nor general. By extension, he reasoned that the values used to make choices about biological needs would be complex, contradictory, and domain specific. Appetite, for example, or the unpleasantness of hot objects play little or no part in making choices about whether to study physics. Even taken singly, they require multiple and competing values. Appetite is not just about the properties of food, for example, its smell, appearance, and texture. It also involves values concerning familiarity, satiation, body image, defiance (cf. formulations of eating disorder dynamics), custom, fashion, and competing interest in other domains (if I eat, will I have time to wash my hair?). In short, even within a given domain, values are multiple, heterogeneous, and often antagonistic. From such considerations, Pugh concluded that many values are at work in the formulation of a single thought or action.

The Classification of Values

Because values are so numerous and heterogeneous, Pugh devised a provisional classification system. The essence of the proposal was that values could be classified along two fundamental dimensions. The first, the developmental dimension, divides values into "primary" and "secondary" values. Primary values are the values one is born with, the fundamental surrogates for biological selection; secondary values are developed out of primary values. The second dimension in Pugh's proposed classification had to do with value domains. Pugh proposed a fundamental trichotomization into *selfish values* having to do with physiological need and self-maintenance in general, *social values* having to do with how we relate to other people, and *intellectual values* having to do with how we determine similarity, difference, probability, necessity, truth, and so on. My purpose in this chapter not being to discuss any particular type of values, I simply note that part of the confusion in thinking about values is that certain common language usages limit values to one domain or another—usually moral or religious—as if value does not permeate all thought and action. The comprehensiveness of Pugh's taxonomy is, perhaps, its most important quality. As is evident, several chapters of this book concern specific value systems lying within one or another of Pugh's domains.

The Resolution of Value Conflicts

The domain specificity of values and their variability and complexity within a given domain lead ineluctably to conflict. Pugh realized that if action and thought are to move forward, there must be some way of resolving conflicts and determining what is most important at a given moment. In that he does not differ from other thinkers. In psychology, the attempt to understand value conflicts has resulted in, among other hypotheses, psychoanalysis's notion of defense, Gestalt psychology's concept of *Prägnanz*, Festinger's propositions concerning cognitive dissonance, and Piaget's theories of cognitive repression, equilibration, and the will. In epistemology and the history of science, it has resulted in Popper's view that a scientist's choice of goals reduces to "an irresolvable matter of taste" (Laudan, 1984, p. 49); in Reichenbach's similar view that "an agent's purposes or goals . . . are not a rationally negotiable matter" (Laudan, 1984, p. 49); in Kuhn's (1977) contention that "choice between competing theories depends on a mixture of objective and subjective factors" (p. 325); and in Laudan's conclusions that "there are principles of empirical or evidential support which are neither paradigm specific, hopelessly vague, nor individually idiosyncratic" and these "are sometimes sufficient to guide our preferences unambiguously" (Laudan, 1984, p. 102). Although interesting in various respects, none of these conceptions completely resolves the problem of how value conflicts are resolved.

Pugh and Piaget

Reasonable allowances made for differences in lexicon, Piaget's and Pugh's descriptions of evaluative phenomena virtually converge. Piaget in his better moments and Pugh consistently saw affective evaluation as a heuristic method used in solving complex problems; both recognized that feeling was the way in which evaluative activities appear in consciousness; both acknowledged that feelings vary in intensity; both agreed that values are diverse, conflictual, and domain specific; and both believed that certain values are inborn and that other values develop from these rudimentary affects. However, Pugh was less anxious and less pessimistic than Piaget. Up until *Possibility and Necessity*, Piaget focused on the incertitude and chaos of subjective values and saw them as an obstacle to be surmounted in the march toward objectivity. Although he finally granted them positive value, he continued to conflate evaluative and energetic functions. In contrast, Pugh focused on the speed and efficiency of values and saw them as an important tool in creating probability that might eventually lead to objectivity and certainty. Obviously, Piaget's and Pugh's interpretations differed in a fundamental way. It is instructive to examine how.

Neither in his theory of equilibration nor in his notion of procedural schemes did Piaget conceive affectivity as the functional analog of selection in biological evolution. In clearer moments, he saw that feelings were an expression of values and assigned affectivity the role of deciding which assimilations would be performed. In murkier moments, he conflated, as many theorists of emotion still do, the evaluative-motivational role of affectivity with the energizing role of arousal. This confusion is evident in his unfortunate metaphor: "[A]ffectivity would play the role of an energy source on which the functioning but not the structures of intelligence would depend. It would be like gasoline, which activates the motor of an automobile but does not modify its structure" (1953–1954/1981, p. 5). The great shortcoming of Piaget's functional analysis of affectivity is that it does not appreciate the need for a surrogate selective system that makes use of subjective values and that occupies an intermediary position between biological and rational selection. He only admits psychological selection of the latter type in which evaluation is accomplished "objectively" either by success and consistency with existing schemes (procedural selection) or by necessity and truth (presentative or operatory selection). Moreover, Piaget did not consider rational selective criteria to be affects (although he always spoke of the feeling or *sentiment* of necessity). For him, the *objective* qualities of necessity and truth were simply the psychological realization of the same functional stability that explained survival. It was an important part of his explanation of why reality and knowledge structures correspond.

For his part, Pugh realized that affects fulfill the selective function in mental evolution and recognized that truth and necessity are feelings. He also observed, correctly, that the latter are rather rare commodities, that one does not jump from ignorance to certainty in one fell swoop, and that it is not possible to reproduce adaptive functions psychologically in the direct way that Piaget imagined. Biologically, manifold new possibilities are created at the time of reproduction, but it takes lifetimes or even generations to play out their full effects and determine their ultimate value in reproductive or survival terms. If the whole functional idea of intelligence is to speed up evolution, direct analogs of biological selection like necessity and truth can only play a limited role in psychological processes. For that reason, Pugh interposed a heuristic selective system between biological selection and exact or rigorous or real psychological selection. He envisioned affectivity as an elaborate system of surrogates for adaptive value that is used to approximate solutions to complex adaptive problems. Although he agreed that values play a role in motivation, he did not believe that affectivity's role was simply to fuel the structures of intelligence as they grind out exact solutions. For Pugh, affectivity was not energy. It was structure; it was knowledge; it was an instrument of intelligence; it was a system of tricks and ruses that intelligence uses to discover partial or provisional equilibria, to create structures that will work until truth and necessity can be found.

All of this leads to a curious situation. On the one hand, Piaget created a theory of how empirical and formal knowledge develop, whereas Pugh greatly clarified the functional role that values play in constructing knowledge. On the other hand, Piaget's and Pugh's theories taken together do not tell us how values themselves develop. Piaget did, however, provide a clue. In fact, his account of the intellectualization of feelings into normative scales of values and his work on possibility and necessity led him to the brink of understanding the way in which values participate in the developmental processes of intelligence and how they are constructed. Unfortunately he never integrated these two lines of thought. I, therefore, attempt to do so now.

AFFECT-TRANSFORMING SCHEMES AND AFFECTIVE DEVELOPMENT

Piaget's point of departure in explaining development of any kind was the Wallace–Darwin theory of organic evolution. In that view, biological, psychological, and social entities are constructed through the interaction of organisms, people, societies, and environments in every conceivable combination. Physical, psychological, and social structures vary and are functionally selected. That being the case, explaining affective development requires that the structures of affectivity be identified, that their functions be specified, and that some version of variation and selection be invoked.

Schemes of Action

Recall in this respect that in Piaget's theory the source of all knowledge is action, and that action results from assimilation of sensory input to schemes of action. Schemes of action are a form of knowledge, but only of knowing how. They are structured, but in the sense of feedback regulations, not in the sense of "operations."[2]

> There is, of course, an immense class of structures which are not strictly logical or mathematical, that is, whose transformations unfold in time: linguistic structures, sociological structures, psychological structures, and so on. Such transformations are governed by laws ("regulations" in the cybernetic sense of the word) which are not in the strict sense "operations," because they are not entirely reversible (in the sense in which multiplication is reversible by division or addition by subtraction). Transformation laws of this kind depend upon the interplay of anticipation and correction (feedback). (Piaget, 1968/1970, pp. 15–16)

Cognitive functioning, Piaget (Piaget & Inhelder, 1963/1969) further argued, has both figurative and operatory aspects. The figurative aspect is linked to consciousness. Its function is to monitor the results of action. The operatory aspect is unconscious (but in many cases can be consciously conceptual-

---

[2]Toward the end of his career, Piaget made a number of changes in his theory that cannot be discussed adequately here for want of space. I have opted, therefore, for a simpler presentation using Piaget's earlier concepts, at the same time attempting to be consistent with later developments. To begin with, I have avoided framing the simple division between schemes and structures in terms of the presentative, procedural, and operational schemes introduced in Piaget's last works and discussed previously. I speak simply of schemes of action and knowledge structures. Also, I speak simply of action, without differentiating comparative and transformatory action, so important in understanding Piaget's (1990/1992) mature theory.

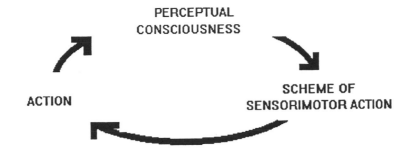

FIG 7.1. Sensorimotor assimilation.

ized). Its function is to organize action. Because different systems of knowing become evident during development, one needs to look at how figurative and operative aspects interact in each system.

Sensorimotor Schemes

On the sensorimotor level, the feedback loop between figurative and operative aspects of knowledge might be schematized as shown in Fig. 7.1. In that figure, *perceptual consciousness* corresponds to the figurative aspect of sensorimotor functioning and the *Scheme of sensorimotor action* corresponds to the operative aspect. By comparing or transforming what is perceived, sensorimotor schemes control the flow of perceptual consciousness. There are, however, other kinds of consciousness and other kinds of action.

Semiotic-Operational Schemes

A central tenet of Piaget's theory is that thought is internalized action. With the advent of the semiotic function, the child becomes capable of representing himself, the world, and his actions on and in the represented world. The great advantage of semiotic-operational reduplication of the sensorimotor world is that actions can be tried out in the represented world before they are actually carried out. This allows mistakes to be corrected in advance—Ashby's definition of operations. By analogy with Piaget's term *sensorimotor,* which indicates both the figurative and operative aspects of assimilation to knowledge structures in the preverbal period, I use the term *semiotic-operational* to designate assimilation to knowledge mediated by signs and symbols. I then posit a feedback loop between figurative and operative aspects of semiotic-operational knowledge as schematized in Fig. 7.2.

In this figure, the figurative aspect of semiotic-operational assimilation takes the form of the conscious awareness of meanings. It is how we "see" represented rather than perceived objects and events. The operative aspect of semi-

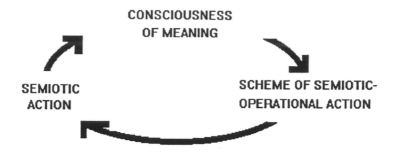

FIG 7.2.   Semiotic-operational assimilation.

otic-operational assimilation acts on meanings, and the flow of semiotic consciousness is controlled by its "actions."

Affect-Transforming Schemes

Piaget said relatively little about affective structures and, apparently, had no notion of affective schemes. I start then from two simple facts: (a) Piaget thought that feelings were conscious, and (b) Piaget believed that objective values result from action. Suppose, therefore, that subjective values present in consciousness in the form of feelings result from what I call *affect-transforming actions*, that such actions are regulated by affect-transforming schemes, and that the functioning of such schemes exhibits figurative and operative aspects. We would then arrive at the schematization shown in Fig. 7.3.

This figure recognizes that feeling is a form of consciousness that, although present in the sensorimotor period, is not perceptual in nature. Further, it suggests that feelings can be acted on by affect-transforming schemes, just as perceptions can be acted on by sensorimotor schemes. Affective-transformational schemes would, then, control the flow of affective consciousness or feeling. On Pugh's hypothesis that feelings are surrogates for adaptive values, that they dichotomize into bad and good, and that intelligence is driven to search out and intensify good feelings, then affective-transforming schemes, by always creating better feelings, more often than not drag adaptation in their wake.

Feeling, the figurative aspect of affective functioning, differs from perception in two essential ways. The first difference may be illustrated as follows. If I look twice at a tree, I twice perceive a tree, but I do not necessarily feel the same way about the tree each time I see it. When it is hot and I am seeking shade, the tree is seen as a welcome haven; when my kite is caught in its upmost branches, it is seen as a nuisance to be cut down. Feeling, then, has something to do with me, the subject, in relation to the tree; it is not a property of the tree.

The second way in which feeling differs from perception is that it can arise from semiotic-operational meanings, whereas perceptions cannot. For example, interest, fear, hesitation, anger, joy, and so on—a whole range of feelings and emotions—can be provoked by something that I learn about symbolically, by, for example, reading. Such feelings are direct, immediate, and real. They are not different from the feelings stimulated by sensorimotor action. In contrast, meanings cannot provoke perceptions. The "perceptual" experience I have when imagining a tree is decidedly different from my experience in perceiving it. I conclude, therefore, that here, too, affectivity reflects something about me in relation to a symbolized reality. The reason that feelings can be experienced directly as a result of semiotic-operational assimilation is that I am present in the situation.

With regard to the operative aspect of affective functioning, it is a bit disconcerting to discover that whatever it is that transforms feelings appears to be the same as whatever it is that transforms perceptions or the objective aspects of meaning. For example, if I lay down *Child Development* and take up *Opera News,* I transform the perceptions and meanings coursing through my consciousness but at the same time I transform boredom into interest. Or if my pregnant sow stumbles on a bed of truffles, I not only get a whiff of their glorious odor but discouragement transmogrifies into glee. In these examples, the actions carried out, that is, reading, trudging through the forest, derive from sensorimotor and semiotic-operational schemes. As commonly conceived, such schemes have as their function to compare and transform perceptions and meanings. What is it then, that transforms feelings?

One factor necessary for answering that question lies in recognizing that assimilation is never purely sensorimotor or semiotic-operational. It always and without exception involves affect-transforming assimilation as well. (That is why Piaget said that there is no such thing as purely cognitive or purely affective behavior.) When, therefore, I assimilate inky little figures on a piece of paper into knowledge structures that permit their comprehension, I also as-

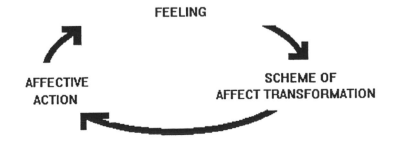

FIG 7.3.   Affect-transforming assimilation.

similate the meaning assigned by that assimilation into knowledge structures that permit value to be assigned to them. As a result, a study aimed at fathoming the mysteries of adolescence by correlating pimples, pubic hair, and school grades results in despair, anger, and disgust. To alleviate such feelings, I lay down the journal and turn my mind to other things.

A second factor necessary for understanding feeling transformation lies in maintaining strict analogies between sensorimotor, semiotic-operational, and the affect-transforming assimilation proposed in Fig. 7.3. (For the sake of simplicity, I consider only the analogy with sensorimotor functioning, but it is not difficult to make the analogy to semiotic-operational functioning as well.) Recall that in the sensorimotor assimilation, schemes of action transform perceptions in two ways. Either they transform the subject's physical relation to the object (changes in perspective), or they transform the object (causal action). By analogy, affect-transforming schemes transform feeling in two ways. Either they switch the point of view—the value structure—from which something is evaluated, or they transform the situation being evaluated through direct action. In both cases, the maneuvers employed may range from the very simple to the highly complex. The change in perspective might be so simple as to decide that it is not really all that important to have a haircut before the weekend, thus relieving unpleasant stress. Or it might be as complicated and painful as giving up the superordinate value that all physical events must be determined (cf. Born, 1971). Similarly, direct affect-transforming action may be so simple as turning the shower valve toward "cold" to relieve unpleasant warmth or as complex as Medea murdering her children to mitigate her fury and assuage the pain of Jason's infidelity.

Schematic as they are, the notion of affect-transforming schemes makes clear how affective consciousness is regulated. If space permitted, I would examine the important implications that this idea has for epistemologies of psychology and sociology. All that I can point out here is that all perceptual and all semiotic information is assimilated to affective structures. Akin to Piaget's presentative structures, those structures allow value to be assigned both qualitatively and quantitatively. The resulting values are afferents to a control system that composes affective, perceptual, and semiotic information into intentional schemes of action. Such actions are organized around the principle of optimizing positive feeling, not around the principle of optimizing equilibrium. Because positive feeling is a heuristic surrogate for equilibrium, this orients action toward better equilibrium—but that is a secondary effect. Objective values are only one among many value structures. When they are invoked and action formulated under their aegis, true or necessary knowledge may result, but confusion and failure are also possible, in which case other value systems will have to be employed. As a general rule, objective evaluation is possible only for action on relatively simple objects like electrons or numbers. It is much harder to apply it to complicated objects like people.

AFFECTIVE DEVELOPMENT

There can be no doubt that something about affectivity develops. Babies who vehemently spit out anchovies come, in the decay of middle age, to crave *tapénade* and crackers. Yuppies once swathed in fur volunteer as dowagers to care for homeless cats. Senators committed to the right to choice, turn up 10 years later at demonstrations for the right to life. How, then, are such changes effected?

It is extremely important not to mispose this question. Although Piaget created an elaborate theory of sensorimotor development, he did not speak of *perceptual* development; although Piaget created an elaborate theory of semiotic-operational development, he did not speak of *semiotic* development. In other words, development is not something Piaget associated with the figurative aspect of knowledge. For Piaget it was the motor and operational aspects of cognitive activity that develop. In strict analogy, I do not claim that it is the figurative aspect of affective activity that develops. What changes in affective development is not feeling; feelings remain more or less the same (Izard, 1984). What changes are the schemes and structures by which feelings are compared and transformed.

From that point of view, I fear that what I have to say about affective development is a bit of an anticlimax. Clarifying affective concepts and positing affect-transforming schemes simply leads back to (but also profoundly changes) Piaget's developmental theory.

> It appears to us that in explaining cognitive development, whether accounting for the history of science or psychogenesis, the concept of improving or optimizing equilibration imposes itself as fundamental.
>
> Since every reequilibration involves actions with a teleonomic character, we must explain how goals, new as well as old, are chosen and account for how the means used to reach a goal are improved or why the means applied succeed. In this regard, the distinction between three broad forms of equilibrium provides the beginnings of a solution . . . the equilibrium of coordinations between the subject and objects, the equilibrium of coordinations between schemes and sub-systems of schemes, and the general equilibrium between the whole and its parts. . . . The third type of equilibrium appears to orient the finality of actions. In effect, it is always when a lacuna turns up, and because of the perturbations that are either its source or its result, that a new endeavor is undertaken. The finality of that endeavor therefore arises from the system as a whole in its incomplete state and tends to complete it by differentiating it. Relationships between subject and object and coordinations among schemes of the same rank, on the other hand, provide means whose particular goals are subordinated to the goal determined by the need for equilibrium between the whole and its parts. (Piaget, 1975/1985, p. 139)

The only change that I would make is to revise Piaget's conception of the third type of equilibration as follows: The third type of equilibrium appears to orient the finality of actions. In effect, it is always when positive desires or bad feelings turn up that a new endeavor is undertaken. The finality of that endeavor therefore arises from affective structures and always works to increase positive feeling. Relationships between subject and object and coordinations among schemes of the same rank, on the other hand, provide means whose particular goals are subordinated to the goal determined by the need for feeling good. If that is achieved, equilibrium between the whole and its parts will usually follow.

Apart from these minor but theory-shaking changes, I would leave Piaget's account of equilibration unaltered. I would even posit that Piaget (1976a) gave unwitting voice to the accuracy of these revisions when, in his *Autobiographie*, he wrote "Fundamentally, I am an anxious person whom work alone assuages" (p. 21, fn 17). His search was obviously for affective not cognitive equilibrium. I would also posit that Piaget suspected the role affectivity plays in equilibration in his syncretic fusion of feeling and motivation, although he never grasped exactly how it worked. But contrary to his intuitions and, in the manner of the philosophers he mistrusted, he made a *subjective evaluation* that people—whom he always confused with epistemic subjects—must, above all else, be rational. That was his great mistake.

Piaget's theory of equilibration is realizable—one can build an equilibrating machine out of blood and bones—only when one sees clearly that human intelligence cannot always aim at equilibrium directly because it takes too much knowledge, too much intellectual power, and too much time to evaluate possibilities after the fact in terms of necessity and truth. In fact, logical necessity and its bedfellow empirical truth arise from the functioning of a more general and affectively organized system. The construction of true or necessary knowledge arises from value-guided evolutions in which a rigid, narrow set of values is made to play the deciding role. Because of its enormous cost, construction in this manner is not practical in many cases, most of which have to do with the profoundest concerns of the human race, but nature found a way around this difficulty. By creating a system organized around a superordinate value of feeling good and by making feelings surrogate indices of adaptation, intelligence can, most of the time, advance toward adaptive equilibrium even though it has no exact knowledge of it.

The suggested changes made, Piaget's theory of equilibration is so clear and converges so completely on the idea of affect-transforming schemes developed previously that further discussion is unnecessary. One is born with innate value structures that assimilate input from the sensory organs and from internal sources as well. The output of their activity is presented to consciousness as feelings. The conscious system uses this and other inputs to formulate intentions and assign schemes in a manner that will transform feelings in the positive direction. When schemes do not succeed in doing that, Piaget's compensation mechanisms (construction of negations, etc.) come into play. The results are judged heuristically, with feelings standing in for equilibrium. Thus, success means moving not just the objective feelings linked directly to equilibrium but feelings in general toward feeling better. In most cases, that will work. As new schemes are developed, they can be organized to produce more complicated ways of inducing feeling. There is always a developmental line for rationality, but many higher level organizations remain heuristic. For example, a taste for Proust's elaborate reminiscences is neither inborn nor rational.

To make these assertions more concrete, consider Pugh's attempt to make busing decisions by designing a value-driven system. In that case, his first attempt was unsuccessful, even though it did achieve the goal. The trouble was that the solution arrived at fell into conflict with other values. Parents did not want one child traveling 20 minutes, another 50. Parents did not want their children going to schools on opposite sides of town. In truly Piagetian equilibratory fashion, Pugh compensated for these "errors." By weighting possibilities with positive or negative value as judged by parents, he was able to come up with solutions that achieved acceptable levels of integration without disrupting family life or violating other value structures. What changed, what developed, and what evolved in Pugh's experiments was not the cartographic structure of the towns in which the children lived nor the mechanical structure of the buses on which they would be transported. Rather, it was the axiology of the decisions. There can be no doubt that it was the simulation's affective structure that had changed. (Completely analogous examples relative to the axiology of science appear in Laudan, 1984.)

CONCLUSION

In contrast to most of the chapters in this book, I have said little about particular value structures. One implication of the present position, however, is that, in certain cases where feelings like perceptions are constant from one subject to another, it is possible for feelings themselves to be evaluated objectively and axiologic truths discovered. This is certainly the case with the intellectual values of possibility and necessity—both feelings. It is also not uncommon with Pugh's selfish values. We all develop extensive knowledge of what causes joy or suffering in the human race. If we did not, neither art nor torture would be possible; nor would morality, a system of affective truths based on the universality of human pain. It is much less certain that such construction can be effected for social conventions such as the sanctity of marriage, high fashion, the political correctness of nonsexist language, and so on. As both Piaget and Pugh suggested, values are a system for evaluating possibilities of action and are linked to the affective system. What Pugh saw better than Piaget is that although affectivity admits of quantity and plays a role in motivation, it is not an "energetics of behavior." It is, rather, a form of knowledge. By knowing how to transform feelings and by being generally biased toward feeling good, the subject remains oriented along the path to adaptive equilibrium in everything attempted. This makes affectivity the functional analog of biological selection in mental evolution. Although most feelings are not true measures of adaptation, they are surrogate adaptive measures, and, in most cases, they are good enough. For the most part, exact determination of adaptation in terms of objective values is neither necessary nor achieved. Because I agree with Piaget that all knowledge comes from action, I have sought the roots of axiological knowledge in the functioning of affect-transforming schemes. This accounts not only for certain properties of feeling but also makes axiological knowledge accessible to Piaget's theory of equilibration as revised herein. Through the processes of knowledge construction set forth by Piaget, the subject is able to develop new affect-transforming schemes and, in certain cases, to abstract affective structures from them. The latter are abstract systems of shared affective transformation integrated into systems of mutual compensation. Insofar as their structure has been evaluated objectively, that is, in terms of probability and necessity, they constitute affective or axiological truth. Such truth is rare, however, for the simple reason that many values are themselves developed, either individually or collectively, using subjective values and start, therefore, from suspect premises. However useful they may be, value systems of this kind remain only a form of knowing how to regulate one's personal feelings. They do not achieve the universality of presentative schemes.

REFERENCES

Blanchet, A. (1986). Rôle des valeurs et des systèmes des valeurs dans la cognition [The role of values and value systems in cognition]. *Archives de Psychologie* (Geneva), *54,* 251–270.

Block, N. (Ed.). (1980). *Readings in philosophy of psychology* (Vol. 1). Cambridge, MA: Harvard University Press.

Born, M. (1971). *The Born-Einstein letters* (I. Born, Trans.). New York: Walker.

Bringuier, J.-C. (1980). *Conversations with Jean Piaget.* Chicago: University of Chicago Press. (Original work published 1977)

Brown, T. (1980). Foreword. In J. Piaget, *Adaptation and intelligence: Organic selection and phenocopy* (S. Eames, Trans.). Chicago: University of Chicago Press.

Brown, T. (1988). Why Vygotsky: The role of social interaction in constructing knowledge. *The Quarterly Newsletter of the Laboratory of Comparative Human Cognition, 10*(4), 111–117.

Brown, T. (1990). The biological significance of affectivity. In N. L. Stein, B. Leventhal, & T. Trabasso (Eds.), *Psychological and biological approaches to emotion* (pp. 405–434). Hillsdale, NJ: Lawrence Erlbaum Associates.

Brown, T. (1994). Affective dimensions of meaning. In W. F. Overton & D. S. Palermo (Eds.), *The nature and ontogenesis of meaning* (pp. 167–190). Hillsdale, NJ: Lawrence Erlbaum Associates.

Brown, T, & Weiss, L. (1987). Structures, procedures, heuristics, and affectivity. *Archives de Psychologie* (Geneva), *55,* 59–94.

Inhelder, B., & Cellérier, G. (1991). *Le cheminement des découvertes de l'enfant* [Children's journeys to discovery]. Neuchâtel, France: Delachaux et Niestlé.

Izard, C. E. (1984). Emotion-cognition relationships and human development. In C. E. Izard, J. Kagan, & R. B. Zajonc (Eds.), *Emotions, cognition, and behavior,* (pp. 17–37). Cambridge, UK: Cambridge University Press.

Kuhn, T. S. (1977). *The essential tension.* Chicago: University of Chicago Press.

Laudan, L. (1984). *Science and values: The aims of science and their role in scientific debate.* Berkeley: University of California.

Mays, W. (1982). Piaget's sociological theory. In S. Modgil & C. Modgil (Eds.), *Jean Piaget: Consensus and controversy* (pp. 31–50). New York: Praeger.

Piaget, J. (1915). *La mission de l'idée.* Lausanne, Switzerland: Édition La Concorde.

Piaget, J. (1918). *Recherche* [Seeking]. Lausanne, Switzerland: Édition La Concorde.

Piaget, J. (1941). Essai sur la théorie des valeurs qualitatives en sociologie statique «Synchronique» [Essay on the theory of qualitative values in static sociology]. In *Publication à l'occasion du XXV anniversaire de la fondation de la faculté des sciences économiques et sociales de l'Université de Genève* (pp. 100–142). Geneva: Georg.

Piaget, J. (1950). *Introduction à l'épistémologie génétique: 1. La pensée mathématique* [Introduction to genetic epistemology: 1. Mathematical thought]. Paris: Presses Universitaires de France.

Piaget, J. (1965). *The moral judgment of the child.* (M. Gabain, Trans.). New York: The Free Press. (Original work published 1932)

Piaget, J. (1966). Débat: Psychologie et philosophie [Debate: Psychology and philosophy]. *Raison Presente, 1, 4.*

Piaget, J. (1968). Explanation in psychology and psychophysiological parallelism. In P. Fraisse & J. Piaget (Eds.). *Experimental psychology: Its scope and method. I. History and method* (J. Chambers, Trans.). New York: Basic Books. (Original work published 1963)

Piaget, J. (1970). *Structuralism* (C. Maschler, Trans.). New York: Basic Books. (Original work published 1968)

Piaget, J. (1971). *Insights and illusions of philosophy* (W. Mays, Trans.). New York: World. (Original work published 1965)

Piaget, J. (1974a). *La prise de conscience* [The grasp of consciousness]. Paris: Presses Universitaires de France.

Piaget, J. (1974b). *Réussir et comprendre* [Succeeding and understanding]. Paris: Presses Universitaires de France.

Piaget, J. (1974c). *Understanding causality* (D. Miles & M. Miles, Trans.). New York: Norton. (Original work published 1971)

Piaget, J. (1976a). Autobiographie [Autobiography]. *Revue européene des sciences sociales et Cahiers Vilfredo Pareto, 36–39,* 1–43.

Piaget, J. (1976b). Le possible, l'impossible et le nécessaire [The possible, the impossible, and the necessary]. *Archives de Psychologie* (Geneva), XLIV, *172,* 281–299.

Piaget, J. (1976c). Le développement, chez l'enfant, de l'idée de patrie et des relations avec l'étranger [The development in children of the idea of country and of relationships to foreigners]. *Revue Européene des Sciences Sociales et Cahiers Vilfredo Pareto, 36–39,* pp. 124–147. (Original work published 1951)

Piaget, J. (1981). *Intelligence and affectivity: Their relationship during child development* (T. A. Brown & C. E. Kaegi, Eds. & Trans.). Palo Alto, CA: Annual Reviews. (Original work published 1953–1954)

Piaget, J. (1985). *The equilibration of cognitive structures* (T. Brown, Trans.). Chicago: University of Chicago Press. (Original work published 1975)

Piaget, J. (1987a). *Possibility and necessity: Vol. 1. The role of possibility in cognitive develop-

ment (H. Feider, Trans.). Minneapolis: University of Minnesota Press. (Original work published 1981)

Piaget, J. (1987b). *Possibility and necessity: Vol. 2. The role of necessity in cognitive development* (H. Feider, Trans.). Minneapolis: University of Minnesota Press. (Original work published 1983)

Piaget, J. (1992). *Morphisms and categories* (T. Brown, Trans.). Hillsdale NJ: Lawrence Erlbaum Associates. (Original work published 1990)

Piaget, J. (1995). *Sociological studies* (L. Smith, Ed.). Hillsdale, NJ: Lawrence Erlbaum Associates. (Original work published 1967)

Piaget, J., & Garcia, R. (1989). *Psychogenesis and the history of science* (H. Feider, Trans.). New York: Columbia University Press. (Original work published 1983)

Piaget, J., & Inhelder, B. (1969a). Mental images. In P. Fraisse & J. Piaget (Eds.). *Experimental psychology: Its scope and method. VII. Intelligence* (pp. 85–143). (T. Surridge, Trans.). New York: Basic Books. (Original work published 1963)

Piaget, J., & Inhelder, B. (1969b). *The psychology of the child* (H. Weaver, Trans.). New York: Basic Books. (Original work published 1969)

Polya, G. (1957). *How to solve it: A new aspect of mathematical method* (2nd ed.). Princeton, NJ: Princeton University Press.

Pugh, G. E. (1977). *The biological origins of human values.* New York: Basic Books.

Shweder, R. A. (1984). Anthropology's romantic rebellion against the enlightenment, or there's more to thinking than reason and evidence. In R. A. Shweder & R. A. LeVine (Eds.), *Culture theory: Essays on mind, self, and emotion* (pp. 27–66). Cambridge, UK: Cambridge University Press.

Tudge, J., & Rogoff, B. (1989). Peer influences on cognitive development: Piagetian and Vygotskyian perspecitives. In M. Bornstein & J. Bruner (Eds.), *Interaction in human development* (pp. 17–40). Hillsdale, NJ: Lawrence Erlbaum Associates.

Author Index

Subject Index